yer's
ntial

s Guide
Dream
Co-Op

Dedication

To my wife, Barbara, and my children, John and Olga, who often played second fiddle to the computer when I worked at all hours on the manuscript. To my parents, Colonel J.M. Dubois and Olga G. de Dubois, who continue to encourage books that help the consumer. To my agents, who make real estate fun, rewarding, and forever a learning experience. To real estate buyers and sellers, who make the whole thing happen. To David Conti of Liberty Hall Press, for his great ideas and suggestions. He and his people put on the final coat of spit and polish for a top-notch presentation.

Home Buyer's Confidential

The Insider's Guide to Buying Your Dream House, Condo, or Co-Op

Maurice Dubois

LIBERTY HALL
PRESS™

This publication is designed to provide accurate and authoritative information in regard to the subject matter covered. It is sold with the understanding that the publisher is not engaged in rendering legal, accounting or other professional service. If legal advice or other expert assistance is required, the services of a competent professional person should be sought.
—from a declaration of principles jointly adopted by a committee of the American Bar Association and a committee of publishers

LIBERTY HALL PRESS books are published by LIBERTY HALL PRESS an imprint of McGraw-Hill, Inc. Its trademark, consisting of the words ''LIBERTY HALL PRESS'' and the portrayal of Benjamin Franklin, is registered in the United States Patent and Trademark Office.

FIRST EDITION
SECOND PRINTING

Library of Congress Cataloging-in-Publication Data

Dubois, Maurice.
Home buyer's confidential : the insider's guide to buying your
dream house, condo, or co-op / by Maurice Dubois.
p.   cm.
Includes index.
ISBN 0-8306-3446-0
1. House buying. 2. Condominiums. 3. Apartment houses,
Cooperative. 4. Real estate business. I. Title.
HD1379.D778   1990
643'.12—dc20   90-6243
                                                        CIP

For information about other McGraw-Hill materials, call 1-800-2-MCGRAW in the U.S. In other countries call your nearest McGraw-Hill office.

Vice President and Editorial Director: David J. Conti
Technical Editor: Lori Flaherty
Production: Katherine G. Brown
Book Design: Jaclyn J. Boone

Contents

23 The Tax Implications of Buying a Home   *242*

Introduction

Purchasing a home is usually the single most expensive decision you'll ever have to make. You'll probably be involved in the home purchasing process not more than a few times during your lifetime, and unfortunately, there are many mistakes that can be made.

Buying real estate can be complicated, there are no hard and fast rules, and even if you've bought property before, it's more than likely that you made a mistake—a mistake that cost you money. Whether or not you're buying a home as an investment or one for your own use, you need to be aware of the many pitfalls that can arise during the home buying journey and how to avoid them.

This book is your guide to making intelligent buying decisions. Beginning in Chapter 1, you'll prepare yourself emotionally for the "hunt" by learning to discern your ideals from your needs and how to remain objective about a piece of property, then in Chapter 2, you'll determine what your needs *really* are.

Once you've determined your needs, you must understand what type of housing market you'll be buying in. You'll learn this in Chapter 3. In Chapter 4, you'll learn how to analyze local housing markets and choose the best locations. Chapters 5 and 6 cover the types of housing available—single family, town houses/row houses, condominiums, or co-op's—and what makes for a good design.

When you're ready to begin your search, you'll learn about advertising media—how to read between the lines and evaluate sellers' motivations from the fine print—in Chapter 7. In Chapter 8, you'll learn all about real estate agents—how they work and whether or not to use one.

Chapter 9 lets you in on the secrets of how good real estate agents determine a seller's motivation so you can form a strategy for making an offer and arranging the best possible financing terms.

Chapter 10 alerts you to all of the structural and equipment pitfalls you should be looking for when you first inspect a piece of property.

Chapters 11 through 14 cover buying different types of property, as well as how to buy direct from builders.

Chapters 15 through 19 take the mystery out of financing. You'll learn what a down payment is, what points are, how standard loans work, and what closing costs include. You'll also learn, line-by-line, how to understand standard VA, FHA, and conventional loan forms. Other creative financing is also discussed, including assumptions, buydowns, wraparounds, and owner financing.

Chapters 21 through 22 prepare you for making an offer on a property and coming to ''The Closing.'' Finally, the tax implications of buying a home are discussed in Chapter 23.

Whether you've bought one home or 20 homes, read the book through once, then go back to the beginning when you're ready to start your home search and take the process one step at a time.

The book follows a logical buying process much like an airline captain who goes through an extensive written checklist each time he gets ready to take off. Your checklists are included throughout the book at each step of the house-hunting process. If you skip a step, it could be disastrous. So, like the airline captain, follow each chapter closely so the whole thing takes off together in complete harmony.

Best wishes in all of your real estate adventures!

1

Preparing Yourself Emotionally

"IT'S EASY TO BUY AND HARD TO SELL." NOTHING COULD BE MORE ACCURATE than this adage, and you must make the very best of your buying experience so that when it comes time to sell, you'll not only have an easy time doing so, but you'll reap the rewards of your efforts past when you first purchased your home.

There are two types of purchases in real estate. One is for a personal home—the one you'll live in. The other is investment property. I like to call the first situation Emotional Buying. The latter, I refer to as Technical Buying.

EMOTIONAL BUYING

You're going to live in your personal home day in and day out. Your spouse, if you're married, will have much to say about its purchase, its location, and its amenities. He or she will certainly not let you buy it as you would a piece of investment property, nor will you necessarily want to do so either. It is no wonder then that there is so much emotion involved in the purchase of a personal home.

For the new home seller—the home builder with exceptional model homes—it is easy to play on a buyer's emotions, particularly a first-time buyer. The buyer walks up to a meticulously executed and maintained model home complex, replete with lush landscaping, perfect model elevations, sumptuous colors, and a wonderful blend of brick, siding, and roof. He steps inside. Everything smells and looks fresh, new, and vibrant. The furniture fits the rooms like a kid glove. The high ceilings give him a feeling of space, and there are wonderful gadgets and decorations in all of the rooms, especially the kitchen. It doesn't matter that some of the gadgets and decorations have a sign that says "Decorator Item" and aren't included with the price of the home. He tells himself that soon there'll be a raise at work, and he'll be able to afford that wonderful gadget or decoration for his own little palace. And, there will surely be enough money left over each month to pay for the furniture that must be bought on credit to furnish and decorate the home to look the same as this wonderful model home.

Buying a new home doesn't have to be as bad as this, however. There are many great new homes out there. In fact, some new homes are a better buy than many existing ones. There are also a lot of new homes that are smaller, less fancy, and in a less desirable neighborhood than what our emotions tell us from looking at the model home complex.

TECHNICAL BUYING

On the other hand, if you're thinking about buying an investment home, then your emotions are much more detached. You'll be looking at the purchase from a more technical standpoint. You're buying a piece of property because it is a good deal, and because it makes good economic sense, not because you like it. The rents you will expect to charge will have to justify the selling price. Cosmetic, state-of-the-art appliances and heating/cooling systems won't be as important as low maintenance, economical equipment that is sturdy and functional. This is Technical Purchasing.

That seems easy enough. You look for your personal home with your emotions and investment property with calculator, pencil, and paper, but that's not the way it works. Unfortunately, too many people buy emotionally and too few people use a calculator. Whether you are buying a personal home or a 30-story building, there's always an emotional impulse that urges you to proceed with a purchase. For example, most investors have no problem renting handsome homes for a nifty profit, but what about squalid, run-down houses? There is money to be made renting squalid shacks as well, but few investors are enthusiastic about owning dilapidated houses and making money renting them. I have sold many houses to investors who fell in love with a piece of property in one way or another, even though there were other properties that would have been a better investment, but they were not as attractive, charming, or in as good a location as the one they ultimately selected. They fell into the trap of Emotional Buying.

Are we then lost to the power of our emotions? Yes! Unless you determine your needs and ascertain what you can afford first, then go after only houses that will fit your needs and budget and not let any financing tricks, bells and whistles, merchandising gimmicks, or powerful sales techniques get you into a less-than-desirable real estate purchase.

In Chapter 2, you'll learn how to determine your needs and to understand the basics of qualifying for a loan. Your needs and budget are two of the most important factors to keep in mind when you purchase a home. A third important point to keep in mind, one that might wreak havoc with your emotions, is the time factor of real estate purchasing. If you must move out of your current residence within the next 30 days, and you're determined to purchase a home before the expiration of those 30 days, then you'll have another set of emotions haunting you during your house hunting venture.

Unless you give yourself plenty of time to find the right property, there is only one chance in a thousand that you'll accomplish a smart Technical Purchase. Everything takes time—including home buying. It's hard to tell what a reasonable amount of time should be, because it all depends on your knowledge of the market, the area, and the availability of housing. Keep in mind, however, that a 30- to 60-day wait on a contract is not unreasonable.

When you begin your search, and as you progress at different properties, tell yourself over and over that you will not buy emotionally; that you will fill your needs in accordance with your budget, and work to get the most house, the best quality, and the greatest number of amenities within your predetermined budget.

Most important, stay within your budget, no matter what you see, no matter what ''bargain'' that's ''too good to pass up'' comes your way. Otherwise, you'll be in over your head, and . . . ''It's easy to buy and hard to sell.''

2

Evaluating
Your Needs

AS I MENTIONED IN CHAPTER 1, THE ONLY WAY TO MAKE A NONEMOTIONAL
real estate purchase is to know precisely what your needs are, and understand
what you can afford so you can stay within your budget—in monthly payments, as
well as a down payment.

In this chapter, purchasing a home you'll live in is covered first. Later in the
chapter, purchasing property for commercial use (rental property) is discussed.
At the end of the chapter, you'll find a checklist for each type of purchase. These
lists are helpful in defining your goals, and keeping you on track during the purchase.

PURCHASING A HOME OF YOUR OWN

When you purchase a home to live in, you must first carefully consider your family's most important needs so that you can have an overall picture of where you
need to start in your thinking process. For example, just because your family is
composed of you and your spouse, and two children—a boy and a girl—doesn't
mean that you need to start thinking of three bedroom homes first. Your first and
most important considerations must be the *location*, and your *budget*. For example, if you live in a high-priced area, you might not be able to look at three bedroom properties because of your income or available funds for down payment and

closing costs. On the other hand, if your children require specialized training, because of learning disabilities or need advanced or accelerated studies, then you need to look at areas that offer that type of education before you think about the size and style of housing you must look at.

Let's define the difference between needs and wants. You *need* housing for your family so you can move out of a cramped apartment into larger space and a better neighborhood. You *want* a house on a big lot with plenty of room for the kids to enjoy themselves. So, let's assume your budget allows you to buy property in the $60,000 range, and let's say that, in your area, property in that price range is only available as attached housing in the form of row houses or condominiums. You'd get a very limited backyard, or no backyard at all, just a common area for everybody to use. Obviously, you'll fill your needs with this scenario, but you'll only partially fill your wants.

Your first step will be to determine exactly what you can afford, and then to find out what's out there within your price range. If your buying ability is $600 per month, then you can't be looking at property that costs $1,000 per month. You'll be way off base, wasting your time in what is so aptly called fantasyland. By the same token, you won't want to be looking at property in the $300 per month range. That would also be a waste of time.

When you start looking at your financial position, you might want to know exactly how much of a monthly payment you can comfortably live with. If you want to be precise, then you should talk to a lender. You won't have to go through all the motions with the lender at this point—no need to fill out all his forms yet—but by giving the lender's agent information about your income and your expenses, he can give you a very close idea of what price range you can afford. The lender might tell you to look at houses that are no more than $90,000 for example.

The next step is to determine general location. If you need special schooling, proximity to work, to play, to churches, anything that affects your particular life-style, look only in those areas that will work for you and your family.

Your next step is to decide what type of housing will best fit your needs that is within your budget and within your acceptable locations. Is it a large house on a large lot? Is it a house that's squeezed into a postage-stamp-sized lot? Or is it a townhouse in row housing, or even a condominium in a large, multistory building, or perhaps a co-op? Be realistic about what you can afford. If your budget restricts you to a modest home on a small lot in the city, automatically rule out areas that have only large lots and expensive homes. And if your budget allows you a good size house with a generous lot, and that's really what you want and need, then search only in those areas that have that type of property.

Once you have determined what you can afford and separated your wants from your needs, you can begin to get more specific on the structure itself: the

Personal Home Buying Checklist

Maximum price $_____   Maximum down payment $_____
Maximum monthly payment (PITI) $_____

Minimum Needs

Bedrooms #_____	Game room_____	Basement_____
Baths #_____	Den_____	Library_____
Garage #_____	Utility room_____	Guest bedroom_____
Carport #_____	Study_____	Guest bath_____
Formal living room_____	TV room_____	Attic_____
Formal dining room_____	Darkroom_____	Home office_____

Other rooms _____

Essential Amenities

Small yard_____	Sprinkler system_____	Refrigerator_____
Medium yard__	Fireplace_____	Central heating_____
Large yard_____	Range_____	Central cooling_____
Fenced yard_____	Dishwasher_____	Central system humidifier_____
Pool_____	Disposer_____	Central vacuum system_____
Spa_____	Microwave_____	Covered porch/patio_____
Trees_____	Compactor_____	Outside Storage Building_____

Other Appliances_____
Other essential amenities_____

Fig. 2-1.

size of the home, the amenities, the number of bedrooms, baths, and other rooms and areas. You won't be able to get too specific unless you have a house custom built for you. Homes vary considerably, and there must always be some compromise when you purchase a house from existing stock.

By using the checklist in Fig. 2-1, you should be able to stay on track despite pressure from a real estate agent or a new home salesman. If you begin house hunting with the list completely filled out, when you see a property that really doesn't fit what you've told yourself that you must have, then it'll be much easier to pass it by. Use the list almost as a contract between yourself as a *technical* person, and yourself as an *emotional* person. Or perhaps between yourself and your spouse.

With this list in hand, you can walk into a builder's nicest model home, and if what he's got doesn't match most of what you've got on your list, you can move on, unswayed by the temptation to purchase what isn't in your best interest. Then again, if you stumble onto a super deal, let's say a property that's within your budget but has a swimming pool at the price that other homes don't, then you can purchase without feeling guilty of needless splurging.

From the very beginning, make a promise to yourself that you will abide by your contract—the purchase list. You'll then make a very intelligent purchase.

PURCHASING INVESTMENT PROPERTY

When you are purchasing investment property, consider every rental house or multifamily unit as a business. When you buy a house to rent, you buy a small business. If you buy another property a few months later, you are adding to your small business. At some point, your small business might grow to be big business. No matter, it is always a business. You don't buy rental real estate for recreational purposes—for fun. You don't buy it for tax breaks, you don't buy it to just break even for a few years then sell it at an inflated price. You buy it to make money *now*. If you can't make money on it right away, then it's not a good investment. If anyone tells you otherwise, don't believe what you hear.

For years, I've seen investors purchase property for the wrong reasons. Some wanted to pay less taxes. However, many suffered when the tax laws were changed in 1986 and their tax breaks vanished. Some bought rental property to break even for the short-term in hopes of making a killing when prices went up. Unfortunately, when prices went down, some went broke. Some wanted to say they had a huge net worth and weren't really sure why they were buying rental property. Experts were telling them to do so, so it was okay to do so. There is only one reason to buy investment real estate: to make money, and to make money right away.

By following the checklist for investment property shown in Table 2-1, you won't buy property for any reason other than to make money. It will keep you on the straight and narrow, and lead you only to properties that are profitable and that make good economic sense.

Investment property is discussed in more depth later in the book, but keep these thoughts in mind: If you were buying a McDonald's franchise, would you buy it just to save on taxes? Would you buy it to operate at no profit for seven years, then sell it at an inflated price a few years down the road? Would you buy it just because you love to serve hamburgers even though you'd make no profit? Of course you wouldn't! You'd buy it to make money right away. You *must* buy investment property only for one reason: to make money right away.

As with a personal home, the most important consideration is the budget. Your budget will determine your needs insofar as the size of home, type of layout, specific neighborhood, and other factors, and you must be certain to stay within your allowed budget. It goes without saying then that, your needs with respect to investment property are met if:

- The property is affordable to you, and;
- You can make money from its ownership.

_____Table 2-1._____

Investment Home Buying Checklist

Maximum acceptable monthly payment	$_____
Maximum acceptable cash investment	$_____
Minimum acceptable monthly cash flow	$_____

Property address_____

Property Description

Bedrooms #__	Library__	Dishwasher__
Baths #__	Guest bedroom__	Disposer__
Garage #__	Guest bath__	Microwave__
Carport #__	Small yard__	Compactor__
Formal living room__	Medium yard__	Refrigerator__
Formal dining room__	Large yard__	Central heating__
Game room__	Fenced yard__	Central cooling__
Den __	Pool__	Central system humidifier__
Utility room__	Spa__	Central vacuum system__
Study __	Trees__	Covered porch__
TV room__	Sprinkler system__	Covered patio__
Darkroom__	Fireplace__	Outside storage building__
Basement__	Range__	

Other rooms_____

Notes_____

1. Comparable neighborhood rents	$_____
2. Less total PITI payment	$_____
3. Less vacancy factor (minimum = rent/12)	$_____
4. Less repairs (minimum = rent/12)	$_____
5. Monthly cash flow	$_____

Certainly, there are other factors that can be considered when an investor purchases rental property, such as tax savings (there are still advantages, though not as many), asset appreciation, quick payoff to allow future retirement income. But for the new investor, the two reasons stated above should be the only reasons for investing in rental real estate.

There are two very poor reasons for buying investment property. The first is to just fall in love with a house—because it's pretty, in a quaint neighborhood, has a great floor plan, or is in first-class condition. The second is because everybody is buying; the market's hot, get it while you can before it's all gone. If it's a sellers' market, that's the worst thing you can do. You make the most money if you buy when everybody's selling, and sell when everybody's buying.

3

Understanding the Home Market

IN ORDER TO GET THE VERY BEST, AND THE MOST FOR YOUR MONEY, YOU MUST become familiar with your local home marketplace. Not only must you be familiar with the area, such as where the good and poor neighborhoods are located, but you should also know what type of market you're in: whether it's a sellers' market, a buyers' market, or a normal market.

KNOWING YOUR AREA

You'll make a truly intelligent purchase if you're very familiar with your local area. If you've lived in the same city for the last five or ten years, you should be well informed. But if you're just moving to town, unless it's a very small town, you might be better off to rent for a while, say six to twelve months, so you can get familiar with the territory.

When you're new, a certain part of town might seem attractive, but only when you live there, when you talk to the neighbors and others from different areas of town, will you really know whether that certain area is what you want or need. Only then will you be able to decide if the schools are okay here, or better over there; if shopping is more convenient in one place or another because of traffic, prices, or better store selections.

If you're being transferred by your company from Los Angeles to Kansas City, and you're allowed only a few weeks or months to purchase a home in order to receive some of your moving and purchasing allowances, your company might be doing you a disservice. If you're allowed 12 to 18 months, however, then your company has sharp management. Rent for a year, then you can make your purchase with more knowledge.

While you're renting, travel the different parts of the city that offer the price range of housing you'll be purchasing. Try not to look at individual houses, but look at the areas, talk to as many people as you can in local shops, supermarkets, and malls about the schools, traffic, local government, local crime rates, police protection, etc. Write it all down. The more people you talk with, the better you'll understand each area. At the end of a year, you'll be a knowledgeable purchaser.

THE MARKETS

There are three types of real estate markets. The best market for the buyer is the Buyers' Market. The most fair market for both buyer and seller is the Normal Market. And the most unjust market for the buyer is the Sellers' Market.

The Buyers' Market

A buyers' market is when more property is placed on the market than the market is able to absorb. In other words, there are more houses for sale than there are buyers. It's a beautiful situation for the buyer. At the time I wrote this book, some cities were experiencing the very best buyers' markets ever experienced. Cities such as Denver, Dallas/Fort Worth, and Houston had such tremendous amounts of excess housing, much of it in the form of foreclosures, that buyers had never seen such bargains in such massive amounts. Houses in Dallas/Fort Worth, and most of their suburbs, were selling at 60 to 80 cents on the dollar, which, with deflated prices, amounts to 40 to 60 cents on the dollar of "normal" housing prices.

Even in a buyers' market, there will be areas that are much more depressed than others, just as there will almost always be parts of town that will not be depressed at all (or very little) because of the type of housing they offer, or because of their proximity to work or play. Housing in most areas, though, should be selling at bargain prices.

The Normal Market

The normal market is a balanced situation. There are about as many sellers as there are buyers. Home builders and multifamily apartment builders will be building at a fair pace. Negotiations for price concessions are probably the trickiest during this type of market. The seller knows his house will sell in a reasonable amount of time, and he can afford to have you go someplace else if you ask for too much of a discount.

As with the buyers' market, there will also be areas that are depressed, and some areas that are hot enough to almost be considered a sellers' market.

The Sellers' Market

As a buyer, you should do all you can to avoid purchasing during a sellers' market. A sellers' market is when there is a scarcity of houses, and plenty of buyers to compete for that scant supply of homes.

During a sellers' market, home builders will be building at an alarming rate, and some of the housing product will, more than likely, be shoddy. In the early 1970s when Houston had its building boom, I saw many homes in nice neighborhoods that were blatantly poorly constructed. I remember a whole row of rather large homes whose concrete garage floors were not finished, only bull-floated, leaving a sorry-looking, uneven finish. That type of finish saved time and money for the builders. Nobody cared about the buyers. They were standing in line ready to buy. They needed a place to live.

There are times when it's better to rent than to buy. I hate to make this statement because I'm sold on home ownership. If you go out into the home marketplace and play the bidding game for a scarce supply of homes, however, you'll probably be sorry later on. Home markets can resemble a sine wave, such as the one shown in Fig. 3-1.

Some home markets work basically in the order of this sine wave. At the bottom of a cycle is the buyers' market. There is an oversupply of housing,

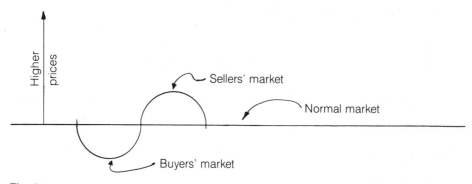

Fig. 3-1.

therefore, prices are at their lowest. As the market moves up the wave, prices start to rise. The time to buy is at the bottom, or as the rise is beginning. Towards the middle of the upgrade is a normal market, which can still be a good time to buy. At the top of the wave prices are at their highest. This market condition might last months, a year or two, even several years. A market might take a long time moving to the top; perhaps a couple of decades. Meanwhile, prices are always rising.

If the rising part of the wave has taken a long time to climb, then the bottom probably will never reach the lower level of the first curve. It will look like the curve in Fig. 3-2.

What you want to avoid is buying a house at the very top, or when the curve is coming down. When it's coming down, you will probably have a house that's worth less next year than the year you bought it. If you keep the house a good many years, you won't be hurt. By the time you sell, prices will have come up again. Perhaps they'll even be above the price you paid.

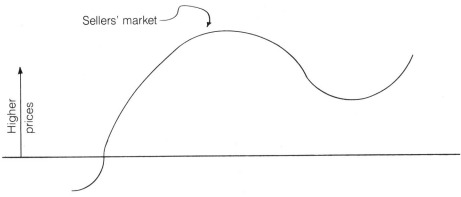

Fig. 3-2.

When to Disregard the Market

Probably the only time you shouldn't worry about the market is when you're building or buying an existing custom home in exactly the area you like, and you're paying all cash because you're almost certain you'll not move again for many years to come, if ever again. You'll get what you want, when you want it, and you can afford it. Even if home prices were to plummet, and your income were to be interrupted for some time, you'd have no payments to worry over other than taxes and insurance.

BUYING A NEW HOUSE

Generally, the best time to buy a new house is in a normal market. The builders won't be flooded with orders, nor will they be starving for lack of buyers. While you won't get any great bargains, most builders will want your business and will do a reasonably good job of constructing your home. In other words, they'll truly want to please you.

In a sellers' market, you're going to pay top dollar for a new home. But you'll pay top dollar for an existing one also. Either way, you'll come out on the short end of the stick. If it looks like your market is at the peak of a sellers' market, then just rent and wait until supply and demand are more normal.

If you're in a buyers' market and don't find what you want in existing housing stock, then you might want to consider new. Find a home builder who's economically stable with a solid, long-standing reputation. He'll want and *need* your business. You'll get a reasonably good deal, and a well-constructed home. Just beware of the builder who's in financial trouble. There will be plenty of those in a weak market. He might get your home started but not finish it if he goes out of business during the process.

UNDERSTANDING VALUE THROUGH APPRAISING

There are three basic approaches to appraising real estate:

1. Reproduction
2. Market
3. Income

Each approach is important to understanding the marketplace.

Reproduction Cost Appraising

Determining value through reproduction cost, in my opinion, is the most important form of appraising for the buyer. With this system, you determine the value of a property by what it would cost to reproduce it as a cost per square foot, then make adjustments for location, condition, and amenities.

Naturally, it's easier said than done, as there are so many variables in construction costs that, even for an experienced builder, it would be nearly impossible to come up with exact figures. But by visiting model homes of several local builders and using the Reproduction Cost Appraising Sheet in Fig. 3-3, you can get a good idea of cost per square foot for most of the homes in your town. You can then use this figure to determine the value of existing housing.

Make several copies of the sheet. Take the price of several new homes in the builders' standard pricing schedule. Add the amenities you wish to have in your home, such as a fireplace, fenced yard, etc. Add those figures to the base price and divide the total by the number of square feet the house has. Now you

Reproduction Cost Appraising Sheet

Property address _____

Add or deduct an estimated amount for the following:

Bedrooms #__$__	Spa $__	Central heating $__
Baths #__$__	Trees $__	Central cooling $__
Garage #__$__	Sprinkler system $__	Central humidifier $__
Carport #__$__	Fireplace $__	Central vacuum $__
Covered porch/patio __	Range $__	Other $__
Small yard $__	Dishwasher $__	Other $__
Medium yard $__	Disposer $__	Other $__
Large yard $__	Microwave $__	Other $__
Fenced yard $__	Compactor $__	Other $__
Pool $__	Refrigerator $__	Other $__

Price of Home $_____
Add or subtract for amenities $_____
Base Price $_____
Divide by s.f.   _____
Price/s.f. $_____

Fig. 3-3.

have a price per square foot. When you get ready to look at existing houses, you do the same, but make adjustments for amenities that are extra or that are missing.

The following are a couple of examples for finding a base cost per square foot of new housing. Assume you're looking for a house with no amenities whatsoever:

1. Property #1 is a 3-2-2 brick home, no amenities. It's priced as follows:

Price of Home	$ 98,000
Add or subtract for amenities	$ 0
Base Price	$ 98,000
Divide by s.f.	1,800
Price/s.f.	$ 54.44

2. Property #2 is also a 3-2-2 brick home, but it has a $400 range, a $300 dishwasher, and a $2,500 fireplace.

Price of Home	$ 107,000
Add or subtract for amenities	$ 3,200

Base Price	$ 103,800
Divide by s.f.	1,900
Price/s.f.	$ 54.63

Now add the price/s.f. of both and divide by 2 = $54.54. That's the average cost per square foot. You would, of course, have perhaps 20 examples, so you would add all of them together and then divide by 20.

Now let's assume you've found an existing house as follows:

3. Property #3 is a 3-2-2 brick home, with a range you estimate to be worth $200, a dishwasher you estimate to be worth $200, and a fence you estimate to be worth $1,200.

Price of Home	$ 88,000
Add or subtract for amenities	$ 1,600
Base Price	$ 86,400
Divide by s.f.	1,400
Price/s.f.	$ 61.71

This little exercise tells you the existing house you're looking at is not quite the bargain the new homes are, but still not a complete rip-off. If you'd come up with $90/s.f., then you might not want to consider the home, or you would make a lower offer to keep the price more in line with the market.

Remember, if you start comparing large houses to very small houses, you'll have highly varying figures. It is much cheaper per square foot to build a large house than it is to build a smaller one, assuming the quality of the houses are fairly equal.

To get the square footage of an existing home, you'll have to measure the length and multiply times the width of the exterior walls (including brick). You do not measure the square footage of each room and add all the figures together. That's not how the builders or appraisers do it, so your figures would vary wildly.

Market Value Appraising

Market value appraising is the favorite method used by real estate people. They do what is called a comparative market analysis to determine the value of a property. To make it work, you have to know the selling price of homes that have sold in that area. For example, assume that within a general area of town there were 16 sales in the last three months of properties similar to what you're looking for. They all sold for between $160,000 and $180,000. You would add all of the figures together, then divide by 16. Assume the answer is $174,000. That means you should be able to find a home in your area, equipped as you want it, for about $174,000.

This method has one big problem, however. Assume the houses are all about 1,800 s.f. If you divide $174,000 by 1,800, you'll get $96.66/s.f. If those homes are equal in quality of construction, amenities, and neighborhood to the new ones we just looked at, then the existing homes are a poor buy. Just because 16 people paid that much per square foot for their homes doesn't mean they got a good deal. The real estate agent can justify the high price through market value appraising and get future buyers to pay the high prices.

Another problem with this method is that you don't have the information available to you that real estate agents do. You certainly don't want to use the asking price of homes on the market as your basis, because, for all you know, sellers might be allowing a $10,000 reduction in price to buyers. Market value appraising only works with properties that have actually *sold* and *closed*. You also must consider financing, which is discussed later in Chapter 15.

Income Value Appraising

If you're purchasing rental property, you need to use income value appraising to decide if a property is correctly priced. When it comes to rental property, it doesn't matter what the market says a property is worth, or how much it is selling for per square foot. The only things that matter are the income stream it can produce, the liability exposure you will take on, and what return on your investment that income represents.

There is a rule of thumb that says, if you rent a house for $700 per month, then it's worth $70,000. That's an easy appraisal method. Simply add two zeros to the monthly rental figure. This might work in some cases, but in others it might disappoint you. It can, however, give you a quick idea of whether you're on the right track or not. If you see that a certain $90,000 house will make a great rental property, you'll know not to give it much consideration if the most you might rent it for is $750, because more than likely your payments will be $900 to $1000 per month.

With some practice, you will be able to determine what your own rule of thumb should be. Personally, I would never buy a piece of property using the above rule of thumb. My own rule is to take the monthly payment, divide by two, and add two zeros. If I can rent for $700 per month, then it's worth $35,000 to me.

4

Deciding on a Location

AS EVEN THE MOST NOVICE REAL ESTATE SALESPERSON WILL TELL YOU, THE single most important consideration concerning real estate is location. You might have heard the old cliche, ''The three most important aspects of real estate are location, location, and location.''

Certainly, the Empire State Building is worth a lot more in Manhattan than in the middle of a wheat field in central Kansas. But there is a lot more to location than value, which is what the old cliche above refers to. The Empire State Building might not be worth as much in the middle of a wheat field in central Kansas, but to many folks, it just might be a more pleasant place to work.

Consequently, when real estate people talk about location, they usually are thinking dollar value. When you think about location as an aspiring landlord, you must also think dollar value. When you think about location when looking for a homestead, however, there are other, just as important, considerations. For example, you'll be thinking of breathing space, crime rates, convenience to schools, shopping, entertainment, recreation, etc. The best parts of town, in other words, might not be the ones with the most valuable property. The most expensive areas of town might not be best for your particular needs.

FINDING THE BEST PARTS OF TOWN

If you live in a relatively small community, there might not be much difference between the best and the worst parts of town. There will, undoubtedly, be better parts and worse parts, but the differences won't be as easily defined as in larger cities such as Chicago, Kansas City, Los Angeles, St. Louis, etc. Consequently, the smaller the city, the less differences you're likely to find. This holds true for the suburbs as well. A city of 5,000 in the suburbs will, more than likely, be quite balanced. A suburb like Arlington, Texas, however, with a population of more than 250,000 can be radically different. Even so, those differences are not as clear-cut as what you'd find in adjoining Fort Worth or nearby Dallas.

All this means is that the larger the city, the more familiar you must be with it. If you are not familiar with an area, it's always better to rent for a while before you buy.

If you've lived in a city for some time as a renter, you might not have paid that much attention to the different parts of town. Now, as a buyer, you have to do a little homework. Drive around and talk to people in the areas that appeal to you. Many of the points in this chapter pertain to investors as much as they do to those buying a home to live in.

The ideal parts of a town are those that offer plenty of inexpensive, modern housing, a lot of open space, good schools, parks, recreation, shopping, proximity to work, and little in the way of crime, traffic and population density. There are such places. In fact, I've seen a few in my lifetime, but they're not the norm. So, when you start your search for housing, if you don't find the ideal, strive for something close to it. To help you find the best location, use the Area Detail Sheet in Fig. 4-1. Fill out the information that best meets your needs, then use the sheet to find the areas that will best fit your requirements.

Proximity to Work

In a large city, it is rare to find housing that requires very little commuting time, especially if you work downtown. Let's take a look at commuting time and what it means to you in annual hours spent commuting. There are 52 weeks in a year. If you take two weeks vacation, and another two weeks for holidays and sick days, that means you'll be traveling to work 48 weeks per year. Multiply 48 by 5 and that gives you 240 trips to work and 240 trips back home. If it takes you 15 minutes to drive to work, then you'll drive 15 (minutes) × 2 (trips) × 240 (days) = 7,200 (minutes). Divide 7,200 minutes by 60 (minutes in an hour), that means you'll drive 120 hours per year getting to and from work. Now divide that by 24 hours and you get five 24-hour days of driving.

Area Detail Sheet

Subdivision_____

His work_____miles_____

Her work_____miles_____

Universities_____miles_____

High school_____miles_____

Jr. high school_____miles_____

Elementary school_____miles_____

Day care_____miles_____

Hospital_____miles_____

Fire_____miles_____

Police_____miles_____

Crime_____

Traffic during rush hour_____

Traffic at night and weekends_____

Accessibility_____

Freeways_____

Price range of homes_____

Age of subdivision_____

Food stores_____

Convenience stores_____

Neighborhood shopping_____

Shopping malls_____

Notes_____

_____

_____

Fig. 4-1.

One-hundred and twenty hours of driving might not mean much to you, but if you consider the value of your time, it should make you think twice about living too far from work. If you earn $10 per hour, that means you're not making $1,200 each year for every 15 minutes you drive to and from work. If you make $20 per hour, then you're foregoing $2,400 per year.

If that isn't enough, think about the cost you'll incur commuting. If you get on an expressway to drive the 15 minutes, then you'll probably drive 12 miles. That means you'd drive 24 miles per day times 240 days, which equals 5,760 miles each year. Assume that gas, oil, maintenance, and depreciation on your vehicle will run 25 cents per mile, then your cost to drive to and from work each year on a 15-minute trip is $1,440. If you're worth $10 per hour, then each 15 minutes that you drive one way to work is costing you $2,640 per year. If you divide that by 15, you can easily assume that every minute it takes you to get to work will cost you $176 per year. So if your dream is to live out in the country in your own little estate, but you must drive an hour to work, then that little estate will cost you an additional $10,560 each year you own it and work at your present job.

Proximity to work can be put another way. If it costs $176 per year for every minute you are farther from work, then if you divide $176 by 12 months, you'll spend $14.67 per month for each minute you drive. Normally, $14.67 will cover the payment on $1,000 worth of mortgage. So if you can afford a $150,000 home within walking distance to your office, then don't pay more than $90,000 for your little estate out in the country, 60 minutes away from work.

Schools

If you don't have children, or won't have children in the future then you might want to skip this portion on schools. Otherwise, it's a good idea to check out the school systems in the areas that interest you. In addition to the quality of the schools, proximity of your home to schools can be almost as important as proximity to work. If you have three children, one in grade school, one in junior high, and the other starting high school, and if you're not within walking distance, unless there's bus service for all three, you'll have a tough job as a taxi driver each morning and afternoon.

Traffic

Some areas of town are blessed with relatively calm traffic. Other areas might be between large housing developments and business or shopping districts. In the evenings and during weekends, these areas might seem quiet, but during morning and afternoon rush hours during the week, they might be a disaster.

Subdivisions that are close to work and shopping, and have narrow, winding streets can be unusually quiet, especially if main thoroughfares or expressways go around them. Nobody wants to drive from one part of town to another through narrow, winding streets. That's too frustrating. But it's great for the residents.

Crime

The amount of crime in an area can be very important. For information on crime, go to the local police station and ask about crime in areas that interest you. Most of the time you'll get a straight answer. You'll find out if there's a strong drug problem in a certain neighborhood or at certain schools. There are neighborhoods and schools that are much more prone to crime than others. Many people don't think much about the impact of crime, but even minor crimes against you or your home could make a drastic difference in your happiness and well being.

FINDING DESIRABLE SUBDIVISIONS

A desirable subdivision does not need to be a rich subdivision with large, expensive homes. I've seen desirable subdivisions with homes in the price range of $30,000 on up. No matter what price range the homes are, there are certain attributes that set a good subdivision apart from a mediocre or bad one. The most obvious sign is the appearance of the yards and the exterior of the homes. During the warm months, the yards should be watered, the grass and shrubbery neatly trimmed, and the lawns should be free of vehicles and other clutter. The homes should be neatly painted and the roofs in good condition. There shouldn't be loose boards, broken windows, broken doors, or failing garage doors. If the majority of the neighborhood has poorly maintained yards and homes, then you either have a subdivision of owners who don't care about their homes, or a majority of the people in the neighborhood are tenants. Renters tend to do less yard maintenance. Many landlords don't care about their property. Stay away from this type of subdivision.

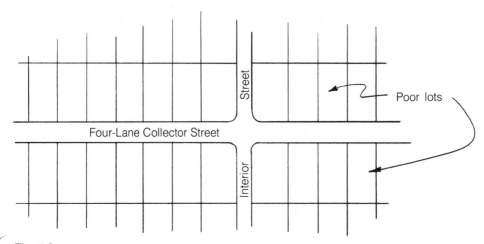

Fig. 4-2.

Some subdivisions don't have enough parking space. If the streets are narrow, then you'll find a parking jam just about any time of the evening, weekends, or a holiday. If you drive by during a working day, you might not notice it. Always look at a subdivision during the evening, weekend, or on holidays.

Pleasant subdivisions do not have busy streets (collector streets) running directly through them, as shown in Fig. 4-2. A dead-end subdivision, such as the one shown in Fig. 4-3, is best. All of the traffic from other areas goes around the subdivision.

The Best Subdivision Lots

The best lots in a subdivision are the farthest ones from the entrance of the subdivision, the ones closest to parks, and the ones on a cul-de-sac or other dead-

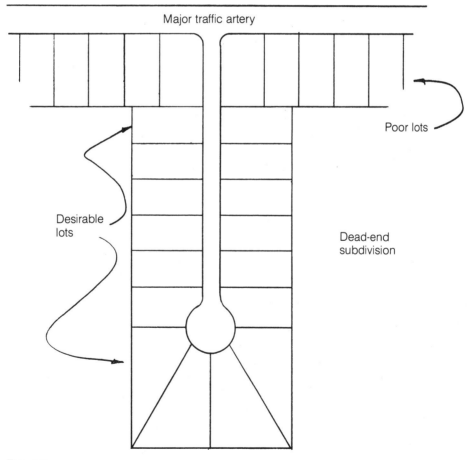

Fig. 4-3.

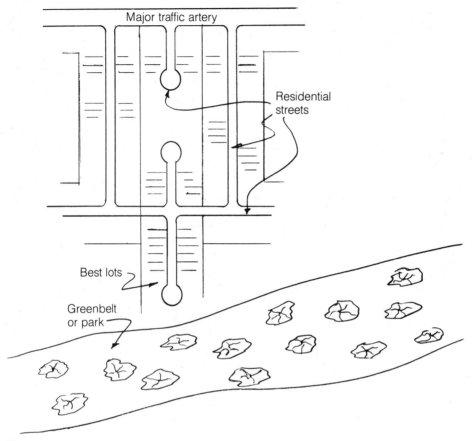

Fig. 4-4.

end street. If you have children, the most desirable lots are the ones closest to schools, to green areas, or other recreation. See Fig. 4-4.

Country Subdivisions

Many Americans dream of a home in the "country." The country to a condominium dweller in Chicago might be quite different from what it means to the owner of a townhouse in Phoenix, however. One person might think a country home is a large lot, perhaps half an acre, out in the suburbs. Another person might imagine 10 acres five miles away from the nearest housing subdivision.

Both are right. We all perceive the world through minds made up of many different backgrounds. A home in the country can be in a subdivision with somewhat large lots, complete with concrete streets, storm sewers, all utilities, and police and fire protection. It can also mean a subdivision with very large lots—two to ten acres—with gravel roads, rural electricity, private water wells, and septic systems, and little or no police and fire protection.

There are extremes to everything. Think seriously before you let the great American dream of living in the country mesmerize you into the type of country living that is far removed from civilization, has many hardships, and few modern conveniences. Too many people have made that mistake. If you move 20 or 30 miles away from a medium-sized city you can often pick up an acre or two on a gravel or dirt road for a song. The local rural electric co-op will bring you electric power. You can dig your own water well and septic system, buy a used mobile home, and presto, you have your place out in the country. Don't do it. The disadvantages can be many. If yours is the first or second mobile home, it will all seem so much like the country. But after several dozen homes have been placed, you'll find yourself the owner of a future country slum. Property values won't escalate appreciably, and you'll be stuck with all the inconveniences of remote living.

If you have the money to buy a country lot in a well developed subdivision, with plenty of deed restrictions to protect the residents from adverse construction, and if you have the money to build a well-designed and executed home, and if you're not too far from work and play, and if you have all the conveniences and safety services you can have in the city, then the country life is for you. Otherwise, do your best with housing in town.

LARGE CITIES AND GENTRIFICATION MOVEMENTS

One of the prominent handicaps that most American cities have suffered is the vast difference in the race and language of their populations. People of different backgrounds, of different races and religions, of different economic conditions, think, live, and act distinctly. Although there are desirable neighborhoods composed of people of diverse backgrounds, most are composed almost entirely of people of the same race or religious affiliation. What can so often happen in this type of neighborhood is that when an influx of people of a different race or religion begin to move in, jaundiced homeowners will begin to sell.

The worst case is when people of a lower economic level begin to move into a neighborhood above their level. Property values can plummet, the condition of properties can deteriorate rapidly, and unhealthy elements of society—drug addicts and dealers for example—can move in and ruin what was once a pleasant area.

Some areas take a long time to deteriorate while others deteriorate quickly. Some might change for the better. The ones you have to be apprehensive about are the ones that are going down. If you talk to neighbors, the police, local merchants, you can avoid buying in a neighborhood where property values are plummeting.

As populations overrun city limits, complex problems can arise that can't always be solved effectively by the city government. Outlying areas and adjoining smaller cities resist annexation or consolidation. How serious are these problems? New York's metropolitan area extends into three states; Dallas', all the way to Fort Worth, including several counties; and Chicago's covers two states. In larger metropolitan areas of the country, nucleus cities have been declining in population while nearby suburbs are increasing, sometimes dramatically.

This spectacular movement to the suburbs is caused by the aging and obsolescence of housing in the nearby areas of the nucleus cities, the slow decay of old residential neighborhoods, and the ease afforded by public transportation, and especially, the automobile. Improved highways and automobiles allow people to live miles away from work in the central cities. The result is the spread of blight, slums, crime, drugs, and other major problems in the central cities.

How does all this affect you as a buyer? The answer is twofold. On the one hand, if you live in a large city, you probably will want to live close to work. In this case, you might not have many choices for decent housing that is close to work and still leaves some space between you and your neighbor. You might have to lower your privacy and space standards to find housing you can afford. On the other hand, you could drive or ride 60 minutes one way to work—not much of a choice.

In a big metropolitan area, your most prudent decision might be to buy a townhouse, condo, or co-op. If you really need to get away from it all during weekends and holidays, there are plenty of places you can drive or fly to out in the country. If you do something constructive with the time you save commuting, you might make enough money to purchase a *nice* place in the country where you can escape, or retire to later in life.

New Subdivisions

I was a homebuilder for years, and this question would sometimes be posed to me: "How do I know your subdivision will turn out to be a nice neighborhood?" The question came up often enough to bother me. In my mind, there was no way my subdivision would have anything but the best homes, the best owners, and the nicest look. As I looked around different areas of the country, and as I got into the resale of existing housing, however, I realized that this was a very valid consideration.

I've seen many subdivisions that held great promise when they were first started, but which deteriorated considerably by the time they were built out. I've seen this happen in expensive as well as inexpensive developments.

When buying a new home, you never know what type of people will move in, whether the original developer will go bankrupt and sell out to one with less stringent requirements for his builders, or whether all the homes will be built to the same standards or of the same size.

In an area that is building out very rapidly, this might not be a problem. Some subdivisions in California have sold out on opening day. There's not much chance the developer will go broke with such heated demand. If a subdivision is begun at the beginning of a housing slump or at the beginning of a major economic downturn, however, then you're better off to forego buying new.

The biggest problems with new subdivisions can be found in the more modest subdivisions that are constructed by small and underfinanced developers and builders. Your best bet when buying a new home is to purchase after many of the homes have been completed, and you can get a thorough idea of what the completed development will be like at the end of construction.

5

Understanding Basic House Design

HOUSE DESIGN AND MATERIAL SELECTION FOR HOME BUILDING CAN EASILY TAKE several books to describe thoroughly. One chapter can't do complete justice to these subjects. But understanding the fundamentals can make your life much easier once you're living in your newly acquired home, whether it's new or old.

One of the unfortunate aspects of American home building is that a large proportion of housing has been, and is designed by, individuals who either have no real insight into what is a truly functional dwelling, or by those who are influenced mostly by profit motives.

In smaller communities, many homes are built by individuals who have not had proper training in house design. A good many of these designer-builders are carpenters who decided they could make a lot more money by acting as general contractors. Many found they could, and many others have gone out of business for lack of good business sense.

I've also seen electricians, plumbers, insurance adjustors, lawyers, and countless other tradesmen and professionals get into home building. Some were wise enough to seek help in their designs, purchasing plans from architects and professional house designers. Others built homes from a rough sketch on a piece of notebook paper. I knew one fellow who sold houses that way. He'd sketch a home as he sat with his buyers, then he'd give them a square foot cost. They'd sign a simple contract, and he'd build the house. About three years after he went into business he went bankrupt.

Inadequate Designs

Years ago, during the height of my home building career, my wife and I were looking at the competition's model homes. We were looking at a two-story, single family unit in Des Moines, Iowa. It was really a pleasant plan. But when we got to the utility room, adjacent to the kitchen, I couldn't believe my eyes. The builder had used a standard bathroom door (24″ wide) for the entrance to the utility room. I placed my feet across the doorway, measuring with my nearly-foot-long shoes, and found that they wouldn't fit in at the doorstop trim. It meant that normal appliances would not fit through the doorway. I laughed then, but I see no humor in it now. Obvious design mistakes like this are too often seen in housing.

A home is generally a person's or a family's most important, and most expensive, possession. There is relatively little control of who designs and builds houses in most places of the country. Can you imagine having a hand operation performed by a lawyer? How about having an obstetrician repair the fuel injection system on your airplane engine? Or your licensed plumber defending you in a civil lawsuit? All of these areas of human endeavor are strictly controlled by laws, but home building is not. The one redeeming value of our system is that the structure itself must be inspected by relatively knowledgeable individuals at city hall. Still, most inspectors don't bother too much with the design aspects of the dwelling.

A depressing number of moderately priced homes have inadequate kitchens, bathrooms, and storage spaces. The layouts of some of these dwellings are abominable. As the price of the house goes up, the situation gets better, but it is amazing how many higher-priced homes still don't have truly functional kitchens, bathrooms, and closets. Many people buy homes like some buy sports cars, not for the practicality of design, but for the pizazz, for the statement it can make to friends and neighbors. Only when dealing with relatively expensive homes does the situation change, because the sophisticated buyer requires that his design be produced by a true professional. That is, a professional home designer or an architect who *specializes* in residential design.

Some modern, large home builders are doing an outstanding job of producing moderately priced housing that incorporates good kitchen, bathroom, and storage design, along with fine room layouts. Unfortunately, those builders are in the minority.

So, are there any homes that are really well designed? Of course there are. I'd say 50 percent of the nation's dwellings boast outstanding designs, the rest go from mediocre to downright worthless. Many custom-built homes, that is, homes of any price range that are built for individuals to meet their demands, have generous kitchens, bathrooms, and closets as well as good room layouts, because the owners demanded them from their designers and builders. There have also been some good plans that have been copied time and again.

Perhaps the biggest stumbling block to good design is money. Those who can't afford good designers are forced to make do with whomever claims to be able to design and build a home. Those who can't afford the best layouts will accept what's available. And, of course, ignorance is a great stumbling block. If you don't know what's best, then anything will do.

WHAT MAKES A GOOD DESIGN

Whether you're planning to have a house built or are looking for an existing dwelling, if you understand good, practical design, you'll be able to insist on the best your money can buy. Before we go into specific design ideas, let's look at ideas on the age of a dwelling.

Age of Structure

Unless a home has been extensively updated during the last few years, be very wary of purchasing an older home. It is very expensive to update, repair, and recondition an old house. Even if you're nostalgically wanting to tackle your own project every time you watch *This Old House* on Public Television, think long and hard before you plunge into that type of project. Do you have the time, the ability, the tenacity, the tools, or the money to carry it through to completion? I've seen a lot of people start and not finish. I've seen much fewer start and finish.

Many older homes have a lot of charm and large, mature shrubs and trees. They can even have plenty of inside floor space and huge outside porches. But most of these older homes also have outmoded designs, small and inefficient kitchens, minuscule bathrooms, old plumbing systems, inadequate electrical systems, uncomfortable heating and cooling systems, layers and layers of old paint, even unhealthy leaded paint, warped floors and walls, shifted foundations, leaky roofs, drafty windows and doors, and maybe, even no insulation. I could make this list last many more paragraphs, but you get the picture.

If this isn't enough to convince you to stay away from very old housing, then think of this example. Just imagine the Los Angeles police department deciding that it would be cost efficient and nostalgic to use 1939 Fords for their squad cars. Of course, they'd have to install larger motors, better transmissions, larger tires, better batteries, air conditioning, seat belts, emission control systems, and they'd probably have to do a bit of patching on some of the rusted panels. Hard to imagine, isn't it? This analogy fits the dream of owning a home that was built in 1948 or 1935 well.

Exteriors

Frank Lloyd Wright stated that, "Form follows function." What he meant by that was, if a great design resulted in an ugly house, so be it. It was better to have the functional, ugly house, than a pretty but unworkable plan.

A good designer can do justice to form and function. It's not impossible to make slight changes to the floor plan to come up with a pleasing exterior. If you're trying to imitate a beautiful colonial home in a smaller scale, then scale everything down so that everything is correctly proportioned.

Shutters are constantly depicted wrong on less expensive homes by less experienced designers. Remember, in the old days most windows had two shutters, one on either side. When you close them, they *must* close the window completely.

In some parts of the country, brick is used extensively. In others, it is so expensive that builders will simply splash a little on the front to make the house look more expensive. If done right, it can look good. Just a dab to call the house a brick home, however, just doesn't look right. The best way to use brick where it'll only be used partially is to do the front and "wrap" it around the sides one or two feet beyond the front.

Traditional designs should emulate the originals as close as possible to be "right." Very contemporary designs, on the other hand, can be just about anything that pleases you.

Square Footage

As I've mentioned before, square footage is measured by multiplying the length times the width of the exterior walls. A knowledgeable designer can make a room or an entire house seem larger by the way he places the openings to a room, and by the volume in the room. For example, a rectangular bedroom will look larger if you come in facing the smaller dimension of the room rather than looking at the long end, as shown in Fig. 5-1.

Any room will look larger if the doors or entryways are placed like this. Provided the room doesn't have too many doors breaking up the wall space, the following are some absolute minimum dimensions for different types of rooms.

- A bedroom smaller than $8' \times 10'$ is not a bedroom, but a fancy closet (see Fig. 5-2).

- A master bedroom needs to be at least $11' \times 14'$ to comfortably take a king-size set of furniture (see Fig. 5-3).

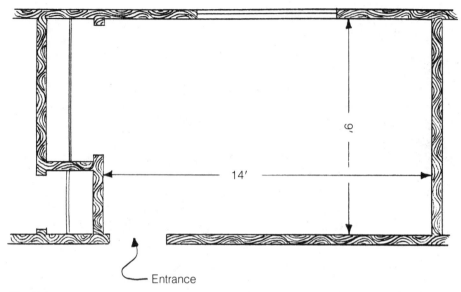

14'

9'

Entrance

Fig. 5-1.

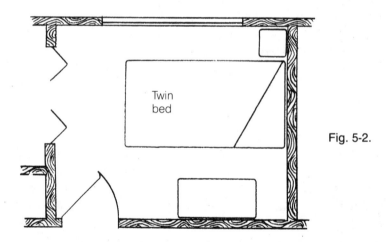

Twin
bed

Fig. 5-2.

- A living room should be at least 11' × 14', otherwise you can't get a complete set of living room furniture in it, and you might as well only consider it a small den. See Fig. 5-4.

- The minimum dimension for a dining room is 10' × 10'. Anything smaller is just a small breakfast area. See Fig. 5-5.

- The smallest dimension in a kitchen should be 8' if there will be cabinets on both sides of the 8' dimension. See Fig. 5-6.

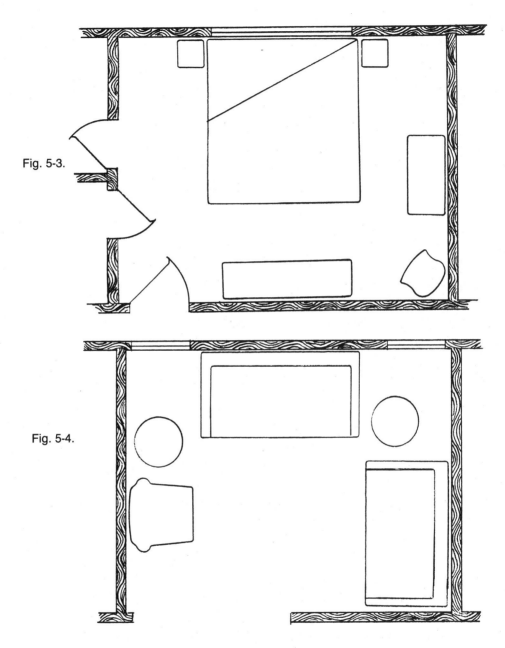

Fig. 5-3.

Fig. 5-4.

- Kitchen cabinets must have 4' between the front of a cabinet and any wall or other obstruction. If you like island kitchens, then to do it right, you must have a very large room, as shown in Fig. 5-7.

- The smallest full-sized bath should not be less than 5' × 7'. This leaves

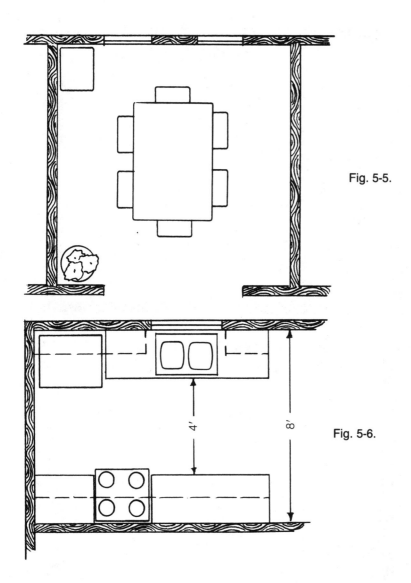

Fig. 5-5.

Fig. 5-6.

enough space for a $5' \times 2^1/2'$ standard size tub, and a minimum of $2^1/2'$ for the stool, and $2'$ for a minimum sized vanity. See Fig. 5-8.

- The narrowest width of an entry hall should not be less than $4'$. See Fig. 5-9.

- The narrowest width of an interior hallway should not be less than $3'$. But if you add just $4''$, you can increase the spacious look and feel of the hallway tremendously. See Fig. 5-10.

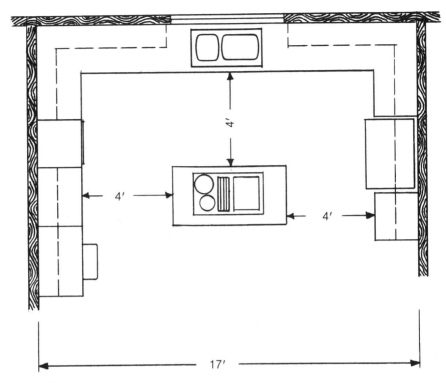

Fig. 5-7.

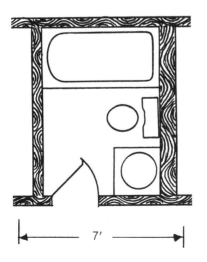

Fig. 5-8.

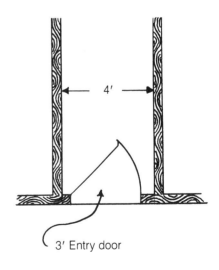

3' Entry door

Fig. 5-9.

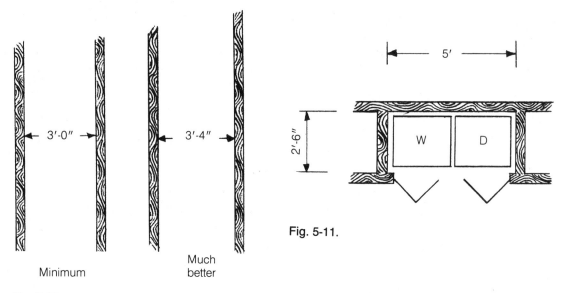

Minimum

Much better

Fig. 5-10.

Fig. 5-11.

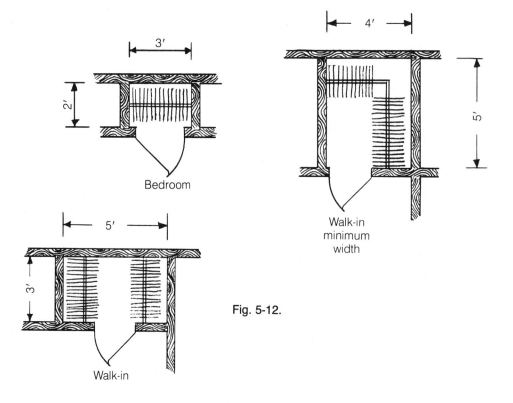

Bedroom

Walk-in

Walk-in minimum width

Fig. 5-12.

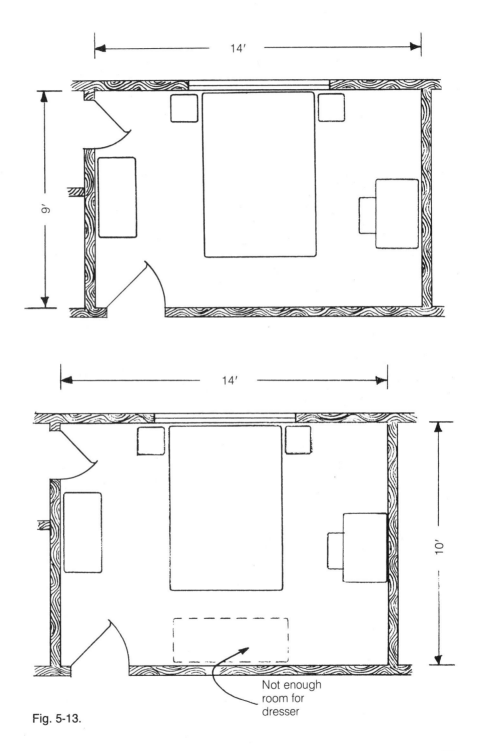

Not enough
room for
dresser

Fig. 5-13.

- The smallest size for a utility room is $5' \times 2^1/2'$, with a full door at the 5' dimension, preferably a set of bi-fold doors that fold completely out of the way. See Fig. 5-11.

- The dimensions shown in Fig. 5-12 are minimum sizes for different types of closets.

If you simply add 12″ to the dimension of some rooms, you'll increase their usefulness tremendously. There are some rooms, however, that aren't helped with a slight increase. For example, a $10' \times 14'$ bedroom is not any better than a $9' \times 14'$ bedroom, as can be seen in Fig. 5-13. In this case, save the 12″ for another area that might benefit by the extra space.

On the other hand, 12″ added to the 10×14 bedroom makes all the difference in the world, because, as illustrated in Fig. 5-3, furniture can now be placed on both walls of the 11' dimension.

Volume

Volume is important to large rooms. A $15' \times 18'$ room can look balanced with a standard height ceiling, but a $20' \times 30'$ room needs at least an additional 12″ of height. A $30' \times 40'$ room needs at least 24″ more. Only in large rooms do you actually need more volume through ceiling height. See Fig. 5-14.

Modern builders realize a house doesn't need to be made large to make it feel big. All that is needed is volume. The standard height of a ceiling in a home

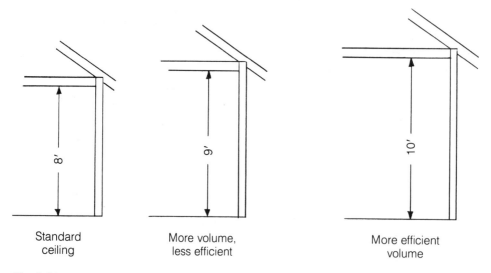

Standard
ceiling

More volume,
less efficient

More efficient
volume

Fig. 5-14.

is 8'. If the ceiling is raised to 9', it gives the home a more spacious feel without the addition of costly square footage. There is one problem, though. The studs have to be cut to 9' from 2 × 4s 18' long, because most lumber comes in even lengths. The logical step would be to go to 2 × 4s 10' long. The cost is increased somewhat when standard 8' walls are not used, because most lumber, as well as most siding and trim, is designed and manufactured to work with 8' walls. Still, it's cheaper to make the house feel bigger than to actually make it larger in square feet.

To give the feeling of size with volume without resorting to taller walls can be done more economically by leaving out attic spaces when the attic isn't being used to run ductwork or other mechanical work as shown in Fig. 5-15. I've seen some modern designs that did a wonderful job of expanding the house with vaulted ceilings in all of the major rooms of the house.

In Iowa, some of the homes I built were not "stick-built" from plans, but produced in a factory and erected in wall, ceiling, and roof sections. We had a plan that was 24' × 42' (1008 square feet). All of the rooms had vaulted ceilings except the bathroom and central hallway, where the heating/cooling unit resided (see Fig. 5-16). It was a great seller, because it felt like a 1300 s.f. home.

Don't be fooled by volume. A 2,000 s.f. home with vaulted ceilings can feel like 2,500 s.f, and the builder or smart home owner might charge close to the

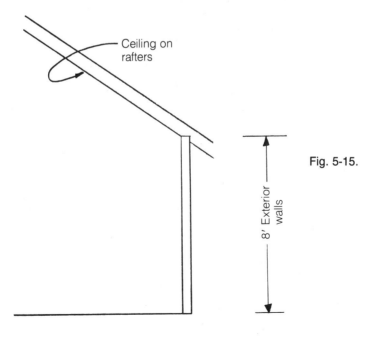

Ceiling on rafters

8' Exterior walls

Fig. 5-15.

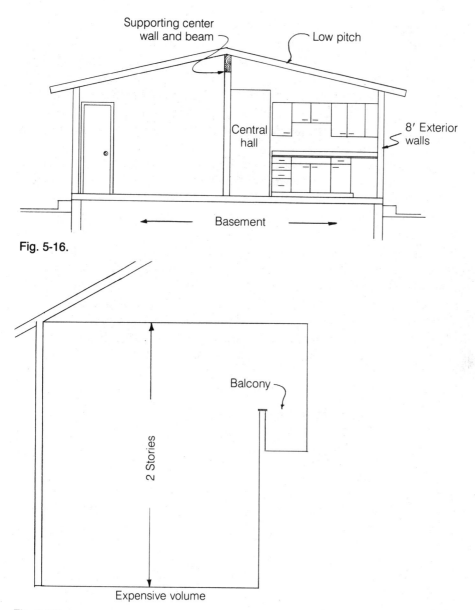

Fig. 5-16.

Fig. 5-17.

same price as a 2,500 s.f. home. It's smart merchandising on the part of the seller. The cost to build volume is considerably less than the cost to add square footage, with only one exception. If you build a room that's two stories high, as shown in Fig. 5-17, then you'll only save the cost of the floor that could double the actual size of the room.

Dimensions

As I explained earlier, in the case of the narrow door leading to the utility room, dimensions can be vital, and if you look at the dimensions of the many items in the house you're considering, you'll find out if the builder or designer was conscientious and talented, or if he was simply a cost-cutter.

Doors. Most doors are 6'-8" high. The minimum width for different rooms can be seen in Fig. 5-18. These are minimum sizes. For much more comfort, the walk-in closet door and bath door should be 2'-4", doors to bedrooms and living areas should be 2'-8", the rear door should be 3'-0", and the front door 3'-6". A 2' deep closet should always have a door that opens all the way across the closet, otherwise you'll have clothes that are hard to get to (see Fig. 5-19).

Windows. Every functional room should have a window. There are very few people who like dark houses, so the more windows a house has, the better.

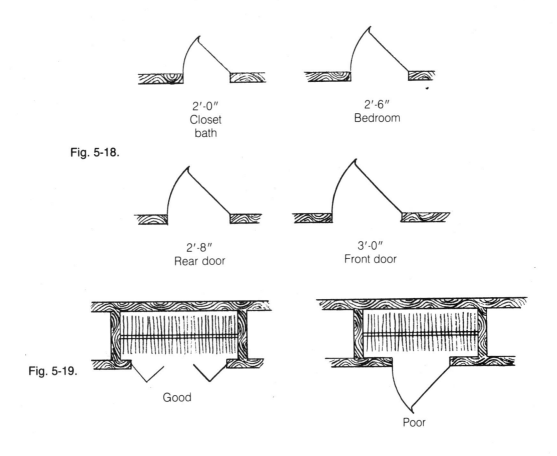

2'-0"
Closet
bath

2'-6"
Bedroom

Fig. 5-18.

2'-8"
Rear door

3'-0"
Front door

Fig. 5-19.

Good

Poor

Windows are expensive, so the more windows, the more you'll pay. The bottom of a window should be no more than 4' off the floor for safety and aesthetic reasons. There are some older houses that have long, narrow windows in the bedrooms, the bottom of which is 5' off the floor. You can't see much out of them, and in case of a fire, a child would have a hard time getting out.

Stairways. A stairway should not be less than 36" wide, the rise from one tread to another is most comfortable between 7" and 8". There are stairways built with tread rise over 9", but they are less comfortable and more dangerous. The most important dimension on a stairway is the depth of the tread. Most male adults have a foot that's about 12" long with a shoe on. If the tread is much smaller than the 12" needed to accommodate the entire foot, then there is danger of falling when coming *down* the stairs (see Fig. 5-20). A drastic example is when a person tries to come down a ladder facing forward. I've seen many stairways with 9" deep tread, and some even down to 8". The illustration below shows the danger. One slip of the foot and down you go.

Another important point concerning a stairway is the way a turn is designed. Figure 5-21 shows a dangerous and a safe example of a turn. A turn with too many steps makes the tread too narrow at the inside of the turn.

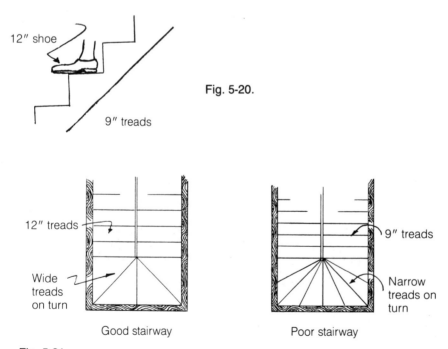

12" shoe

9" treads

Fig. 5-20.

12" treads

Wide treads on turn

Good stairway

9" treads

Narrow treads on turn

Poor stairway

Fig. 5-21.

Kitchen Cabinets. As you've guessed earlier in the chapter, kitchens are one of my pet peeves, not only in many older houses, but in so many of the moderately priced, and even not-so-moderately priced modern homes. First, I think many kitchens don't have enough cabinets. Second, many cabinets are poorly designed or very cheaply constructed. I'll give you a few ideas below that will show you what to look for in existing and new homes.

- **Bottom Cabinets.** Most bottom cabinets are constructed 24″ deep and 36″ high. It's hard to store a quantity of items in a 24″ deep space. You have to dig for the items at the back. The most practical way to deal with bottom cabinets is to bring the items at the back forward when you need them, which can easily be done with drawers. There are two types of drawers. There are standard drawers that you simply slide out from the front of the cabinet and hidden drawers, which have a cabinet door covering them. The most practical drawer is the exposed one. It doesn't make much sense to have to open a door, then pull out drawers. The more drawers a kitchen has, the more expensive it is, and usually the better it functions.

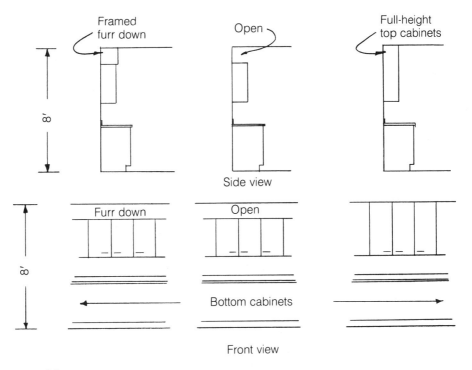

Fig. 5-22.

- **Top Cabinets.** Top cabinets are about 12″ deep and anywhere from 12″ to 48″ high. A well-designed kitchen either leaves the top of the cabinet to the ceiling open, or better yet, makes full use of a cabinet that extends all the way to ceiling. Figure 5-22 shows three common layouts. The first is the normal layout, with a ''furr down'' on top of the cabinet. The second shows a space between the top of the cabinet and the ceiling. The final one shows the best and most expensive: a tall cabinet. Adjustable shelves in kitchen cabinets are extremely useful both at upper and lower cabinets.

Baseboards and Trim. The narrower the baseboard and trim at doors and other areas, the cheaper it was to build. Some of the old, well-built homes had massive trim boards, inside and outside. I've seen cheap baseboards and door trim narrower than 2″ (see Fig. 5-23). In my opinion, if the builder cut corners on trim boards, he must have done so on structural and mechanical systems as well.

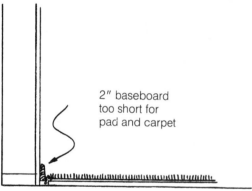

2″ baseboard too short for pad and carpet

Fig. 5-23.

GETTING THE MOST LIVING AREA FOR YOUR DOLLAR

The most inexpensive house to build is one that has 8′ ceilings throughout the house, as shown in Figure 5-14. Another method of building is placing the sheetrock directly on the rafters. It's not much more expensive, because the cost of the ceiling joists is eliminated. This makes up for most of the additional cost of the extra rafters and sheetrock needed for a vaulted ceiling, such as the one shown in Fig. 5-16.

Remember, you can only tell how many square feet you're getting by measuring the house, and not by how it feels. Raised and vaulted ceilings will always fool you into thinking you're in a much bigger house.

Square footage in a house is the least expensive amenity, if you can call it an amenity. When it comes to square footage in closets, I would call it a necessity. Moderately-priced houses are notoriously short on storage space.

The reason square footage is a bargain can be seen from the following example. Let's assume you buy a house that's worth $150,000. The house has 2,400 square feet. Simple arithmetic suggests that the house is worth $75.00 per square foot, or $75/s.f. But let's see what plain raw square footage is worth, and why, if you were building this house, you should be able to add square footage for much less than $75/s.f.

If the lot is worth 20 percent of the value, then we can take $30,000 off the cost, to give us $120,000 for the structure. Now assume that the driveway, sidewalks, landscaping, garage, water lines, sewer lines, and gas lines cost another $20,000. Now we're down to $100,000 for the structure. Finally, we can delete the cost of the kitchen and the bathrooms (cabinets, fixtures, appliances, rough and finish plumbing). That should be somewhere around $10,000. Now our cost for the structure is down to just $90,000 for 2,400 s.f. Notice that I've left everything else in the cost, because an increase in square footage will raise the cost of the electrical, heating, cooling, paint, carpet, etc.

Now the value of each square foot added to the house as raw square footage is only $37.50/s.f. Therefore, adding 500 square feet to this house would be a real bargain at $18,750. Or look at it another way. The builder could add two generous 5' × 8' walk-in closets, a total of only 80 s.f., and increase the present cost only $3,000. Unfortunately, after this house is built, you won't be able to get a remodeler to come out and add two closets to your house for $3,000— $10,000 to $15,000 would probably be more like it.

Houses with space in the attic that can be finished off, or that has been finished off, can give real value for the cost per square foot. A basement is also an ideal and much-used space for adding living area to a house. Sadly, I've seen too many wet basements to be thoroughly enthused about adding living space below. A basement might go for years without leaking, then one year of monsoon rains it floods.

You can't compare the cost of a 2,000 s.f. house with no finished basement or attic with one that's the same square footage that has a finished basement or attic. Rather, you must compare the cost of that 2,000 s.f. house with one that has 2,500 s.f. to include a finished basement or attic. The best value is probably going to be the 2,500 s.f. one.

THE BEST FEATURES IN A HOME

Look for a home that has well-designed areas. Dead-end rooms rooms that have only one entry are the best. They afford the best use of space because there's much more useable wall space, and you don't have a hallway effect through part of the room. Figure 5-24 shows a good example of poor use of space and good use of space.

Pass up a house that has few or tiny closets. If you're young and single, or newly married, you might not have many belongings. Just give yourself a couple of years, however, and you'll long for ample storage space.

The kitchen should have plenty of cabinets and counter space. It doesn't have to be large. In fact, kitchens that ramble are not necessarily the most efficient. You can walk your feet off if the range-sink-refrigerator triangle is too large.

Corners can be a waste of cabinet space unless you have lazy susans at the corners. A lazy susan is an excellent storage vehicle, because it holds a multitude of items and has adjustable shelves that rotate.

The kitchen should have a generous pantry. A pantry is actually a walk in

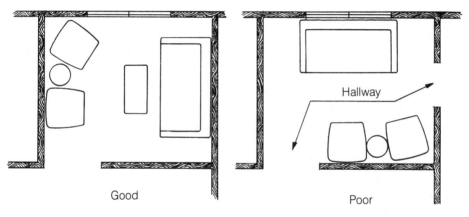

Good   Hallway   Poor

Fig. 5-24.

closet with shelves on the sides and at the end. Next to a walk-in pantry, a large, flat pantry is best, because everything is right in front as you open the doors. This type of pantry is usually 4' to 6' wide and 7' or 8' high, with shelves only 6" to 8" deep. Another great pantry is one with a lazy susan. These are usually 24" × 24" × 7' high.

Bathrooms should also have plenty of storage space. Even small baths can have a cabinet above the commode for towel, paper, and toiletries storage. Larger baths can have linen closets. The ideal is a walk-in linen closet with shelves similar to the pantry described above. Regular clothes closets inside a bathroom are common in larger homes, so it's particularly pleasing to have a closet(s) in the bathrooms of a smaller home.

Exterior storage space is an often overlooked necessity for most people. If a home has a garage, many times it won't hold the cars as was intended because there are too many other items—lawnmowers, patio equipment, tools, boxes—taking up space. Outside storage makes a lot of sense, and more often than not, the selling price of a house won't reflect the value of outside storage in existing dwellings.

Garages are substantially better than a carport, and are usually not much more expensive. If you're considering buying a house with a carport, it is safe to say you can deduct substantially from the price for the lack of a garage.

PROBLEM ELEMENTS

There are certain materials and system designs that can be problematic or expensive to maintain, and you need to be aware of some of these.

Roofs

Flat roofs, gravel roofs, and wood roofs can be a problem—in that order. Flat roofs, I can almost guarantee, will leak. Look at any commercial building with a flat roof, and most likely it will have stains inside on the ceiling from past leaks. Most flat roofs have a gravel roof. There are some older houses that have a very low pitch on the roof, and are built with the same gravel materials as found on a flat roof. Because they have a pitch, they are a bit better than the flat roofs, but they're still a problem after they've weathered a few years. Wood roofs are expensive to install and replace. The shingles tend to warp after a few years, and even the fire resistant ones are a real fire danger.

Sidings

Wood sidings that do not come in plywood form are tough to maintain. Even with the best finishes, they can warp, split, and refuse to hold paint for any length of time. Pressboard sidings are a little better, but they quickly go to pieces if they're not repainted often enough. The best siding is vinyl, and the best wood siding is a plywood siding.

Eaves

Homes with very little or no overhang—the section of roof that comes beyond the exterior wall line—can pose a water problem at the tops of windows and doors. If the flashing or caulking at the top of the openings is not installed correctly, the overhangs can be of great help. Without them, faulty openings generally leak first at the top.

Flood Areas

Be absolutely certain that the house you're contemplating is not in a flood area. Some houses are in designated flood plains, but others are in marginal areas. Do some research if you suspect, or if you hear from neighbors, that there are water problems in the neighborhood. If your house is in a flood plain and you must purchase flood insurance, you're better off to pass on that property. Nothing will ruin your day worse than to have to swim away from your home as you watch your belongings float along with you. I've seen it happen, and no amount of insurance will make up for your pain and suffering, assuming you don't drown in the process.

Heating

All electric homes should have a heat pump for heating except in the very coldest parts of the country. The heat pump is a drastically more efficient heating apparatus than the strip heating that makes an electric furnace work. A heat pump is basically an air conditioner that runs backwards in the winter.

Electrical

There was a time a few years ago when there was a rage over aluminum wiring. It has major drawbacks, and you're better off to stay away from properties wired with aluminum wiring. Aluminum wiring has caused fires, and even if you never experience anything that severe, there can be failures in switches, light fixtures, and outlets with taxing regularity.

MATERIALS AND EQUIPMENT

There are *palaces*, there are *houses*, and there are *dwellings*. In the somewhat facetious *Dubois Standard Dictionary of Housing Terms*, a *palace* is a work of art, you might say a piece of fine real estate furniture. Everything is constructed by craftsmen using the finest materials. A *house* is what most of us live in. It's comfortable, with reasonably good materials, put together by good workmen. A *dwelling* is a place used to stay out of the rain.

If you're looking for an existing house, or even a palace, then most of the structural materials will be hidden to you. The finish items that are visible, both inside and outside, can give you a dependable clue on how well the structure was built or how well the previous owners took care of it. The rest of this section discusses those items that constitute the best materials for different parts of the finish work in a house.

Roof

The best roofing material is concrete tile and slate. It will last just about forever, and the only thing that can hurt it is hail. Concrete tile comes in either a flat pattern, or it looks like Spanish tile. It is somewhat thicker than real spanish tile, which is made of clay, and it will outlast Spanish tile. Tile and slate are very expensive, and you'll find them mostly in very expensive homes, though there is a small percentage of moderately priced homes with the concrete tile.

Spanish tile, aluminum, and standing-seam metal roofs, especially the copper ones, are close behind in quality and durability. It is rare to see a standing-seam copper roof, even in very expensive homes, because of its cost.

Composition roofs that come in very heavy shingles, and look almost like wood roofs, are next in line. They are excellent in quality and longevity, similar to Spanish tile. They are relatively fireproof and only excessively large hail stones will hurt it. Dollar for dollar, this is the best buy.

Standard composition shingles are last in line. They're practical, inexpensive, and will last 12 to 15 years. Moderately large hail will hurt them, and high winds can sometimes pull a few loose, but for the price, this type of roof is a bargain.

If you're set on wood shingles, then look for one that has hand-split cedar shakes. They're rough in texture, and vary in thickness from shingle to shingle because each one is hand split. Their thickness makes them more stable and durable.

Exterior Wall Finish

Most residential structural construction starts off with a wood stud framework. There is relatively little in the way of poured concrete and concrete block which, if done correctly, is far superior to wood construction. On top of the wood studs is placed a sheathing board that is either a thin, inexpensive aluminum-foil-covered cardboard, asphalt impregnated fiber board, or foam insulating board of varying thicknesses, or best of all, $1/2''$ plywood.

The finest exterior wall covering is brick or stone, although on frame houses, it has no structural value. Wood framing actually keeps the bricks or stones from falling off. Stone is normally the more expensive of the two.

Brick or stone needs to be placed around the entire perimeter of the house, all the way up the walls, including the gables. Otherwise, it does little to save on maintenance, such as painting. A builder can save money by not using brick on certain portions of the exterior, but any siding you can see has to be painted, and can warp, crack, chip, peel, and fall apart unless made of vinyl, aluminum, or steel.

A good stucco finish is next in line. It can be as long lasting and good looking as brick if it is installed correctly. A good stucco finish will have a three-coat process with plenty of metal expansion joints. The stucco is trowelled onto a heavy metal lath (not chicken wire) that is nailed to the exterior walls. A thick, *scratch* coat is put on first. After that sets, a thinner *brown* coat is applied, Finally, a thin *finish* coat with color mixed in completes the process. The three-coat process will keep the stucco from cracking. The scratch and brown coats do the cracking as they set and cure. The finish coat is thin enough not to crack.

The expansion joints are placed in straight vertical lines every 15 to 20 feet and at the ends—top and bottom—of every window and door opening. Because it expands and contracts (stucco is a concrete) and is prone to cracking at the weakest points. Breaking it up with expansion joints allows it to expand and contract at the expansion joints and not in the middle in rough, ugly cracks.

Vinyl, steel, and aluminum finishes, in that order, are next in line. Vinyl has the color all the way through, so if it gets scratched or hit, the color won't come off. It's also flexible, so it can give on impact. Steel and aluminum have a vinyl or paint coating, but steel is a better base because it isn't quite as flexible. It won't readily dent, but if hit hard with a baseball or other object there will be a dent.

Even if a house is made entirely of brick or stucco, the eaves are still a problem if they are covered with wood or fiberboard. The best solution is to use vinyl or aluminum for the soffit, the bottom part of the eaves, and the fascia. Then there's no painting at all to contend with.

The best wood siding is made of $1/2''$, $5/8''$ or $3/4''$ plywood. It is the most stable of the wood sidings and tends to hold stain and paint better. Sidings that come in horizontal or vertical boards, unless extremely well cared for with frequent coats of paint, are prone to cracking and warping.

Fiberboard sidings are the least desirable. They must be painted often or they'll warp and chip away. They also must be kept well caulked at all joints, such as the edges, because if they're not painted they will swell and come apart.

Windows

The best windows are constructed of vinyl-covered wood. They seal tight and keep out the cold or heat. They don't stick and they operate easily. The best of these windows have insulated glass plus a third glass for triple insulating.

Aluminum windows are satisfactory in the warmer climates of the south and west, but if they don't have insulated glass, storm windows should be installed. Single-glazed aluminum windows will leak air, heat, and cold. The older ones are hard to open and close. If you're contemplating a home fitted with these anachronisms, your heating and cooling bills could force you to spend a pretty penny for storm windows later.

Jalousie windows, horizontal pieces of glass that tip up with a crank, are alright for enclosed patios and porches. Stay away from a house that has them for main windows, however, because they leak a lot of air.

Doors

Foam insulated, steel-clad exterior doors are the best for the money. Fancy wood doors, if exposed to the weather, can get nasty looking in only a few months unless they're refinished a couple of times a year. Hollow core exterior doors are a joke. If you're looking at a house with wood exterior doors, rap on each one. If they sound hollow, deduct the price of each hollow core door from the price of the house, because you'll end up replacing them in a very short while.

Aluminum, sliding patio doors are not too bad in the temperate parts of the country. In colder areas they can freeze up and cause heat to escape. Wood patio doors are much better insulators, but they are considerably more expensive. They also have to be refinished often to keep them in good shape.

Atrium and french doors made of wood are sometimes sold as the ultimate in beauty, practicality, and thermal efficiency. While most of that is true, you still must consider them a constant-care item. They need plenty of paint—often. The most practical french doors are steel clad with foam insulation and insulated glass.

Kitchen and Bath Cabinets

The best and sturdiest cabinets are made of 3/4" plywood, with 3/4" plywood shelves and dividers. You can tell the quality of a cabinet by just opening a door and looking at the thickness of the door and shelves. The cheapest cabinets have very thin shelves made of fiberboard, and doors that have a wood frame with a large and very thin insert in the middle. They might look good, but they'll not last long.

The best countertops are made of precast, smooth marblelike substances. In the bathrooms, the sinks are integral with the countertop. In other words, they're poured in the same mould as the top. Of equal quality, and perhaps a bit more expensive, is ceramic tile. It is gorgeous and sturdy, but the grout joints are a real tiger to keep clean. Plastic laminate (Formica) is the least expensive, and almost universally used in kitchens. For the money, it's quite a good bargain.

Sinks and Bathtubs

The best sinks and tubs, aside from the marble units, are made of a cast-iron base with a porcelain finish. The cheaper units are made of steel with a porcelain or plastic finish. The latter will chip easily when something heavy is dropped on top, because the steel will give and allow the finish to come off. You can tell a cast-iron unit from a steel unit by tapping on it. If it sounds very solid, it is cast iron. If it sounds like you're tapping on a barrel, then it's steel.

One-piece fiberglass tubs and showers are not the most aesthetic units. Nothing can beat the look of ceramic tile, but they are supremely practical, and in my opinion, are the units of choice for someone who treasures cleanliness. There is no tile or grout to scrub.

Ceramic Tile

There are two methods for installing ceramic tile. The best method is the one where a stucco base is placed on top of a layer of sheetrock. Once the stucco sets, then the tile can be glued to the stucco and grouted. When the grout cracks, and as sure as the sun comes up in the morning, it will crack, water that gets behind the tile won't affect the stucco.

The cheaper method starts with a "waterproof" layer of sheetrock on top of the layer of sheetrock that covers the studs. This is called the "thinset" method. The tile is then glued onto the waterproof sheetrock and grouted. When the grout eventually cracks, however, water gets behind the tile and the "waterproof" sheetrock proceeds to fall apart from daily soakings. The more showers that are taken each day, the sooner the tile will begin to fall off. You can sometimes tell what type of tile a house has by tapping on the tile. If it sounds hollow, it's thinset. Most of the cheaper homes have thinset tile. If it sounds almost like concrete when you tap on it, then you have the real thing.

Faucets

The best faucets are not necessarily the prettiest. The best faucets usually have only one handle. They don't contain the same internal systems as the cheap units. They'll last a lot longer before they fail to seal properly. The cheap ones are easy to spot. When a valve is turned off, the rubber washer can be felt. The lever can then be forced beyond the point where the pressure of the rubber washer is felt. The better units simply stop when you lower the handle or turn the dial. There's a definite stop.

Carpet

The best carpet has the most fiber. Carpet quality is generally measured by the weight of the fiber that you walk on. Eighteen-ounce carpet is relatively cheap, while 40- and 50-ounce carpet is quite good, although expensive. When you walk on carpet, you can usually feel how heavy the pile of fiber is. Still, you should stoop down and put your hands through it to make sure you're not walking on cheap carpet with a very thick pad. While cheap carpet with a thick pad is infinitely better than cheap carpet with little or no pad, heavy carpet with a moderately thick pad is the best and most expensive.

Hard Flooring

The finest hard flooring is either a ceramic tile, generally Italian tile, or quality, strip-wood flooring. The ceramic tile is easy to maintain and extremely tough, though it can crack. Wood flooring is more difficult to maintain, and it's not very tough. You must be gentle with it.

Parquet wood flooring is a cheap second choice to wood strip flooring, and I believe a good, heavy sheet vinyl is better. A bit better than sheet vinyl is solid vinyl tile, which is made with the color being all the way through. The solid vinyl tile is so good that it'll fool you in its imitation of slate or brick. When I was fresh out of college, I worked for a builder in San Antonio who used quite a bit of "used" brick. He'd buy it from an old fellow who would deliver it, then charge us after he had counted it after it was installed on the exterior walls. He once gave us a bill for several thousand more bricks than we had used on the walls. When we objected, he insisted that he was right, and that maybe we weren't counting the brick we'd used on the floors. He was disappointed to discover that he'd counted a few thousand vinyl tiles.

The cheapest tile is the one that comes in thin squares. Asphalt tile is the cheapest of the two, it's about $1/8''$ thick, and requires the most care. It's great in grocery stores where it's waxed and buffed often, but quite troublesome in the home. The other is known as composition vinyl, formerly vinyl asbestos. It's $1/16''$ thick and a bit easier to care for. It's generally too thin for commercial use, because it will wear out soon under heavy traffic.

Interior Doors

Most modern homes have hollow core doors. They're made of a wood frame with interior cardboard spacers. If you find a home that has solid wood doors, you've either found a very old home, or a very well-built modern one. The better homes have hollow core doors with a wood veneer so they can be stained and varnished. Most hollow core doors are equal in quality. Some will look better than others depending on the veneer, but in a heated and air conditioned environment, they'll all hold up quite well. If you're in a very cold climate and don't use a humidifier, you could experience some problems. Unless the doors are painted or varnished all the way around, including the edges, they can warp considerably when they dry out in the winter.

Mechanical Equipment

The quality of a home generally reflects the quality of the equipment (that is, heating/cooling, electrical, and appliances) the builder or previous owners installed in it. Always check the location of the furnace. If it's placed in a closet next to the living room, you'll have a very noisy time watching your favorite television shows or listening to your stereo. The best furnace location in terms of noise is in the attic. The basement is the next choice. The more expensive units have relatively quiet fans. The cheap ones are terribly noisy.

SEPARATING THE STEAK FROM THE SIZZLE

Many houses have a lot of sizzle but very little steak. You can buy a house like you buy a car. A Cadillac is a fancy Buick, but some Cadillacs are just fancy Chevrolets. If that's your style, then a house with a lot of trim, vaulted ceilings, gold faucets, and wallpaper will appeal to you. They come with a lot of sizzle, and with either a large price tag, or scant few square feet. There are a lot of homes out there with plenty of lean meat, however. They are well built and well designed with few fancy gimmicks such as jaccuzzi tubs, hundred-pound chandeliers, or central vacuum cleaners—a waste of money.

6

Types of Housing

THE AVAILABILITY AND COST OF LAND DETERMINE THE TYPES OF HOUSING builders select to construct and merchandise. I don't remember ever going through a very small town in a rural area that had anything other than single family dwellings. As you get very close to metropolitan areas, however, even the small towns begin to show signs of space-saving designs by using multifamily units.

There are three distinct types of housing. The first is the single family, detached home, which sits on its own lot, separated from other homes. The second are town houses or rowhouses. They are attached to each other, but each unit has its own parcel of land below it and its own portion of air above it. Finally, there is the condominium, which is not only attached to other units horizontally, but vertically as well. Some people may call town houses condominiums, and vice versa, but for ease of explanation, I'll use single family, town house and condominium to explain the differences to you.

SINGLE FAMILY HOMES

Single family detached housing is built on lots of varying sizes with the structure usually centered on the lot, as shown in Fig. 6-1. The advantage of the single

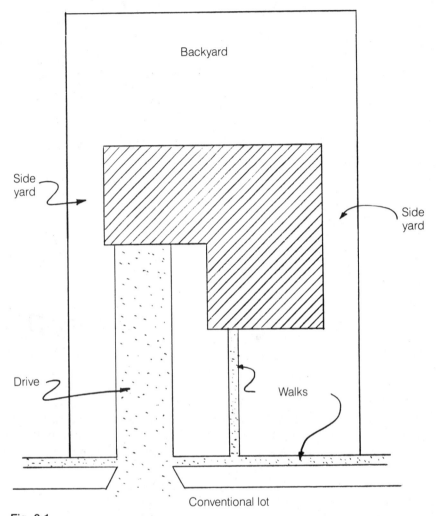

Backyard

Side yard

Side yard

Drive

Walks

Conventional lot

Fig. 6-1.

family home is the complete separation of one house from the other and the availability of yard space, depending on the size of the lot. The big disadvantage is that the larger the lot, the more maintenance involved. I've known folks who spent most of their weekends working on yard maintenance, whether they wanted to or not. Although, people with large yards usually either really like to work on them, or they hire the work out.

Another method of placing homes on separate lots is by using zero lot-line design such as the one shown in Fig. 6-2. If the lots are small, zero lot-line homes are an excellent way for a homeowner to have full use of his yard. In fact,

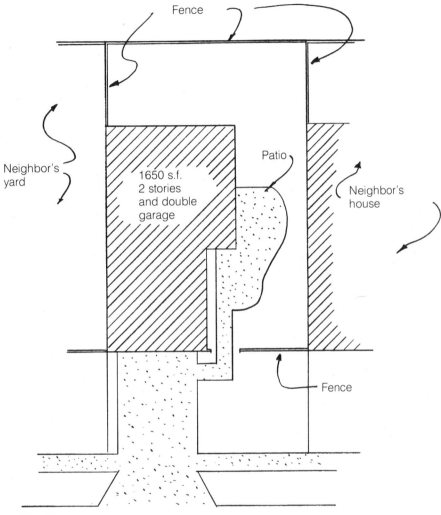

Fence

Neighbor's
yard

1650 s.f.
2 stories
and double
garage

Patio

Neighbor's
house

Fence

Fig. 6-2.

there are zero lot-line homes with small lots that offer homeowners more use-able yard space than many subdivisions with medium-size conventional lot lay-outs. A zero lot-line home can be built on lots platted specifically for that pur-pose, or on ordinary lots.

In zero lot-line subdivisions, the homes are placed with one side of the house exactly on the property line. Thus the homeowner has use of front, side and rear yard. On a standard subdivision, houses can be placed in the center of the lot, but one side of the yard is deeded to the neighboring house as a "recrea-tional easement." This is done all the way down the street, and the side and rear yard fences are placed accordingly to allow each homeowner one generous side yard in addition to the normal front and rear yards. If you think about it, even when there are relatively ample-sized lots, the zero lot line design makes a whole lot of sense. Very few people use their side yards for anything.

The best designs for zero lot-line houses require brick, stone, or stucco on the entire side of the house that faces the neighbor's useable side yard. This reduces the maintenance and entering the neighbor's yard is kept to a bare minimum. Most home builders will also design the house so there are windows and openings to the useable side as well as rear yard so that the side and rear yards flow into one large recreational unit. There are no windows on the neighbor's side yard. Naturally, the yards must be fenced to allow privacy. The zero lot-line concept has all of the advantages of the standard lot development, but with the advantages of better yard use and less waste of land. The only disadvantage, and it's a small one, is that the homeowner must enter his neighbor's yard to maintain that side of his house. This can be minimized by using low-maintenance materials, at least on that wall.

Some home builders developing standard, single family houses on very large lots will use a variation of the zero lot-line concept. Instead of centering the house on the lot, they'll place it as far as possible to the side building line, then design the house with one side yard similar to a zero lot-line house. The homeowners then have a generous side yard that flows into the rear yard. The other side yard is small and unusable. The yards can also be fenced as with the zero lot line designs.

TOWN HOUSES

Town houses are designed in buildings that have two or more units. Some developers will lay out lots in pairs by taking a standard lot, say a $70' \times 120'$ lot, and splitting it into two smaller lots of $35' \times 120$. They then build a duplex designed so that the common wall, also known as a party wall, lies directly at the 35' line that separates the two lots. They call these units *single-family attached* houses. For our purposes, we'll call them town houses, because the only difference between two town houses built in a building of two, and these single-family attached units is that the latter have no homeowners association, whereas the former do. In other words, the single-family attached units are owned, insured, and maintained as individual homes. Each owner cuts the lawn, paints the walls, and fixes the roof to his own side. And therein lies the big disadvantage to single-family attached houses. If you happen to be unlucky enough to buy next to a bum, and that bum lets the weeds take over his yard and doesn't maintain his side of the structure, you've got real problems. Even if you buy next to Mr. Perfection, you never know who he'll sell to in the future.

Builders of true town houses solve that problem by setting up a homeowners association at the start of the development. The association, made up of a governing body elected from the homeowners, either hires a manager, or directly runs the maintenance of an entire group of town houses in a development. You could have an association for each building of two or more units, but that generally is not the case. Usually, the entire development is set up into one association for economy of numbers. The association then takes care of all exterior maintenance and repairs to the buildings and all amenities in the complex, such as pools, tennis courts, clubhouses, etc.

Town houses can be laid out the same way houses are on any street. In other words, one house after another, each one having access to the street through its front yard, and each one having a backyard, usually completely fenced off. Older town houses set up in large buildings were often laid out like single-family attached units. In the older parts of some large cities you'll still find many of these town homes without homeowners associations. But most modern developments incorporate a homeowners association.

In new developments, more often than not, the land is owned by the entire community of town houses, and each individual purchases his unit along with the right to exclusive use of his front and rear yards. This is especially true in developments that have building and lot layouts with unusual twists and turns.

CONDOMINIUMS AND CO-OPS

There is sometimes a fine line between condominiums and co-ops in my definition of town houses and condominiums. Condominium refers to a form of ownership in which there are individually owned units in a multiple-unit project. Unit ownership is a specific cancelling of the common-law doctrine that, ''He who owns the soil owns everything below to the center of the Earth and everything to the heavens.'' You can say that about some town house projects, depending on the way ownership is set up. Some clusters of town houses are built almost like condominiums.

Condominium ownership is often described as horizontal property ownership, or more accurately, a freehold interest in a horizontal piece of vertical air. My definition of a condominium is actually a town house with no separate front yard and backyard for each unit. Normally, a condominium will not only be without yards, but also will either have no sky above it, or no land below it, or both.

A typical, well-defined condominium is in a multistory building among dozens or even hundreds of other units, with no land or sky available to it. It often has a balcony on one end, and always a front door leading out to a hallway on the other end.

There are different forms of condominium ownership. The owner might purchase his unit and have equal ownership of the land, amenities, and hallways with the other owners. Sometimes a nonprofit corporation purchases the building and every stock owner will have a right to the use of one unit depending on how much he paid for his stock. The latter is called a co-operative, or *co-op*. So when someone says he owns a condo, he could be talking about a co-op. With a co-op, each unit has its own price, the buyer purchases that unit, but legally only purchases stock that gives him an exclusive right to his unit.

7

Starting the Search

ONCE YOU'VE DETERMINED WHICH AREAS WILL WORK FOR YOU, YOU MIGHT WANT to start your search by driving around the neighborhoods that interest you. See what's for sale or just see what's happening in those neighborhoods. Some areas might look a bit run-down, and you'll discard the thought of buying there. Other areas might pleasantly surprise you, and you'll concentrate your search for a home there.

Take a look at builder model homes in areas that interest you. You'll meet some good salesmen who'll do their best to sell you. At this point, however, it probably isn't in your best interest to buy until you become very familiar with your market area.

Begin looking in the newspaper classifieds. This can be confusing though. You might find hundreds of ads, some simple with little detail, others very grandiloquently boasting about every detail of the little mansion the owner's selling. No matter, you're looking at advertising: Signs at existing houses, model homes (which are simply live, exciting advertising), and newspaper ads.

SIGNS

Advertising can tell you a lot, not just in what it says, but in how it says it. For example, a very nice real estate broker's sign, well placed and in good repair, can mean the property is being sold by professionals. An old, beat up broker's sign might mean a tired out, careless broker is selling it. If it's an old, beat up, rusted FSBO (For Sale By Owner) sign, it might mean the property's overpriced and the owner's had his sign out for months, even years. A shiny, new FSBO sign might mean the owner just started trying to sell his house, or he's read my book *Sold by Owner*, where I explain the necessity of a nice sign when property is for sale. Shiny FSBO signs usually mean you're dealing with a rather savvy seller. If you see a little hand drawn cardboard FSBO sign, you're dealing with a rank amateur. He might have his house overpriced, or even much underpriced. Some sharp negotiating might snag you a good catch.

MODEL HOMES

Model homes that aren't absolutely sharp in every respect can mean one of three things. Either the builder is about to wind down the subdivision and has only a handful of houses to sell, and he's concentrating on his new subdivisions, or he's in financial jeopardy, or he's a sloppy builder. The signs leading to a builder's models or his subdivision can also be a telltale sign of a builder's character.

NEWSPAPER ADVERTISING

Newspaper advertising, while it will always look neat, can also give you some hints on seller motivation. It can tell you something about the agent, the builder, the builder's interim lender, how the property may be bought and financed, and what condition of repair or disrepair the property enjoys. Because there are so many ideas hidden between the lines of newspaper ads, let's dissect a few.

> NICE 3-2-1 Today! $2,400/dn. Owner finance.
> New roof. $585/mo. Call 555-5555.

This ad from a major Dallas newspaper tells you that the house has three bedrooms, two baths, and a one-car garage. The Today describes a floor plan that FOX & JACOBS, the biggest builder in the Dallas area, built in great numbers. Many people are familiar with the plan, the size, and its layout. The $2,400 down payment might not be all the money you need to buy the house. It could just be the amount the buyer wants for himself, then you, or he and you, will share in the closing costs. It might also mean that he'll pay for all of the closing costs out of that $2,400. Its got a new roof, then the $585 per month is probably the entire payment for principal, interest, taxes, and insurance. Keep in mind, however, that it might only mean the principal and interest, in which case the taxes and insurance could cost another $80 to $120 per month.

$750 DN-ASSUMABLE
Lease/option to buy. 3-2-1, only 4-yrs old.
214-555-5555.

This fellow wants to dump his house for a number of reasons. Perhaps the payment's too high for him, or maybe it's too high for the size and condition of the home, or he's being transferred and he must leave soon. It might also be a landlord with a good gimmick for renting his house. The $750 down might be all the desperate seller needs to move on, and if he's being transferred, it could be a good deal for you. Keep in mind that these ads are from the Dallas area at a time when it's probably one of the best buyers markets in decades. You won't see an ad like this from a home seller in a sellers market. The "lease/option to buy" is a popular landlord phrase, but desperate sellers wanting any small equity rather than to just walk out and not get a penny of equity also use it. The rest of the ad is self-explanatory.

* HUD - VA *
$0 Down — Low Down. E-Z qualify. These sell
fast, so hurry! Authorized broker.
555-5555

HUD-VA means this broker is selling only VA and FHA foreclosed properties. There were thousands of these homes in the Dallas/Fort Worth area at the time of this writing. This ad is misleading to the novice. First of all, the only people who can buy with absolutely $0 down are veterans who purchase using their VA eligibility and get a VA-guaranteed loan, or those who borrow 100 percent of the purchase price from Aunt Millie, or Mom and Dad. Low down can mean $100 to some people, and $5,000 to others. E-Z qualify might mean there is no credit or employment check, or that the lender will take someone with a weak credit rating, or even with no job. "These sell fast, so hurry!" means there aren't that many available, so hurry or you'll miss your chance to buy. An authorized broker means that he's one of only a few who can sell these homes.

But here are the facts. The $0 down this ad refers to is the down payment. Buyers will have to come up with an average of $800 to $2,500 in closing costs to get into the property, plus any repairs, decorating, and cleanup that might be needed. Some of the houses sell fast, the real steals, and they are more often than not bid up near current market prices. Other homes sit around for many months before they're sold. In 1990, HUD was sometimes acquiring 900 repossessed houses a month in the Dallas/Fort Worth area but only selling 500. Hardly a situation where they're selling fast. Authorized broker means he or she has signed up with VA and HUD and joined the majority of his peers in his selling area. In other words, he's one of many. This is a very effective ad. Is it illegal and immoral? Not really. It just means that for those buyers who haven't informed themselves of their market, it's an easy fishing expedition for the broker.

> Grand Saline/Canton Area
> Nice Cedar home surrounded by trees; 7 acres,
> no restrictions, fenced & cross fenced, 2-
> barns, nice pond, deck, huge den/formal
> dining, 5-ceiling fans, 2-full baths, int.
> paneled/papered. See to appreciate! Owner
> moving out of state. 214-555-5555/444-4444.

Canton and Grand Saline are two small towns about 100 miles east of Dallas. This is a good ad, probably written by the owner, because real estate laws oblige brokers and agents to indicate in the ad that they're in the real estate business in one way or another, although some brokers and agents still leave out that information. This ad might mean that, if someone's interested in a little place way out in the country, he can probably get a good deal on it from this owner.

There are times when the more information an ad has, the more noble are the intentions of the seller. This next ad gives you all the information you need to know about this house and the seller.

> By owner, 3/2/2, 2 living areas, spa, wbfp,
> other extras. Assume 10% fixed, no down
> $84,500 555-5555 eve

This is a great ad for the buyer. It tells him many things, except value. For example, it says that the home is being sold by owner, which means no agents to deal with. It has three bedrooms, two baths, and a two-car garage. It has a living room as well as a den or game room. It has a spa, probably in the backyard. It has a wood-burning fireplace and other extras that usually are part of homes a step or two above entry level, single family homes in the area. The loan is at a 10 percent fixed rate, it's apparently assumable, probably an old VA or FHA loan. The seller wants out. If he doesn't sell, he might walk out on his loan, but he's doing all he can to save his credit and have someone take over his payments. This is an ideal situation for someone who wants to own his own home and has bad credit. The only drawback is that he'll be paying full price for the home. And that full price might be more than the home is presently worth. Because there's no such thing as a free lunch, this owner is giving such a good deal only in desperation. If the house goes into foreclosure, either HUD, VA, or some lender will end up with it. This $84,500 house might sell on the foreclosure market at $70,000. But there's no down payment, the buyer can have bad credit and still buy a house, after a few years the market could change and this house might sell for $150,000. If the buyer doesn't like the house, he can just walk away from it.

Better yet, he can stop payments for six months until it's foreclosed and he's forced to move out. That's six months of free rent.

Most ads by real estate brokers are strictly fishing expeditions. They're trying to get either buyers or sellers. Their real aim is rarely to sell one particular house. Even open houses work that way. While the agent at the open house would love to sell the house he's showing, he or she knows that what will come along is buyers and sellers. Neighbors and lookers will come through who might want to list their own homes. Buyers will come by who might not like that house but will work with the agent on the purchase of another property.

The very big display ads by some of the larger real estate firms are public relations ploys. They're looking for buyers. But they also want sellers to notice. That gets property listings. Listings can get more buyers through the agency's signs on listed properties. Signs mean ad calls. Ads and articles congratulating million-dollar producers are used to make agents feel good and stick it out with the company. They also attract other agents who might want to work for the company.

RESPONDING TO ADS

While real estate agents often offer some very good deals, the very exceptional ones should come directly from sellers. Here's why. If a seller owes $80,000 on his home that's worth $120,000, and if he sells it for $110,000 with a real estate commission of 6%, then all he'll get is $103,400, or a net of $23,400. With no commission, he'd get $30,000. With no agent, you might be able to negotiate with the seller for $106,000, which will net him an additional $2,600 over the $110,000 that includes a commission. It would save you $4,000. Of course, if you're dealing with a very good real estate agent, he might get you to pay the full $120,000 for the house, which will help the seller but certainly not you.

There are certain questions you need to ask the seller when you call on a house. Answers to these questions will give you the seller's motivation and attitude about selling. You'll also get enough information about the house to know if you're still interested in it enough to make the trip to check it out. The questions to ask are in the Telephone Calling Questionnaire in Fig. 7-1. Make copies of it and use them when making calls. Have the sheets ready when you start going through the newspaper. Write down the telephone number of ads that show some promise. Cut out the ad and tape it to the sheet, and place all of your sheets in numerical order, using the telephone numbers as guides. Later on, when you have a lot of sheets, you can leaf through and not bother with repeat ads by the same individual.

If you reach an individual who controls the conversation, suspect a pro or someone who's read up on salesmanship, because the one who asks all of the

Telephone Calling Questionnaire

Telephone #_____   Publication_____   Date_____

(ad copy)

Name of seller_____

Address of property_____

Reasons for selling_____

Time on market as FSBO _____ Asking price _____

Length of previous listing _____ Asking price then _____

Assumable loan, yes _____, no _____. Loan balance _____ Int. rate_____

Assumable second lien, yes ____, no ____. Balance _____ Int. rate _____

Owner financing, yes _____, no _____. Amount _____ Int. rate_____

Bedrooms ____, Baths ____, Garage ____, Carport ____, Den ____, Game Rm.____

Bkfst. Rm. _____, Covd. patio _____, Cov. porch_____, Fenced yard_____

Type of home _____ Style of home_____

Appliances _____

Amenities _____

Flood plain, yes _____, no _____. Near unacceptable noise _____

Living area s.f._____, Lot size _____

Notes_____

_____

_____

Fig. 7-1.

questions is the one who controls the conversation. As soon as you call, have your sheet ready and start asking questions. Avoid chitchat, or it will take you forever to go through the ads in a major newspaper. As soon as you find out that there is one point about the property that is completely unacceptable to you, stop the conversation, thank the seller for his time, and hang up. For example, if you're looking for a home that has a two car garage, and the seller tells you that the garage has been converted to a den and that there's no garage, then you don't need to go any further unless the house is so well priced that you can build a garage and come out ahead, assuming there is room on the lot to build one.

The most important aspect of this questionnaire is to get from the seller his true motivation. Just how strong is it? Does he really need to sell, or does he simply want to sell to move to a different house or a different neighborhood. A truly motivated seller will sound anxious. You'll hear it in his conversation. He'll often spill the beans and tell you his whole story. An agent rarely does that. I've seen deals close where the seller walks out with a nice sum of cash after he was a week or two away from foreclosure, because an agent was smart enough to keep his mouth shut tight about the seller's dilemma.

If you call someone who has a fair amount of equity, and he tells you that if he doesn't close on the house by a certain date he'll lose it through foreclosure, then you might be looking straight in the face of a great deal. Here's an example. Let's assume Agent Smith had Joe Blow's house listed for $100,000. It's worth $110,000 but the market is tight, and his loan balance is $80,000. But Joe Blow hasn't made a payment in five months because he was out of work. With Texas' easy foreclosure laws, for example, Joe might be on his last month before foreclosure. His back payments amount to $4,000, so the balance due on the loan is $84,000. If Agent Smith's a nice guy and lists Joe's house at 3 percent commission, and if he gets full price for the listing, Joe will still come out with $13,000. Agent Smith would say nothing to the buyer about the foreclosure. He'd do his level best to get Joe his full asking price and save the day for his client. If you find out Joe's on the throes of foreclosure, you can come in for the kill. Even if you have a heart and give him $90,000, you'll still get a good deal, and it's not all that bad for Joe either.

8

Working with Real Estate Agents

WORKING WITH REAL ESTATE AGENTS IS A VERY INTERESTING SUBJECT. IN FACT, I could write a whole book on it. Although I'm a real estate broker and have some wonderful agents working for me, there is no end to the number of incompetent, undereducated or slightly-to-highly unscrupulous agents and brokers. Not that other professions don't have their share. There are at least as many bad lawyers and bad doctors as bad real estate people. This is a real estate book, however, and I'll stick to real estate agents and brokers.

TYPES OF AGENTS

If you've read my book *Sold By Owner*, some of this might sound a bit familiar. I like to classify real estate agents in three categories:

1. Amateurs. These are the 50 percent who lack experience and knowledge. A great many of whom are part-timers.

2. Taxi drivers. These are the 25 percent who are reasonably competent, though still quite green.

3. Professionals. These are the final 25 percent who are totally competent, full-time agents.

The above figures I've taken off the top of my head. They're certainly not infallible, but I believe that in 23 years of being in and around the real estate business, I'm not far off. Approximately half of the agents and brokers I meet are in the first two groups, which I wouldn't hire under any circumstances. Of the remaining half, those in group #3 above, I'd hire in a minute.

The problem with the real estate business is that there's not a requirement for thoroughly professional training before people are allowed to get into it. Would a lawyer be allowed to practice law with a few weeks of legal training? A physician operate on you after only a year's worth of cutting fetal pigs and human cadavers? Texas is much like most other states, and in Texas, a real estate agent needs only 12 semester hours of real estate education or related courses beyond high school to get his license. A home is too large an asset to allow someone with little education or experience to help you. It's better to do your own dealing than to work with amateurs or taxi drivers. Let me tell you about these two types of agents so you can recognize them and keep a good distance away.

Amateurs

Amateur agents either just got their license, or have had it a while but work real estate part-time. Some may have been in it a while and are full-timers, but their main reason for being in the business is to socialize at the office because they have nothing better to do. I know that's a little severe. I hope you realize I'm being somewhat facetious, but it's too often true. Retirees and well-off spouses can spend useless hours in real estate. It's highly unlikely these folks ever go to a seminar, read a real estate book, or take a salesmanship course. They are totally stagnant.

They do like to work with buyers. Their passion is to take telephone ad calls, grab a buyer, and work him thoroughly until they sell him a house. They sometimes succeed, but too often they connect a buyer with the wrong house.

Most new or inexperienced agents won't have the ability, patience, or perseverance to do a decent job of leading you to the right property—at the best price, with superior financing, and a smooth closing.

New agents come on the scene with very little training, often on a part-time basis, and usually will be almost as ignorant after a couple of years as when they started. It's not surprising to see why this group has a business mortality rate of a year or two at the most. Because you're dealing with what is probably your largest investment, don't leave it in the hands of amateurs.

Taxi Drivers

The next group of agents I call "taxi drivers," because their favorite trick is to take a buyer and drive him and his family in a nice car to 35 houses, one right after the other. After six hours of this torture the buyers are exhausted. They don't even remotely remember the first 30 houses.

When a taxi driver finally wears his buyers down, they'll sign any contract on any house. But when the buyers go for a loan application, the loan officer might discover the husband is looking for a job, the wife doesn't work either, and they filed for bankruptcy two months ago. The taxi driver never qualified them. Believe it or not, this is not a rare occurrence.

Taxi drivers are people who have been around long enough to have received some real estate experience through osmosis. Like the newcomers, however, they also lack a thorough real estate education. Some will graduate to Professionals, others will flounder in the Sea of Mediocrity for years. No matter, you don't want to be the fish they prey on.

A lot of these people have been in the business long enough to get by comfortably with innocent buyers. In lieu of lackluster help, you need True Professionals.

True Professionals

True Professionals have three outstanding qualities:

1. They are full-time professionals.
2. They have been in the business full time for several years and started out with a good education in their profession.
3. They keep abreast of their business by going to seminars at least a few times a year and reading books on real estate law, finance, and merchandising.

FIND OUT WHOM YOU'RE DEALING WITH

Because a good agent can lead you to a wonderful purchase, you need to know with whom you're dealing. The best way to do it is to ask a few simple questions:

- How long have you been in the business?
- Are you full time?
- When is the last time you went to a seminar?
- How many educational meetings do you attend per year?
- Can you show me that you *fully* understand residential real estate financing?
- How much experience and education do you have in your profession?
- What will you specifically do to find me the best deal?

By the way, in all the years I've been selling real estate, I've never had a buyer ask any of these questions, and none of my agents mentioned anyone posing these questions to them either. If the agent is insulted with these questions, it's because he or she is trying to cover up a major deficiency. You have 25 percent of all real estate agents to choose from. Ask enough questions and you'll find the bright ones.

Unfortunately, even if you diligently do all of the above, you might still not get the best agent for your needs. Therefore, it's a good idea to further understand agent mentality.

UNDERSTANDING AGENT MENTALITY

As in all forms of human endeavor, people are in a business to help themselves and their families; they're in it for the income that puts bread on their tables; and they're rarely in it for an altruistic need to help their fellow human beings. In other words, an agent is there to:

1. earn a commission;
2. serve his company;
3. serve his principal; and
4. help you.

All in that order. The truly conscientious agent, though, will understand this to be true, but will also know that if he does his level best for everyone's good, in the end he'll make a good living, because real estate is a repeat business.

Numbers 1, 2, and 4 probably seem quite obvious to you, but you might wonder about number 3. Unless you're in a very progressive area, you'll probably deal only with sellers' agents. That is to say, all the agents you'll work with will be agents for the seller. The seller is known as the principal. This means that legally he owes his loyalty primarily to the seller for whom he's acting as agent through the listing contract. He owes you nothing more than to treat you fairly.

The most confusing part of this whole scheme is the subagency situation. If you're working with an agent who works for ABC Realty, and he finds you a house listed by XWZ Realty, the agent who listed the house is the seller's agent, but your agent is also the seller's agent, and not yours. Your agent is a subagent of the seller. Both the seller's agent, and your agent are working for the seller. The seller is their *client*. You, on the other hand, are your agent's *customer*. You are *not* his client.

Obviously, this is not fair, so I will let you in on a secret. As a general rule of agency, if you tell your agent, who isn't really your agent, that you can afford to pay up to $100,000 for a house, then he has an obligation to tell the buyer this fact. Let's assume your intentions are to offer $95,000 for the buyer's $100,000 property, but you tell your "apparent" agent that you like the house so much that you'll pay the $100,000 if the seller doesn't take your lower offer. The agent has a legal obligation to tell the seller this fact, and by offering $95,000, you'll only be spinning your wheels. That's assuming, though, that your "apparent" agent treats his client as he should, which isn't always the case. So who is your agent?

Just Who's My Agent?

So who's my agent? Nobody. In most real estate transactions, nobody is. As a rule, the buyer's "agent" treats the buyer as his client, even though that's wrong. The seller pays the listing agency a commission for the sale of his house, and the listing agency splits this commission with the selling agency for its part in acting as a subagent. Consequently, if both the listing agent and the selling agent are both paid by the seller, each has a fiduciary relationship with the seller, and owes the seller complete loyalty. Consequently the buyer is out naked in the cold wilderness of home buying most of the time.

In Texas, as well as in some other states, we have to give our customers (the buyers) a paper that explains for whom we're working. We do so at the beginning of our relationship and explain that we'll treat them fairly, that we'll do our very best for them. We hope they forget that little paper, though. Because the system is unfair. Legally, it's completely biased to the seller's side because he's paying the commission. But look at it this way, if there is no sale, there's no commission. In other words, if you don't buy, the agent doesn't get paid.

If all of this seems confusing, let me clear it up with a supposition. Let's say you're divorcing your spouse. Your spouse hires two lawyers. Your spouse will pay both lawyers to handle the divorce, and you're allowed to use one of those lawyers to help you. "Your" lawyer gives you a little sheet of paper—actually makes you sign it—explaining that he isn't really your lawyer, that he's working for your spouse, but that he'll treat you fairly. Not very equitable, is it? Well, that's *exactly* how real estate works.

Before you get completely discouraged with looking to an agent for help, I should say that, in most cases, the buyer is treated fairly. Though it is legally wrong, the "buyer's" agent often treats the buyer like his client. Nevertheless, you should be aware that the system is biased against you.

BUYERS' AGENTS

To remedy this condition, there have sprung up in some forward-thinking areas what are called buyers' agents. These people work strictly for the buyer, owe total allegiance to the buyer, and are paid by the buyer. In effect, though, the seller's commission still pays them. Semantics is the only difference in this situation. The buyer's agent calls the seller's agent and tells him that he's working strictly for the buyer, and won't be working as a subagent for the seller. He does tell him, though, that he will expect to receive his share of the commission, that he's explained this fact to his principal, the buyer, and that he expects the seller's agent to explain the entire situation to his principal, the seller.

If you can find a buyer's agent, and you can ascertain that he's a real professional, then by all means this is your best route. This type of relationship allows *your* agent to work like a tiger for your needs and in your best interest, and not to walk a fine line like a pussy cat on a flimsy fence.

EDUCATING YOUR AGENT

Whether you work with a seller's subagent, or a buyer's agent, you need to educate your agent about what you need and want. Professional agents will ask a lot more questions than they answer, at least at the beginning of a relationship. They must know your needs, your desires, and your financial condition. If you find the agent running at the mouth from the very beginning, and not listening to determine your needs, then find another agent.

A good agent will first qualify you. He'll want to know how much you make, how much you owe, the condition of your credit rating, how large a family you have, and many other pertinent facts. Be specific and be truthful. It's the only way he can help you. A favorite saying among real estate people is that "buyers are liars." Don't say you want a $50,000 house when you know full well that you'll spend $120,000 if you have to. Don't say you're ready to buy even though you can't move for six months. And most important of all, work only with one agent.

Tell your agent that he or she will be the only one you'll work with, as long as that agent works only for you, and not for the sellers. If he's a seller's subagent, tell him you understand the situation and that you want him to act as your agent. Demand loyalty. If he won't do that, then find someone else. Lay it on the line right up front. I don't believe you can get a truly fair deal if your secrets will be shared with the seller. He works for you, or you find someone else. Don't worry about the law. That's his problem. Your problem is to be well represented, and a totally dedicated seller's agent won't do that for you.

After the agent has qualified you as far as your income, expenses and credit rating, he'll tell you how much house you can afford. He might say you can buy a $150,000 house. Or he might say you can afford payments of $2,000 per month. Abide by what he says. He knows his business, is aware of the current interest rates, loan qualifying requirements, and monthly tax and insurance costs. If he's told you $150,000 is the most you can afford, and you tell him you want a $250,000 house, you'll create an impossible situation for him. He can't work miracles.

On the other hand, if he tells you the most you can spend per month on a payment is $1,800, and you know you can get decent housing on your own self-imposed limit of $1,300 per month, then let him understand from the start that he must find you the best deal that fits within your own budget, and not the limit of your ability to pay. A favorite ploy of savvy agents is to show you three houses within your self-determined budget then explain, ''I know this is more than you want to pay, but I'd like to show you just one more home you'll just love.'' He'll take you to one that puts your payments at your maximum paying ability, the $1,800 per month, for example. It'll be a knockout, and naturally you'll love it. Many folks fall for this trick and buy, which raises the value of the sale and provides the agent with a higher commission. Some agents do this when they find you are wanting more than what your self-imposed budget offers.

If you're taking your time at buying—which you should be—then give the agent very specific details of what you want and need. Be flexible about items that aren't of great importance, but be firm about what really matters. You'll be living in the home day in and day out, and a mistake in buying can deprive you of a truly comfortable home for years to come. A smart agent will want to take you out and sell you the first day. That's fine if you get exactly what you need and want. If what you're looking for is not available now, then tell your agent you'll be patient and buy when he finds just the right property. Arnold Glascow reminds us that ''The key to everything is patience. You get the chicken by hatching the egg—not by smashing it.''

WORKING WITH A BUYER'S AGENT

There are several advantages to working with a buyer's agent. Let me go back a little bit to agent mentality, and you'll see what I mean. When you're working with a seller's agent, the agent never really knows that he has your complete loyalty. If he doesn't find you the right house within a reasonably short time, he knows you might find a house through another agent, or through a homeowner, and all of his efforts with you will have meant zero commission for him. Therefore, he'll push and push for a sale, if not on the first day, then soon thereafter. Rome wasn't built in a day, and finding a house, the right house, in one day is often an illusion for both agent and buyer.

So how do you slow the agent down to do his level best? Simply by assuring him of a commission when you buy. You can do this only in one of two ways: by promising to be loyal—fat chance he'll believe you; and by guaranteeing it in writing—your greatest weapon. With a signed agreement guaranteeing that the agent will be paid when he finds you the right house, that agent will go all out to work for you. That agreement is like an exclusive right to sell that a seller gives a listing agent: if the house is sold by anyone, including the seller, the agent collects his commission. With an exclusive right to be your buying agent, the agent will be paid whether you buy from him, from another agent, or from a FSBO.

Because most buyers can't stand still when they're looking for a house, they'll look with their agent and scan the house classifieds in the paper when they're not with their agent. They'll even call other agents for information on other properties. It often happens that they come upon the deal of the century while they're not with the agent to whom they promised loyalty, and they buy from an owner. That's fine for you as a buyer. You haven't lost anything. The agent's lost some of his valuable time. Most buyers use the reasoning that because commissions are so high anyway, the agent will make it up on the next sale. While that's sometimes true, you lose the benefit of your agent's expertise in making sure the deal you're consummating on your own is the very best you can find. If you have a buyer's agent, however, you could simply call him and have him call the seller for details on the property. If it sounds good to him, then he can go with you to the property, make sure it's indeed a good deal, handle the negotiations, and get you the deal of the century.

Figure 8-1 is a contract you can use with a buyers' agent should you have to convert a seller's agent to your side. The best way to work the agent's remuneration is to let him split his usual commission with the seller's agent, if he finds you a house where the seller has a property listed with another agent. And if you find a house on your own, offered for sale by the owner, then negotiate a lower commission that you'll pay out of your own pocket, as you'd pay a lawyer to handle a deal for you. The agent is not in lieu of a lawyer. He's actually better than one, though you might still want to use a lawyer to look at the final papers.

The agent's going to do all he can to get you a house wherein he will receive his full commission, and still be paid for his efforts, though not as handsomely, if you find a property for sale by the owner. If you do this, you'll find the quality of the agent's work, and the success of your relationship with him, will be a rewarding experience for you.

AGENTS' TRICKS FOR GETTING YOUR SIGNATURE

An agent doesn't get paid until he gets his check at the closing. The first step to that pleasant conclusion is your signature on a contract to buy. The absolutely

Buyer's Agent Agreement

The BUYER hereby authorizes the BUYER'S BROKER to locate and/or negotiate for the purchase of real property of a general nature as described below. This Agreement begins on date of signing, and ends on _____, or on the earlier closing of a property under this Agreement.

Buyer's Broker will persevere in professionally locating a property acceptable to Buyer, and assist Buyer throughout the transaction and act in the Buyer's best interest at all times. Buyer will work exclusively with Buyer's Broker for the purchase of a property, and furnish Buyer's Broker all relevant personal and financial information to ensure Buyer's ability to purchase property.

Buyer agrees to pay Buyer's Broker $_____, or _____ % of the purchase price of the property, payable at closing, if the Buyer, or any other person acting in the Buyer's behalf, buys, exchanges for, or obtains an option on any real property of the general nature described below. Buyer's Broker is authorized to negotiate for a commission paid by the Seller, the payment of which will satisfy the Client's obligation to pay a commission under this Agreement. The payment of any commission by the Seller from the sales proceeds will not make the Buyer's Broker either the agent or subagent of the seller.

General Nature of Property

Type_____

Approximate price _____ Location_____

Terms and conditions_____

_____

_____

Buyer's broker_____Date_____

Address_____Phone_____

Signature_____

Buyer_____Date_____

Address_____Date_____

Signature(s)_____

Fig. 8-1.

best agents will sell you the first time out, mainly because they will have done a thorough job with their homework. They'll know exactly what you need, where you need to buy, what you can afford, and they'll be intimately familiar with the home market. They'll show you three, maybe even four houses, and have your signature perhaps at the first or second house, because they will be smart enough to start the search with the very best house, and let you know that's the very best one. You'll like it very much. When you get to the second one, you won't like it quite as much. By the third one, you'll realize the first was the best, that it completely fits your needs, and you'll return to sign the contract in your new home's living room.

Now, I'll give you some tricks that those who aren't the very best agents will use. As I've explained, some will attempt to wear you out. If you look at 100 houses, you're bound to find one you like, or you'll buy just to finish the ordeal.

Some will push you into signing. If your agent senses you don't really know what you want, that a lot of houses will fit your needs—which is entirely possible—she might simply pull out a contract at a house that works reasonably well for you, fill it out, and put it in front of you. She'll give you a pretty smile and say softly, "Now Joe and Mary, you know this house is perfect for you. Just okay the contract here and we can get things rolling to have you moved in this lovely home as soon as possible so you can start enjoying all these great features."

You've found the perfect home. The seller wants $150,000, but you're sure he'll take $140,000. The agent's certain she can get it accepted at $145,000, but hasn't let you in on her secret. You mention $140,000. She tells you the property's very desirable, and that another agent in her office was going to show it early the next morning. Now she's taking it away from you. An excellent trick. She'll get you to at least $145,000 on the first try.

While it might be true that another agent will show it the next morning, if you sense the owner's very motivated—remember, you'll have asked your agent all about the owner by now—you'll make your $140,000 offer and insist that the agent do her level best to see that it's presented that same day and that she push for an acceptance of your offer.

For complete success in obtaining what you want at the very best price, there's one thing you must *never* tell your agent. That's how much you like a house. Go off in a corner and tell your spouse how much you like it, and ask your spouse's feelings about it in private. When you make the offer, be unemotional, even though you're dying for that perfect house. Because if there's one perfect house, there's bound to be another one around the corner if you don't get this one at the right price.

Don't ever quarrel with your spouse about your feelings for a house in front of your agent. If you have a major disagreement, work it out in private. A good agent can sense when one or the other of you has fallen in love with a house and will play that fact for all it's worth to help get a contract.

You can certainly buy a house without the help of an agent, but if you work it right, you might get truly professional help and a great bargain all at once by wisely using an agent to work for you, and not for the seller. Even if you've never bought before, or never worked with an agent before, don't forget that *you* are the boss, *you* are the buyer, and that agents, appraisers, and sellers don't set prices. Only *you*, the buyer, can set prices, because only you can say what you'll pay for a particular property. And without you, there is no sale.

9

Finding Motivated Sellers

THE TYPE OF MARKET YOU'LL BE BUYING IN WILL DETERMINE THE NUMBER OF motivated sellers available in your area, as well as their degree of motivation. A motivated seller is defined as one who *needs* to sell rather than one who simply wants to sell, even if there's a slight amount of need coupled with the desire to sell. This definition might sound confusing, so it'll be easier if we break down motivated sellers into three categories.

MOTIVATED SELLER #1. "I'D LIKE TO SELL."

This seller has a definite need, but he can take his time to get a good price. He might have three children and his wife isn't satisfied with their three bedroom house anymore. They really need a house with more bedrooms, but if it comes this year that's great, and if it happens next year, that's okay.

You might find a variation of the above. An older couple whose children have moved out, and whose house sits on a huge lot might have more than they can handle in maintenance. There's no rush, but there's a definite need. The older the owners are, the greater their want turns to a need.

There are some sellers who might have chewed off more than they can handle. They can afford the house, but just barely. Or they can afford it alright, but the payments dampen their high life-style. They want out, but they're not fools. They'll take their time and get close to full value for their property.

MOTIVATED SELLER #2. "I NEED TO SELL."

These sellers are the tip of the iceberg of buying opportunities. They truly need to sell, but time is still a little bit on their side. For example, a department manager of a chain store outfit gets moved from one end of a large city to another. His company doesn't help him with the move, because he's still in the same city. He now has a 45 mile drive one way to his work place. He'll do it for a while, but the driving gets old fast. Now, he really does need to sell sooner than later.

Another example is the old couple who stayed longer than they should have in their large home. Their health simply doesn't permit them to stay any longer. Then there's the executive or junior executive who gets transferred to another city. He really needs to sell his house before he moves so he can buy at his next destination. If he doesn't sell, however, he won't dump his property for a cheap price. He'll rent it and rent at his new location. He's more motivated than Seller #1, but he's not desperate. He can afford to hold off for a reasonable price.

MOTIVATED SELLER #3. "HELP!"

The truly motivated sellers are the ones who offer you real opportunities. There are sellers who absolutely *must* sell, and those are the ones you need to seek. I'll give you a list of words that should make your ears perk up when you hear them. These words indicate the possibility of a bargain:

1. Divorce
2. Relocate
3. Inherit
4. Layoff
5. Illness
6. Hate
7. Death

There are plenty of other words that can force people to sell their homes, but I think these are the most important. Let's examine each one briefly so you understand their meaning in this context.

Divorce

In 1900, the divorce rate in America was 0.7 per 1,000 population. Today, it's about 5 per 1,000. Such a significant divorce rate causes many wonderful opportunities for lawyers and home buyers. Too many divorces end up in all-out war, and couples breaking up not only want out of their unhappy marriage, they also want to forget all about it. So one of the first things to go is the house they shared together. Many sell because neither partner can afford to keep the house alone. A large percentage of couples buy houses and finance them using both incomes to qualify.

If a divorce is imminent, neither spouse will be able to stay in the house alone. This is especially true of young, childless couples who've only owned the house a year or two. Until there is built-up equity and the payments have become rather comfortable, then neither husband nor wife will be able to sustain the house payments and maintenance costs. If there are children, then the mother might be able to keep the house with her income plus the child support from the father. You should be able to tell what type of situation you're dealing with early in your conversation with the seller.

Relocate

When a homeowner is selling because of a move, you'll find various degrees of motivation. The most motivated are those who are moving because they can no longer find local employment or because they're making a move up the career ladder. When you hear relocation, you need to ask why the seller is moving to determine if he's getting help from his employer. There will be little motivation if the employer will buy the property and pay all closing costs if the owner doesn't sell by the time he must move. On the other hand, if the owner is doing it on his own and he needs to get his equity out of the home in cash he will be highly motivated. Always ask as many questions as you can so you can find out the seller's circumstances.

Inherit

It's sometimes hard to buy from the estate of a decedent, especially if there were many older heirs, but that's where the best bargains are in inheritance cases. If an eighty-year-old owner dies and leaves a house to three children in their late 50s, more than likely those children already have their homes paid for and aren't interested in the decedent's home as a residence. If they all live reasonably close to the property, they might keep it as a rental. If they all live far away, the house will be a problem to them. They won't even be aware of local prices. A low offer from a serious buyer will often get a favorable response.

Layoff

Layoffs are worst for young workers without seniority who have indebted themselves deeply to a large number of lenders. A young couple with good jobs might owe on two new cars, a new home, and several "fully loaded" credit cards. Either one's layoff is a sudden shock to their paying ability. The first thing they'll abandon is credit card payments, furniture payments, boat payments, and other "toy" payments. Then they'll get behind in their house payments. The car is too important to the American way of life, so that will usually be last.

If you find a young couple with the appearance of credit overindulgence, then you can pose a simple question, "Are you behind on any of your payments?" If they are, then a layoff is often the culprit.

Illness

There are times when an illness can cause a change in housing needs. If someone needs special care, perhaps the owner is new in a wheel chair or he needs special equipment, the present home might be obsolete.

Also, the owner might have been ill for a long time, out of work, and unable to earn enough to make the payments. That's a sad time, but you might be helping him out by buying his house. If someone *must* sell, then some buyer will get a good deal when the owner prices his property below market value. You might as well be the one to get the good deal.

Hate

I've seen rare instances where folks develop a hatred for the home, the city, or the state they live in. Sometimes they're transferred from their home state and never acquire a liking for the new area. They might accept the new territory at first, but eventually, home is where the heart is, and in their desire to return, they develop a hatred that causes them to dump their property.

I've lived in Texas, New York, California, Iowa, Illinois and Louisiana, and the first time I encountered this "real estate hatred" phenomenon I was shocked. I liked all the states I'd lived in. I have my favorites, but they all have their qualities and shortcomings. A few years ago, I listed a house for sale that was owned by a couple who wanted to go "home." They were in their 50s and childless. They hated their house, their neighborhood, their city, and their state. She said, "Maurice, I'm going to brush the Texas dust off my shoes on the way home. I'll never come back." Her husband repeated her words.

I was a little upset. I like Texas and couldn't see why they didn't either. I've met a few people since then with the same feelings. I had decided Texas just rubbed some people the wrong way, but after some meditation I realized I'd met people like that all over the country. People with this attitude will often give you a good deal. They want out, and the sooner, the better.

Death

The death of a spouse can cause a compelling need to sell. The need could be economic or psychological. The surviving spouse of a young couple with heavy payments who relied on both incomes to meet those obligations will be forced to sell. The older survivor might have the house paid for, but might not be able to stay. There are too many memories, and he or she might want to get on with a fresh life.

Becoming Sherlock Holmes

You often have to act the part of a detective to find the best deals. Most real estate agents aren't going to lead you to the best deals. They might find you the best property for your needs, but rarely do they combine that with an extremely good financial deal. You have to dig that out for yourself.

That means a bit of hard work, a lot of patience, and the posing of many, many questions to all of the sellers you meet. Don't be timid. The better you know the seller's situation, the better you'll know the seller's motivation, and that's the whole secret to getting a good deal.

10

Inspecting Structures and Equipment

WITHIN THE LAST DECADE, THE ROLE OF THE HOME INSPECTOR HAS TAKEN A more prominent role in the resale market. Years ago, when buyers were contemplating purchasing their own home or an investment property, they'd come to me as a home builder and ask if I'd look for major structural flaws in their selection. I never charged for a service like this. It was always a favor for a friend.

A few years later, I found some "out-of-work" builders hiring out for house inspections. Soon, other, less-knowledgeable individuals started offering their services. In the last couple of years, Texas began licensing home inspectors through the Texas Real Estate Commission. Other states have done the same, and I'm certain in the very near future all states will have regulations for licensed inspectors.

I dislike excessive government regulation. There's too much of it now, and the regulation of the home inspector is both a blessing and a great disservice to home buyers. First, most real estate agents now push the service as a complete necessity. Inspectors are supposed to be infallible because of their license. Now, instead of just giving a clean bill of health, the inspector assumes he must find every little flaw in the structure. I guess it's to justify his existence. He comes up with pages and pages of insignificant items that cause the buyer to be overly cautious and often increases unreasonable requests for repairs from the seller.

You don't have to use an inspector, just like you don't have to use a real estate agent, a lawyer, or even a title or escrow company. The nature of the purchase will dictate whether you should use any of these people. If you're "stealing" a property, with little or no cash invested, then you might not need any of them. I've had people "give" me their house, where I took title to the property subject to the loan—I didn't assume the loan, I just kept making payments. A quick walk through and around the property, and a bit of figuring with the calculator were enough to tell me if it was a reasonable deal. I prepared the paperwork, had them sign the contract and deed, and we had a deal.

If you're buying a property cash, then the use of every available expert is wise and inexpensive insurance. Even if you're getting a steal, when you're plunking down cold, hard cash, there's no turning back. If there are major systems failures in the structure, you have no choice but to pour more money into the purchase for repairs. Normally, a buyer puts the minimum amount of money down for the purchase of a relatively new structure, and a careful inspection by the buyer is sufficient.

WHAT NEIGHBORS CAN TELL YOU

Once you've decided on a particular dwelling, before you make a firm offer, talk to the neighbors. The information about your selected property from one neighbor shouldn't dissuade you from making a purchase unless you find it to be exceedingly derogatory and you can prove the accuracy of information given you. Just the other day, I was with some of my agents previewing a repossessed home for sale by a federal agency. An old retired neighbor followed us into the house with a plethora of information about the previous owners. It seems the husband had shot and killed his wife, a couple of his kids, and wounded his sister-in-law before turning the gun successfully on himself. He showed us the bullet holes in the walls—they were barely discernible—as well as some slight blood stains that remained on the hardwood floors.

He spoiled our sale of the property. As agents, anything we know about the property we must pass on to the buyer, and this information was too vital to delete in any showing of the house. We knew we wouldn't be the ones to sell it.

From a neighbor in another area we found out that the backyard of a very nice house with a large, level lot was the lowest point on the block and water accumulated there when it rained. That point was also the very location of the septic system for the house. We checked with the city's engineering department and found that it would take $3,000 to connect to the city sewer system and that the city was considering denying the water to be reconnected for the new buyer until the public sewer connection was accomplished. We didn't sell that one either.

USING PROFESSIONAL INSPECTORS
VS. DOING YOUR OWN INSPECTION

If you're working with a real estate agent, you might be persuaded to use a professional inspector, either in lieu of your own inspection, or in addition to it. My feeling is that you should first do your own inspection, then hire an inspector if you're still in doubt about some items. Figure 10-1 is a worksheet you can use to help you do your own inspection, which is discussed later in the chapter.

There are several types of inspectors. If you're buying a very large and expensive home, with the outlay of a substantial amount of cash up front, then hire a termite inspector to look for any wood-destroying infestations; a licensed mechanical engineer to look over the mechanical systems; an architect or general contractor to inspect the structure, though a better alternative would be to have a plumber look at the plumbing, an electrician the electrical system, a heating contractor the heating/cooling system, and a home builder the structure. Most people who use inspectors use only a termite inspector and a for-hire building inspector.

One inspector most people are apt to use is a surveyor. A surveyor can find the corners of the lot and determine if the house is within the city's required building boundaries. He'll map out a *plot plan* with details of easements, fences and encroachments of your improvements onto the neighbors' lots, or of theirs onto yours.

WHAT TO LOOK FOR DURING AN INSPECTION

Whether you do your own inspection or use the services of a professional, there are specific things you will want to look for. Many of these are red flags that should immediately alert you to an unsound structure or potential costly problems. If you use a professional inspector, be sure he has checked for all of the points in the remainder of this chapter, if not, do your own inspection. It is always a bad idea to leave it to strangers to ensure the success of your own investments.

Lot Layout

Find out right from the start if the house is in a flood plain. If it is, then don't buy it. There is just no way to cure such a liability. Some houses are not in flood plains, but might still have drainage problems. Ask a lot of questions, because you'll want to avoid those homes as well.

The most desirable lot is the level one that rises slightly all the way around towards the house foundation. Very steep lots can be a disaster. They're dangerous and inconvenient to mow. In cold climates the driveways are impassable,

Home Improvement Checklist

Exterior

Driveway: OK ☐   Fix _____ Cost _____

Sidewalk: OK ☐   Fix _____ Cost _____

Lawn: OK ☐   Fix _____ Cost _____

Shrubs: OK ☐   Fix _____ Cost _____

Trees: OK ☐   Fix _____ Cost _____

Sprinkler
   system: OK ☐   Fix _____ Cost _____

Brick: OK ☐   Fix _____ Cost _____

Siding: OK ☐   Fix _____ Cost _____

Eaves: OK ☐   Fix _____ Cost _____

Windows: OK ☐   Fix _____ Cost _____

Doors: OK ☐   Fix _____ Cost _____

Roof: OK ☐   Fix _____ Cost _____

Fence: OK ☐   Fix _____ Cost _____

Exterior
   buildings: OK ☐   Fix _____ Cost _____

Other: _____

   OK ☐   Fix _____ Cost _____

Fig. 10-1.

Fig. 10-1. Cont.

Interior

☐ Entry   ☐ Master bedroom
☐ Living Room   ☐ Bedroom #2
☐ Dining Room   ☐ Bedroom #3
☐ Den   ☐ Bedroom #4
☐ Game/Exercise Room   ☐ Other _____

Floors: OK ☐   Fix _____ Cost _____

Walls: OK ☐   Fix _____ Cost _____

Ceilings: OK ☐   Fix _____ Cost _____

Trim boards: OK ☐   Fix _____ Cost _____

Doors: OK ☐   Fix _____ Cost _____

Windows: OK ☐   Fix _____ Cost _____

Door knobs
  and hardware: OK ☐   Fix _____ Cost _____

Light fixtures: OK ☐   Fix _____ Cost _____

Closets: OK ☐   Fix _____ Cost _____

Cabinets: OK ☐   Fix _____ Cost _____

Other: _____

                     OK ☐   Fix _____ Cost _____

Fig. 10-1. Cont.

Kitchen

Floors: OK ☐   Fix _____ Cost _____

Walls: OK ☐   Fix _____ Cost _____

Ceilings: OK ☐   Fix _____ Cost _____

Trim boards: OK ☐   Fix _____ Cost _____

Doors: OK ☐   Fix _____ Cost _____

WIndows: OK ☐   Fix _____ Cost _____

Door knobs
  and hardware: OK ☐   Fix _____ Cost _____

Light fixtures: OK ☐   Fix _____ Cost _____

Closets: OK ☐   Fix _____ Cost _____

Cabinets: OK ☐   Fix _____ Cost _____

Countertops: OK ☐   Fix _____ Cost _____

Sinks: OK ☐   Fix _____ Cost _____

Range: OK ☐   Fix _____ Cost _____

Ovens: OK ☐   Fix _____ Cost _____

Refrigerator: OK ☐   Fix _____ Cost _____

Dishwasher: OK ☐   Fix _____ Cost _____

Other: _____
                    OK ☐   Fix _____ Cost _____

Fig. 10-1. Cont.

	Bathroom: ☐ Master	☐ #2	☐#3

Floors: OK ☐   Fix _____ Cost _____

Walls: OK ☐   Fix _____ Cost _____

Ceilings: OK ☐   Fix _____ Cost _____

Trim boards: OK ☐   Fix _____ Cost _____

Doors: OK ☐   Fix _____ Cost _____

Windows: OK ☐   Fix _____ Cost _____

Door knobs

    and hardware: OK ☐   Fix _____ Cost _____

Light fixtures: OK ☐   Fix _____ Cost _____

Closets: OK ☐   Fix _____ Cost _____

Cabinets: OK ☐   Fix _____ Cost _____

Countertops: OK ☐   Fix _____ Cost _____

Mirrors: OK ☐   Fix _____ Cost _____

Faucets: OK ☐   Fix _____ Cost _____

Water closets

    and seats: OK ☐   Fix _____ Cost _____

Shower and

    enclosure: OK ☐   Fix _____ Cost _____

Tub and

    enclosure: OK ☐   Fix _____ Cost _____

Other: _____

    OK ☐   Fix _____ Cost _____

Fig. 10-1. Cont.

Mechanical

Fireplace: OK ☐   Fix _____ Cost _____

Heating system: OK ☐   Fix _____ Cost _____

Cooling system: OK ☐   Fix _____ Cost _____

Central vacuum

  system: OK ☐   Fix _____ Cost _____

Other: _____

          OK ☐   Fix _____ Cost _____

hard to clean, and dangerous. Even in warm months they pose numerous problems. Also, watch for the lot that's at the bottom of a hill, or at the lowest part of the neighborhood. It might be the only one that floods under severe rains.

Trees are pretty, but too many of them can be a hazard to your foundation, as well as to sewer and water lines. Find out where the sewer and water lines are buried. If there are many trees in their path—some of the fast growing trees that require a lot of water, such as willows, can be especially bothersome—you could have hefty repair bills later on. Trees too close to the house can damage the foundation, the exterior walls, and the roof. Near sidewalks and driveways, trees can cause upheaval and severe concrete cracks.

It's hard to tell if a lot will pool rain water. If you have any suspicions, then have your surveyor do a rough topography of the lot. If there are any parts near the house that are lower than the rest of the lot, and the house is on a slab foundation with the framing close to the ground, look inside for indications of water penetration. Slight stains or mold on the walls are a dead giveaway of problems. If that's the case, insist that the problem be corrected before you buy.

Concrete Work and Foundations

Probably the largest single part of the structure that can create major repair bills is the foundation. Whether it's a basement, a slab, or a pier and beam foundation, large movements can cause other systems to be adversely affected. I've seen houses built on ground that was filled and not properly compacted. After a few years the houses were so broken that no amount of leveling and patching could put them back in order.

One of my rental houses dropped 12 inches at the back. When I walked in the back rooms, it felt as if I were on a roller coaster. The house had actually broken in half. The front stayed in place, and the back half fell off. I kept the house in good repair except for that one shifting problem. My tenants didn't seem to mind terribly. It wasn't their house and rent was cheap. They realized repairs would be a costly undertaking and never hounded me for them. At one point, though, the drop caused the commode at the rear bath to back up. I had no choice but to fix the foundation.

I asked for repair bids, and the lowest was $2,500. I decided it was too much, so I bought three, 30-ton hydraulic jacks for $75 each and had several workers dig holes along the back and sides. They poured a footing at each hole and slowly jacked up the back about eight inches—we didn't want to go too far and break the water lines under the slab—until the floors felt reasonably level and the commode once again worked. For $1,000, I repaired a major disaster.

Unfortunately, not all foundation problems are that easy and cheap to fix. I've seen house slabs raise up from the middle, and it's pretty tough to raise the entire perimeter to meet the raised center part of the slab. Pier and beam foundations, as well as crawl space foundations, are a little easier to fix because you can get under the structure and level the house if there's no interference from brick.

To check for a faulty foundation, walk inside the house and see how the floors feel. If they're out of level, so is the foundation. You will see cracks in the drywall or plaster above doors and windows, and along the line where the walls meet the ceiling.

A buckled basement wall is a serious situation and can be expensive to fix. You must dig out dirt from around the buckled area, then allow the wall to come back in. It usually does so rather easily. If you see cracks in a concrete basement wall, or along or through concrete blocks, then place a string line horizontally and vertically at the cracks to see if there is inward buckling. If there is, then expect a large repair bill if you purchase the house.

Good basement drainage is the solution to pushed-in walls and damp or wet basements. If a generous amount of waterproofing has been applied to the exterior basement walls, and there is plenty of drain gravel and tile at the basement footings, with the tile leading away from the house, then you'll never have problems. If the tile leads into a sump pump inside the basement, then a backup pump is a good idea, in case one pump fails during a heavy rain. Unfortunately, in dry weather you can't tell how well the basement waterproofing is performing and how well it's installed unless you dig all around the foundation, which is out of the question.

The only other indications of poor basement drainage can come from a thorough inspection on the inside. Check to see if the basement seems or smells damp, if there are water stains on the walls, and large cracks on the concrete or block. These telltale signs say pass on to a better deal unless you're prepared to spend a few thousand dollars taking care of the problem. If the walls have been covered with sheetrock or paint, look carefully at any wall and floor covering around the edges of the outside walls for clues of movement or moisture.

You aren't likely to find many houses with wooden basement walls, but you'll probably find less problems with them, because builders need to take exceptional care when constructing them. They normally have vast quantities of gravel at the perimeter and base for good drainage. But you still must determine if there are any leaks on the inside.

If you're looking at a fairly old house, and the basement is dry, with very few cracks on the walls, then you'll probably never have problems. If it hasn't given trouble in 20 or 30 years, it's likely not to cause you grief in the next 20 or 30 years.

The integrity of exterior slab and asphalt work can be an indication of the stability of the soils around the house. *All* concrete and asphalt work will crack. Rarely will you see large sections of streets, driveways and walks free of cracks. The more sand and rock in the soil, the more stable will be anything placed on top of it. If you see hairline cracks, don't be alarmed. That's normal. If you see cracks that have opened up wide, that can mean there's some soil instability present. If areas of concrete have moved away from each other, then it means two things: the builder left out the steel reinforcing, and/or there is major movement of the soil on that lot. Both are bad omens. Any builder who doesn't reinforce his concrete has no scruples and might have left other essential elements out of the structure. A major soil movement around the walks and drives means there's a chance of a large foundation settlement. Pass on this one, and find a house on a more stable lot.

Exterior Walls and Roof

If there are problems with the exterior walls, it is usually very evident. Look at all of the brick, stucco, or sidings. Any cracks, loose material, or unusual peeling of paint is cause for further investigation. If it all looks straight, level, and neat, there should be no problems. If paint is very new, look for any type of a cover up, especially if only some walls have been repainted, and not the whole structure.

Roofs are a tougher item. The majority are covered with standard composition shingles. Very new shingles lay down perfectly flat and each shingle is truly distinct. As shingles get older, the edges begin to get rough, and they start to curl. Very old ones are bubbled and have curled into themselves. The edges, especially at the eve, are very rough and broken. Once shingles start to curl up or in, the roofing is very close to the end of its useful life. That's when small leaks start to show up inside the structure. Buying a house with a roof like this is like buying a used car with bald tires. There is no way you'll squeeze much more life out of a worn item. Discount for the cost of a new roof, or have the seller install one prior to closing.

The heavier, multilayered composition roofs are much more durable, and because they're relatively new on the market, you'll find very few on their last breath. Some are so heavy that they'll outlast two or three applications of standard composition shingles.

Concrete tile roofs are almost permanent. If you can see the entire roof from the ground and it looks good, and if there are no telltale signs of leaks on the inside, then you can figure you'll have no trouble while you own the house. The major drawback to this material is breakage. In a giant hail storm, not only can the roof be ruined, but the tiles are so heavy that they'll come crashing through the ceiling and end up tearing everything inside apart.

Wood shingles warp when they're old. They also split and the edges get ragged. If you find a lot of newer shingles stuck between the old ones, it means someone has patched the worst parts, and an entire reroofing job is not far in the future. Wood shingles are supposed to last a couple of decades, but most fall short of that time.

Another problem area can be the eaves. A house with a problem roof, or one that hasn't had total care, will have rotted eaves. If some of the fascia and soffit boards are rotted, then the underlying structure might be damaged. It's an expensive and tedious job to repair such damage. Old and faulty gutters can help cause, as well as hide, rotten fascia boards.

Interior Floors, Walls, and Ceilings

As I mentioned before, uneven floors usually mean deeper trouble than just the floors. Sometimes though, wood, plywood, or pressboard subfloors will warp and buckle. A lot of warping can indicate an underlying moisture condition. Either there's been a leak, or there's a massive amount of moisture under the floors.

The easiest way to spot poor subfloors is to look at areas that are tiled with thin vinyl tile. The warped or uneven subfloors will "bleed" right through the vinyl and show up as lumps, breaks, or cracks. If there are a lot of vinyl floors, and they're level and in good condition, you can be sure you've found good subfloors, especially if the vinyl is old.

Vinyl and hard tile can also indicate problems in slab foundations. If there are major cracks in the concrete, the hard tiles will readily crack along the break lines. The vinyls will tear and distinctly show the cracks.

Carpeted floors are an entirely different matter. For one thing, thick carpet over thick pad can hide some of the most dreadful subfloor and concrete foundation problems. Unless it's an aggravated situation, you'll not feel lumps and breaks under the carpet.

Carpet can also hide old, nasty spills, which might still be deep at the bottom in the backing or in the pad. A few years ago, in one of my rental houses, I had the unfortunate luck of housing the filthiest family I've ever encountered. Contrary to my good judgment, I allowed a fellow and his wife and son to move in, even though they had very bad credit. They looked dirty, which should have given it all away. The fellow's wife and son had had major health problems, and his pleading for the rental house touched my heart.

Surprisingly enough, he generally paid his rent on time. After a year and a half, however, he started to get slow on his payments. One day, he moved out in the middle of the night. One of my workmen asked me to take a look at the house during the cleanup. I asked why I needed to look at it. He said he didn't know how much I wanted to spend for repairs. I shuddered. I went over and found there wasn't major damage, but there was a lot of filth.

The walls were covered with a layer of grime and grease. Most of the house was carpeted, and they must have owned the last of the white wooly mammoths, or at least a very large white dog. There were not only stains all over the carpet, but there was a solid layer of white wooly mammoth hair over every inch of carpet. I don't think they owned a vacuum cleaner. The worst mess was in the dining room. The carpet was covered with dried dirt, and I assumed they'd had a lot of plants and had gotten dirt all over the floor. I later discovered, to my horror, that they'd kept the dog in the dining room and had almost never let him out.

I knew the carpet was ruined. I had the walls painted and other items repaired, then just before I replaced the carpet, I asked my carpet cleaner to take a look and see if he could do anything to help me. He shocked me when he said he could take care of the carpet. Basically, what he did was wash the carpets with huge amounts of water. The carpet in the dining room he cleaned top and bottom. With a bit of dye and very expert use of deodorants, he managed to make the carpet look and smell not new, but quite satisfactory. The only way someone could tell there had been major problems in the dining room was to look at the back of the carpet. The stains in the backing never came out.

I no longer own that house, but personally, I wouldn't live with anything like that, and nowadays, I don't ever ask my tenants to do so either.

You can't tell what's under the carpet, but if you're contemplating buying a house with fairly old carpet, just think of my dog story and consider tearing out the carpet as soon as you buy, or have the seller change it with your selection. If you have him change it, you won't have to come up with the cash for the carpet. It can be included as part of the purchase price and financed in the house loan.

Look at the condition of the walls above windows and door openings. That's where foundation movement will first show up. You'll see cracks emanating from the top corners of the windows and doors up to the ceilings. Hairline cracks aren't anything to worry about. Only a pro can completely patch wide settlement cracks on sheetrock, however, and if the home owner has done the work, you'll see the patches over the cracks.

Peeling paint on the inside walls of older houses can pose a health hazard for young children. Old paint has lead in it, and a child ingesting chips of it can get lead poisoning. You won't usually find the paint peeling off walls, but you might find it coming off door trim, windows, and window casings.

Pay particular attention to ceilings. If there has been a roof leak, you'll see a round discoloration on the ceiling somewhere below the leak. A large leak will pour so much water onto the ceiling that the sheetrock will bow from the weight and the weakening effects of the water. A small leak will only discolor the ceiling. If it's been leaking for a long time, it will ruin not only the ceiling sheetrock, but rot framing members. There are several ways to cover up a leak stain without taking care of the leak or the damaged ceiling. A spray mist of ammonia or matching paint will do the trick. Paint is often noticeable, so unless the entire ceiling has been painted, you'll spot the cover up.

Go into the attic. If the insulation is neat and full, you'll know there haven't been roof problems. Once up there, see how deep the insulation in the ceiling is. Anything less than six level inches is not acceptable. In fact, if the insulation has been poured onto the ceiling and not placed in batts, eight inches is better. Take a good look at the rafters in the attic—they hold up the roof and are the slanted framing members—as well as the ceiling joists—the flat boards you'll walk on. Even if a house is very old, the wood inside the attic should look fairly new: a light wood color as you'd see in fresh material at a lumber yard. Leaks of years gone by, as well as new leaks, will be easy to spot as discolorations on the framing members. A house with wood shingles might show telltale signs of small leaks at many of the rafters. That's normal and shouldn't alarm you. Wood shingles don't seal like composition shingles over their plywood base.

Interior Trim

Interior trim is everything that's installed after the sheetrock is finished. It includes paneling, doors, door and window casings, baseboards, ceiling trim, beams and other such decorative items. Check the fit of all wood joints. If a house has moved, the trim joints will no longer fit.

Look at the doors. They should close neatly on the frame when shut. If they don't catch easily on the metal strike plate, then they might be warped. You'll have to replace them sometime in the future. If hollow core doors aren't finished with paint or varnish all the way around, including the edges, lack of proper humidity during a heating season can warp them. This is a problem more prevalent in northern states.

The finish given the trim work can be an indication of the rest of the workmanship in the house. If the trim and doors are painted, a smooth, shiny finish indicates pride in workmanship. If there's stain and varnish, the smoother it is the better the workmanship. Signs of poor workmanship are nail holes that haven't been filled, or nails that haven't been countersunk.

Cabinetwork

Open and close all cabinet doors. Some of the cheap doors look good, but don't last long. The cheap cabinets have very thin wood on the doors. If you look at the way the doors fit against the cabinet facing you'll see if any doors have warped. Inspect the shelves. Inexpensive shelves warp after a few years. Replacing cabinets is an expensive proposition, and while some remodelers offer cabinet refacing, which is a little less expensive than replacing, it is a poor second choice to complete cabinet replacement.

Countertops made of plastic laminates (Formica types) can buckle away from their backing if water has been allowed to get under the plastic. Look around sinks to see if there are signs of delamination. Tap on the countertop with a fingernail. If it sounds hollow, that's an indication of air between the plastic and the backing.

Plumbing

You might need a plumber for a thorough inspection of the plumbing system. But you can get an idea of plumbing health just by looking under the sinks, in the basement or crawl space, and elsewhere to look at the drain and water pipes. Flush commodes and run water at all sinks. The older the house, the more trouble you can expect. Old cast iron water lines are often corroded and full of mineral deposits. It's not unusual to have to replace all of the water supply lines with new copper—a very expensive proposition. Corrosion in cast-iron sewer lines of an old house can have caused perforation of the pipe walls. That allows sewage to leak out. Expensive replacement might be inevitable. Finally, the old sewer line going to the main city sewer is impossible to inspect because it's underground.

Most of the older homes had clay pipe, and at some point the pipe just erodes away. There's no way to fix it without digging up the yard and installing new iron pipe. If the previous owners have replaced the plumbing lines, that's a big plus for you.

If the structure is old and still has the original faucets and water heater, be prepared to pay for replacements. These items rarely last more than 10 years, especially water heaters. If you see old fixtures, make a note on your inspection sheet. Put down a figure you estimate will cover the replacement.

Electrical

There are two types of wiring to be concerned about: knob and tube and aluminum wiring. Old knob and tube uses two separate wires that run throughout the house. Modern wiring uses Romex—a group of copper wires wrapped with a plastic insulator. You'll only find knob and tube in very old houses. Aluminum Romex wiring was used in the early 70s, but it was blamed for a good number of fires.

In older houses, you'll find fuses instead of circuit breakers. Circuit breakers are switches, fuses look like little flat light bulbs. Fuses burn out when there's an overload in a circuit. They're a nuisance because they have to be changed any time they burn. Sometimes homeowners don't have spares and will bypass the fuse with a penny behind the burnt fuse; a bad idea that has caused its share of fires.

Heating/Cooling Systems

The older the furnace, the more trouble it's apt to give you. A great majority of modern houses have forced air heating, and virtually all cooling units are the forced air type. Look at the duct work in the attic, in the basement, and under crawl spaces, to see what shape it's in. If the furnace looks neat and new, it's probably in good shape. Turn it on and make it work in both the heating and cooling modes. If the furnace or the cooling condensing unit on the outside look old, dirty and tired, you can expect to repair or replace sooner than later.

The same holds true for boilers and radiators that use water heat. Some boilers are so big and obsolete, you'll have trouble getting them fixed. You might not be able to remove one from the house if you upgrade to a modern system unless it is cut up into pieces.

Not only is it time consuming but it's very expensive to modernize the electrical, plumbing, or heating/cooling systems. Take nothing for granted in old houses. Jot down the model numbers of furnaces, condensing units, water heaters, etc. Call plumbers and heating people to get their opinion on reliability and cost of repair and replacement. Lift the lid on a commode. Normally, there's a date on the back of the tank or on the lid. It'll tell you when the unit was manufactured. This will often tell you the age of the house if there haven't been upgrades in the plumbing fixtures.

If you suspect potential trouble with any of the mechanical systems, make a provision in the contract that you have a right to have them inspected by professionals, and to what extent the seller will be liable for repairs. Don't spend any money for inspections, however, until you have a firm contract to purchase.

11

Buying from Builders

IF YOU ARE PURCHASING A NEW HOME, THERE ARE SEVERAL DIFFERENT TYPES of builders you might encounter. Most builders do their own merchandising, meaning that they either sell the homes themselves or they hire salespeople to do the selling out of model homes. A few of the smaller builders list their houses with real estate brokers. If you have a choice, purchase a home that's already completed. That way, what you see is what you get.

If you do have a house built, be aware that one of the hardest times in a new home-purchaser's life are the weeks or months it takes to have a house built. The very best builders can smooth things over throughout the building process. They carry out each step professionally, neatly, and the buyer always feels not only that there is quality construction, but that there's progress every day of the construction period.

Sometimes, you'll hear from buyers about shoddy construction and abnormally extended periods of construction. In some cases, it's the builder's fault. But often, it's the buyer's lack of familiarity with construction techniques, subcontractor scheduling difficulties, materials shortages, and building time scheduling.

When builders talk about "rough framing," they mean the wood structure of the house. The very best framers' work looks like trim work, wherein all joints and cuts are perfect, but most production crews' work is just that, rough framing. Not all framing members meet perfectly and not all cuts are exactly straight. A lot of houses are framed speedily by large crews and, even though they are well built, the knowledgeable buyer should realize that most homes are structurally overbuilt and that rough framing is expected to be less than perfect. If the house has straight walls, roof, and ceilings, then the framing was done correctly. That's the real determining factor.

There are true horror stories. Home building is one of the riskiest of businesses and corners are often cut whenever possible. Don't purchase a house that's only a dream in yours and the builder's mind. The dream for you is a perfect house, but the dream for the builder might only be a handsome profit and a house that will satisfy you just enough to keep you off his back once it's finished. There are countless builders that go broke during construction, and there are many times when subcontractors and materials suppliers don't get paid and later file liens on a property. Building is a loosely controlled business, and anyone can be a builder, no matter what his experience.

Some buyers can't take the psychological strain of construction, and they don't realize that fact until their house is well underway. So unless you must have a home designed and built specifically to fit needs that no other house offers, buy a house that's completed. If you must have one built, do a *thorough* job of satisfying yourself of the builder's integrity, experience, and economic stability. Especially the latter. Don't let a builder's Mercedes fool you into thinking he's economically stable.

Generally, there are three types of builders. First is the large, national or regional builder. Second is the local tract builder. The third is the custom builder.

LARGE NATIONAL OR REGIONAL BUILDERS

Large national or regional builders don't fool with much less than hundreds of homes at a time, often starting a dozen or more foundations simultaneously. They work over a region that can cover one state, several states, or the whole country. Some are even international. They always have professionally decorated and landscaped model homes. That's an absolute must, and the reason for their success. If you're in a smaller city, far away from a large metropolitan area, you'll never see this type of builder. The big advantages to buying from a very large builder is financial stability, expertise in design and construction, control of subdivision development, and tight control of quality and time schedules. You'll almost always end up with a quality, or at least acceptable, product. The disadvantage is that because of building efficiency, the houses all seem to come out of approximately the same cookie cutter molds. Still, the chances of being completely disappointed with a large builder's work are slim indeed.

You won't be able to negotiate much with a large builder. The model home designs, and a few other designs, will be all that's offered for sale. Very little customizing is available. Price negotiation is generally impossible. Most of these builders work with real estate agents. The agent will get a commission, but if you show up without an agent, you'll not get a discount for the commission. That might seem unfair, but the builders figure their profit margins on averages of the whole developments, not individual units. One house might yield a 5 percent profit and another a 15 percent profit. If they're shooting for 10 percent overall, then with enough volume, it will all average out satisfactorily. In a sellers' market, you'll find the builder's prices firm, but in buyers' markets, you'll note some price concessions in the form of specials or in extra ''points'' the builder pays to buy down the interest rate on a house loan.

The tricky element of buying homes from builders using exceptional model homes is that you never really see what your own home will look like. If the models have a lot of ''decorative items'' that aren't included as part of the purchase price of your house, you might be disappointed when you finally see your own house. You can get around this by inspecting the production models before you decide on a particular design, or even a particular builder. Often, the production houses look simpler and smaller than the model homes. This is because the eye can't determine size without furniture. The walls look closer or farther away because there's no furniture to give rooms depth.

Fast production is a disadvantage with large projects. At first, there are a lot of empty lots. The subdivision can look wide open and the lots spacious. How the houses will look once they're all in is an unknown factor. I've seen beautiful areas, even ones with plenty of trees, turned into mediocre subdivisions because the houses were all built two stories high and very close together. The final product can be disappointing, and the only way to get around it is to be one of the last in the subdivision. You'll see the completed house, subdivision, and your neighbors. If there are a lot of unkept yards, very little landscaping, cars on the lawns, dogs, cats, and kids running wild, then continue the search for a better subdivision.

LOCAL TRACT BUILDERS

There are ''large'' local tract builders in almost every sizeable town, including very large cities. They might build anything from a few dozen to a few thousand homes per year. The latter works exactly as large national builders. In fact, local tract builders are very similar to national builders, with a few exceptions.

Local tract builders can be more undercapitalized than larger builders. Don't make a large down payment when buying from them. If they go belly up during construction, you'll lose your deposit. A few hundred dollars in earnest money should be all you have at risk.

Local tract builders will negotiate more than their larger counterparts. Most will treat the real estate agents' commissions the same as the largest builders, so you probably won't get a discount if you buy without an agent. Still, asking for a commission discount is worth a try. A commission discount is not illegal or immoral as long as the lender is aware you're receiving it, and that you're getting it as a discount in price, and not as a kickback at the end of the loan closing. Receiving a discount after closing can be fraud, because you might have entered into a double contract, which is illegal. This is discussed further in Chapter 15.

The local tract builders might have one or two unfurnished and undecorated models. This is good because you're not fooled: what you see is what you get.

Often, you'll negotiate the sale directly with the builder. That's also good because changes to model plans, pricing, and equipment might be available. You'll also know exactly who it is that's behind the operation. They tell you not to judge a book by its cover, but if the builder sounds dumb to you, it's because he probably is. There are very few colleges that offer degrees for builders, so yours could have been a carpenter, an accountant, a lawyer, a shrewd business-man, a snake oil salesman, even a homeless streetwalker before he became a home builder.

Smaller tract builders are on the edge of the fence when it comes to tract building and custom building. In happy times, when all they do is put up for sale signs on their lots and the houses go like hotcakes, they'll be tract builders. There will be little price concessions, and few changes to plans are allowed. In lean years, however, they are strictly custom builders, constructing houses only on signed contracts with strong buyer down payments up front.

CUSTOM BUILDERS

Custom builders work in all price ranges, from the very smallest single family detached houses to the largest condominiums, co-ops, and multimillion dollar estates. A professional custom builder will have at least one well-appointed model home, reflecting his ideas of what is good in design and execution. Smaller ones have their office adjacent to the model home, or even in the garage of the model. Large ones have several models and the office is in another part of town. Custom builders can put into existence your ideas, or change his ideas to meet with your needs and desires. His houses will be more expensive per square foot than those of tract builders because there is less efficiency in building custom homes and because there will surely be more expensive appointments through-out the structure.

Some custom builders work with real estate agents, others don't. When you sit down with the builder or his salespeople, you'll be asked all of the questions a good real estate agent would ask. The builder will first sell you on his work and ability, then he'll qualify you to see what you can afford, ask many pertinent questions concerning your needs, wants, family size, and so forth. If he has models, he'll ask you what it is in those models that you like, and what you want to avoid. If you like one of his models, he'll sketch out its floor plan with changes you request and give you an idea of cost to produce. Once you have a firm price, he'll want you to go on contract for the construction of the house on a lot you select. He'll need a fairly good sized down payment, and might even close on the house before construction begins. If you preclose, he'll receive advances from your permanent loan on cost of materials and labor as the work progresses.

Before you sign a contract and plunk a large amount of money down or preclose on a loan, thoroughly check his references. Talk to his banker, past customers, as well as his major material suppliers, including subcontractors. See how he pays. If you get any bad reports, especially from his banker, then don't do business with him. Buying a home before it's built is a very risky business. Even a builder who's been stable for years might run into challenging economic times, and your house could be the one where his luck runs out. If that's the case, you can end up with an incomplete structure, or with subcontractor or materials supplier liens on the property. They might have performed their work and supplied materials, but never got paid, even though you've paid the builder for the work or materials.

Some builders, anticipating objections from sophisticated buyers, might take draws payable to them as well as the supplier or subcontractor who performed the work or supplied the materials that covers the draw requested. This is a great safeguard and keeps liens from being placed on the property.

If you don't preclose, but simply give the builder a large down payment at the start of construction, you could be asking for trouble. Let's say you contracted to have a $200,000 house built. The builder requests $20,000 up front. In a buyers' market that could be the extent of the builder's profit. As my grandmother always said, prepaid musicians don't play well. It might be best to escrow the deposit in a bank account with a provision that the builder gets it when you sign an acceptance of the property or when you move into it, whichever comes first.

ANALYZING THE PAPERWORK

Having a home custom built takes more paperwork than when buying an existing one. The builder should provide you with a complete set of plans, specifications, and a construction contract. The plans indicate all of the dimensions, door sizes, cabinet locations and sizes, electrical outlet locations, etc. The specifications should specify the quality and types of materials to be used throughout the structure. The contract will set out the terms of the agreement, how the builder will be paid, what happens if there are disputes, how he'll charge for changes. Go over the plans and specifications carefully. Have the builder explain everything thoroughly. If you have to put down any money for preparation of plans and specifications, then have him show you a sample set of plans and specs to see how complete yours will be. I've seen many small builders work off preliminary sketches, and, believe it or not, off rough sketches made on the back of an envelope. That's an unacceptable situation that only courts disaster. If you get a hint of this at the beginning, find another builder.

Once construction has started, changes are often a source of unnecessary expense, delay, and disagreement. Keep all changes to a minimum. Don't make changes that require the tearing down and replacing of materials and equipment already in place. Make sure from the start of plan design that you thoroughly understand dimensions, room sizes, cabinet layouts, and that what's indicated on the plans and specifications will take care of your expectations. If you think you'll need an extra ten inches in a room, say so before the plans are completed, or at least before the walls are framed. No changes should be made without a written order covering price, method of payment, and the specifics of the change, which should be signed by you and the builder. A large national builder I worked for years ago in Chicago first introduced me to VODGs (Verbal Orders Don't Go). They were great. *Never* allow a change to be made without a signed order, even if the builder won't charge you for the change. If your relationship goes sour towards the end of construction, he might give you a bill for what you thought were free changes. He can force you to pay by filing a lien because you had no written understanding about it.

I believe the contract and paperwork for the construction of a house should be completely explicit as well as understandable by any reasonably intelligent adult. Long contracts replete with lawyer mumbo jumbo are a ridiculous waste of paper and ink, as well as a source of confusion for the buyer and the builder as well. If the builder has one of these lengthy documents, go over it with him and have him explain it, sentence-by-sentence.

If you're purchasing a house that's under construction the paperwork should be just as thorough as if you were starting from scratch, but the initial earnest money deposit should be less significant. After all, the builder's already building *his* house on *his* lot with *his* own interim financing. If you don't like the final product and decide not to go through with the purchase, the only damages he might incur are changes and color selections you might have made that are not to his liking. If the layout of the house is exactly like one of the builder's models, then plans and specifications are not necessary. The contract will simply state which specific house yours will copy, and exclude items that you won't get, or include items the model doesn't have.

UNDERSTANDING WARRANTIES

During the 1970s, the National Association of Home Builders decided a Home Owners Warranty (HOW) would be a great selling tool. They set up a separate company to underwrite insurance policies covering certain sections of the structure. I was against adding additional cost to a house, and at the time, home builders in entire areas like Houston, Texas, decided against participating in the program. A lot of builders offer HOW, but I still believe my original feelings were on target. Homes built in cities of any reasonable size are inspected by city inspectors, which doesn't say they'll be perfect, but it's a lot more supervision from a third party than cars or appliances might get. I've seen many cases where HOW didn't stand behind buyer complaints.

Your best assurance is to carefully inspect a builder's work before he gets to your house. Educate yourself a bit on home construction techniques and go out on his jobs as well as those of other builders. Learn what to expect. If the trenches for your concrete foundation footings are neat, the steel reinforcing orderly, and the concrete finish acceptable, then you don't need a guarantee. The house will stand up to the elements like others in the neighborhood. The same is true of other parts of the structure.

A builder's reputation, financial stability, and integrity should all mean more to you than warranties. A reputable builder will acknowledge there's a problem when he sees one. He'll take care of it in a timely manner, because you are his best advertising. If you're happy, you'll recommend him to others. Home building is like the resale real estate market. When we get a referral, we know we have no competition. The prospect will buy from us without so much as talking to other real estate agents.

Most builders offer a one-year warranty on any part of the structure; some will offer a longer warranty. As a builder, I personally would stand behind a house for many years if I'd designed it and carefully supervised its construction, because a house, unlike a car, has very few moving parts, and it sits still all of its life. Once constructed, only the elements or neglect can tear it down.

Having gone through many years as a builder, I can say that if I were buying a home today, I would look for a house that's one or two years old. The design would still be new, all of the systems like new, even the carpet can still be perfect with only one year's wear, and best of all, the little things that can go wrong with the house, and the major items that can fail, would already have failed. If the foundation's just plain no good, there will be hints of that fact after the first year. In a developed subdivision, all the houses will be completed. You'll know which direction the neighborhood is taking, and who your neighbors are.

SELECTING FINISHES

Builders select finishes and equipment for three reasons: because the builder is comfortable using them, because the item is a good buy and exhibits quality, or because of budget restraints. All of this is good, but the latter can influence a builder to go with equipment that's marginal. The best path is to spend money on quality systems, then use more modest finish items. For example, if you're offered gorgeous wood doors but a marginal heating/cooling system, ask your builder to give you less expensive doors with a good paint job, which is less expensive, and to substitute his minimal-comfort heating/cooling system with a better, quieter, more reliable one.

There are many items you can skimp on without affecting quality, but there are some that should be of the highest quality. Some of the items you can skimp on if your budget is constrained include:

- Interior paint finishes
- Interior doors
- Light fixtures
- Carpet and flooring

These and other items that can be replaced with ease and that are relatively inexpensive can be upgraded at a later time. Some of the items you should never skimp on are:

- The foundation
- The framing structure
- Insulation
- Windows
- Electrical and plumbing systems
- The heating/cooling system

Once these items are installed, they are usually permanent. Appliances, cabinets, counter tops, garage doors, roofing materials, and plumbing fixtures can be changed later, but at relatively high costs. There will be tough decisions, but you'll be more satisfied if you opt for higher quality inside the walls and simpler appointments on the exterior.

CHOOSING AMENITIES

Amenities can be defined as any item that enhances the value or attractiveness of a structure. Real estate people consider pools, wet bars, fireplaces, and trash compactors amenities. The more expensive the house, the more amenities it's supposed to have. And the more amenities it has, the more expensive it gets. Some amenities, however, won't return their cost to you when you sell the home. For example, a pool is usually a poor investment. If you spend $20,000 on a pool for a $100,000 home, and you decide to sell the house a few months after you add the pool, you'll sell the house for maybe $110,000 unless you're in a very hot sellers market. Other amenities will actually add more to the house than what the amenity costs. A $100,000 house without a $1,500 fireplace might only sell for $95,000. The $1,500 fireplace can have a $5,000 perceived value.

If you stay with the norm in your neighborhood, you'll make the right decisions. I fly over the Dallas/Fort Worth area a lot, and there are neighborhoods where I see very few swimming pools. In those areas, a pool is a luxury. In contrast, there are other areas where almost every house has a pool. In this case, the pool is a necessity, and you're likely get 100 percent of the pool's value back when you sell the house.

Some amenities will never be of much value at sale time. For example, assume you have two, five-year-old houses, side-by-side, and they are exactly the same plan and size. If one is priced at $80,000, and the other at $80,200 because it has an intercom, forget getting extra for the intercom. Anything extra should be attributed more to landscaping or condition than to the intercom. The same holds true for central vacuum systems, trash compactors, and other non-essentials. That's not to say that you can't get $1,000 more for one house than the other if it has an inordinate number of amenities, but the seller might have paid $7,000 more for those goodies when he bought the house new.

Except for those who are building a very basic house, most builders will sell the buyer on the "sizzle" and not the "steak." The reason they have model homes is to get you so excited about the way your home can look, to get you so involved in seeing yourself in it, that you buy, even if you don't buy all of the extras. There is a little bit of money to be made in amenities, but the big money is in selling the structure itself. Think of the automobile market. Many basic and fairly standard cars sell for around $20,000. In my real estate business, we delve into people's finances day in and day out. We see many folks with $45 to $50,000 annual incomes who make payments on $20,000 cars. Does it make any sense to pay 40 percent or more of one year's pre-tax income for a vehicle that will be very much depreciated at the end of a five-year loan? I don't think it does. There are too many good new cars out there for half that amount, or good used cars for one fourth that amount. These folks bought the sizzle, however, not the steak. They were fooled by the razzle-dazzle on the showroom floor.

The same can happen with model homes. Don't be fooled into buying the sizzle and end up with a tiny, flashy steak. Buy the amount of space you need with the items you feel are essential to your life-style. Keep in mind the expectations of those that might buy your home later on. It is always a good idea to give a little thought about future salability. If everyone in your subdivision has a trash compactor or a pool, then put one in your home.

12

Buying a Single-Family Detached House

ECONOMICS OR CONVENIENCE WILL DICTATE WHETHER YOU BUY A SINGLE family detached house, or go the attached route. A single-family detached house is one house on one lot that is not attached to another structure in any way. In this chapter, you'll learn how to analyze the effectiveness of lot and house layout, the condition of landscaping, walks, drives, and the location of easements, and utility lines when purchasing a single-family house.

HOW THE COST OF LAND AFFECTS PRICE

When buying from a builder, you might want to keep this information on land cost handy. The cost of land is the most expensive item in a single-family home. This is true whether it's a standard, single-family dwelling, or a zero lot-line home. Everything else is minor compared to the land. Naturally, heavy cost in land is the main reason for modern town houses and condominiums, although it was probably less of a reason in the town homes built hundreds of years ago when distance between houses might have been just as important. With the advent of cars, urban sprawl was no longer much of a factor.

One of my college professors explained that the cost of land should equal about 15 percent of the total finished price of a home. That might have been right in the 1960s, but that figure doesn't work in many cases today. Using the formula above, the cost of land for a $200,000 home would have to be around $30,000. That's not a farfetched figure, and if you can do it and still live in a good area, you'll have done an admirable job of purchasing your lot. But $50,000 is probably more like it. This means the cost of land can be 25 percent or more of the finished house price.

I've found that the 15 percent figure is more likely to work in small towns away from large cities. The 25 percent is more the norm in the suburbs of larger cities. In very nice areas inside large cities, the 25 percent figure is often surpassed.

Naturally, these figures won't work if you're paying $200,000 for 150 acres in East Texas and building a $50,000 home on it. Farm land isn't considered a building lot. Also, these figures won't mean much to those of you looking for existing, older homes. There are times, however, when the price of land increases so dramatically that shacks are sold for a tremendous price. If you're trying to buy in an area that has too much demand, you could end up paying more for the land than the house, even though you'll not be aware of it. An example is a house I saw sell for $250,000 in Highland Park (an exclusive area of North Dallas) several years ago. The new owner proceeded to raze the structure and build a large, impressive home on the lot. A $250,000 house in Highland Park is rare—$500,000 and into the millions is more like it. If you really wanted to live in Highland Park, and could afford only $250,000, then you'd buy one of the remaining obsolete structures and live in discomfort.

Its not a good idea though. When you're buying a house, avoid at all cost your desire to impress friends, neighbors, and relatives. Many home builders prey on those vain weaknesses of the human character with their loud sizzle and little steak. Buy within your means, live within your means, and you'll enjoy large, comfortable housing.

The value of the lot is supremely important in all real estate. That's why someone would pay $250,000 for a property and knock down the house and use only the lot. Increases in the value of single-family homes, as well as town houses, condos, and co-ops are due more to the increase in the value of the land than an increase in the value of the structure. It's crazy that housing should appreciate as it depreciates.

In order to separate what you're paying for the land from what you're paying for the structure, you must know what a new structure comparable to the one you're contemplating would cost. When you go look at houses that builders are selling, always ask what the cost of the lots are. Then just delete the cost of the lot from the total price of the house. Divide the cost of the house by the number of square feet in the structure. With that figure, you can determine what people are asking for their houses and what they're asking for their lots. This can help you in the selection process.

WHAT LANDSCAPING REVEALS

The landscaping around a house tells a lot about the people who have lived in it. If it's in good condition, and there is plenty of it, feel comfortable that the inside of the house is probably just as neat, and that the owners have taken pride in keeping everything in top shape. If the yard is a mess, if there is little grass, the shrubs are overgrown or dying, you can expect to find things on the inside equally ragged. With landscaping, you can read the book by its cover. You can also read the neighborhood by the landscaping. If the whole area looks good on the outside, then the neighbors are probably neat people who keep their houses in good shape and who take pride in the way their neighborhood looks.

Don't let the landscaping of the house you're looking at compel you into the purchase of a dwelling in a declining neighborhood, however. The whole area must look neat, not just the one that interests you. Also, don't let the landscaping cover any problems with house exterior walls and its foundation. Pull the bushes back and look carefully for problems.

The lawn is very important. In areas that have shifting soils because of changes in water content, a good lawn means the soil around the foundation has been kept at a constant, moist level, keeping the foundation stable. In those areas, if the soil around the perimeter of the foundation is allowed to dry, the foundation can settle. If rains come pouring in after the drying process, the soil will swell and the foundation goes along for a ride. Of course, that wouldn't be so bad if the whole house moved all at once, but that's rarely the case. Usually, only one side or the other shifts, and the foundation and house walls split.

Trees that are too close to the house can sometimes cause damage. The house walls or the roof are particularly susceptible. Some large trees are expensive to remove, so if you feel the trees are causing damage or could do so in the future, have the seller cover that expense.

EVALUATING WALKS AND DRIVES

If concrete walks and drives are very old, the finish cement layer can scale. The top of the concrete will be uneven, and rocks or gravel will show in lieu of a smooth concrete finish. There might even be rust stains where the top of the reinforcing steel shows through. Concrete this worn comes apart easily, especially on driveways, because of the weight of cars rolling on top. Consider the cost of replacing bad concrete in your offer to purchase. Highly deteriorated asphalt drives and walks are easier to spot, because asphalt comes apart in large chunks with huge cracks.

If there is a common driveway shared by your house and a neighbor's, determine where the lot line divides the driveway. You might see a situation where there is a 16' wide drive leading up between two houses, then it splits into side entry garages. Is the property line directly in the middle of the 16', or is it mostly on one property or the other?

A very steep driveway leading up to a property can pose problems. If the driveway drops into the house, does the rain water pool in front of the garage, or is there drainage to the sides? If the house sits high off the street, is the drive very steep? If it's too steep, you'll see scratch marks where cars scrape going in and out.

Some level driveways shift because of soil movement or through frost upheaval and end up above the level of the garage floor. If the house sits low on the lot, then rainwater might come into the garage and collect there until it reaches the level of the driveway outside. There is no way to cure this problem without removing part of the driveway and regrading some or all of the lot. In this case, you might not even see signs that water has stood in the garage, as most garages have a concrete curb around their perimeter and the water might not reach high enough to stain the walls.

INSPECTING RETAINING WALLS AND FENCES

Old retaining walls made of brick, stone, or railroad ties will tell you how well they were made. If a house is older than 10 years and there's a retaining wall that's still straight and level, then you can assume it will stay that way forever. On the other hand, you can't tell what a new one will do. The best retaining walls—those holding back a certain amount of earth—are built of steel-reinforced concrete with a concrete finish, or covered with stone or brick. These are well designed to carry the weight of the earth behind them.

With freestanding walls, the only problem can come from the foundation holding them up. If there's up and down movement of a brick or stone wall, it will crack and come apart. Wood and metal fences generally don't need a foundation. They can move about with no damage.

With a fence or wall, it's best to determine who owns it. If it's on your property, you must maintain it. If it's on the neighbor's lot, not only must he maintain it, but he has a right to remove it. If he removes it, you might be forced to replace one on your lot.

WHAT SURVEYS REVEAL

Usually, a survey of the lot is done only a day or two before the closing. If you foresee a problem, ask to see a plot plan of the lot from the builder or the last survey from the present homeowner. The survey will show the following:

- Exact location of the house on the lot
- Fences
- Drives and walks
- Encroachments from, or with, adjacent neighbors
- Easements
- Building setback lines
- Pools and patios

I've had resale deals fall through because the survey showed the unexpected. If a homeowner builds a garage on the back of his property and he places it directly on top of a utility easement or halfway into his neighbor's lot, there can be trouble in the future.

A sloppy builder might even build a house across a city-required building setback line or even across the property line. The latter case is not entirely uncommon, and there have been cases where a house had to be moved or torn down as a result.

Any encroachment by you onto a neighbor's lot, or by a neighbor onto your lot, or by any of your improvements onto an easement or setback line, should prompt you to do a thorough investigation to see if it causes problems with neighbors, the city, or utility people. If a pool is built onto an abandoned utility easement, it won't be a problem. If there are utilities under the pool, however, that's serious enough to find another property unless you want to tear out the pool.

UNDERSTANDING BUILDING RESTRICTIONS

To find out if there are any building restrictions on a property, ask for a copy of deed restrictions from the original development. The papers will be filed at the county courthouse. Deed restrictions set forth the following:

1. Uses allowed of and on the property.
2. Types of structures that can be built.
3. Minimum allowable size of the homes.
4. Materials allowed or required for construction.
5. Animals that may be kept on the premises.
6. Vehicles allowed on or in front of lots.
7. Antennas and other appurtenances allowed.

All of the previous restrictions are very important, especially on newer houses. The older a house gets, the less success a neighbor will have of winning a lawsuit to enforce a deed restriction your house might be violating. On fairly new subdivisions, however, success if fairly certain. Let's examine each restriction individually.

1. **Uses allowed.** Most restrictions in single-family developments restrict the use of each lot to one single home, for the use of one single family per lot. There are no multifamily uses, nor are duplexes or other multi-family units allowed. The house must be used by only one family. If you're buying a house for use by your family of four, as well as by your parents, there's a possibility of conflict with the deed restrictions. Home businesses and other commercial uses might not be allowed.

2. **Types of structures.** Sometimes the restrictions are indeed restrictive. They will dictate what types of structures can be built to include the main dwelling and any other buildings allowed on the lot. They might not allow detached garages, carports, or certain types of storage buildings. They will state maximum number of stories high for structures, and even dictate design of houses and accessory buildings. Generally, trailers and mobile homes are prohibited. An attached garage might also be a requirement.

3. **Size of the homes.** There is always a provision for minimum square feet of living space. If the builder doesn't comply, the homeowner can be forced to add enough living space to bring the house within size requirements of the deed restrictions.

4. **Materials for construction.** I've seen several lawsuits over material requirements. Two often-cited requirements are the exterior wall and roof finishes. The restrictions might call for only wood or tile roofs. They might not allow anything on exterior walls except brick or stone. Some might even require a certain percentage of masonry cover, say 75 percent, for example. If your house needs to have 75 percent masonry, and the builder provided only 50 percent, you could be forced to install more brick—a very expensive proposition on a completed structure.

5. **Animals allowed.** Animals that are allowed to be kept on the premises are often cited. You might buy a house on a two-acre lot, but not be allowed to have a horse. You might be restricted to a certain number of dogs or cats. Chickens or quail might not be permitted.

6. **Vehicles allowed.** Many restrictions prevent homeowners from keeping large trucks, recreational motor vehicles, or trailers or boats on the street yard, and even on the sides of the houses. Be sure to check this

restriction if you plan to keep unusual vehicles or even a large number of cars on the property, or even in front of the property at the street.

7. **Antennas and other appurtenances.** Some of the amateur radio station antennas tend to get large and unsightly, and they're often disallowed through deed restrictions. Certain kinds of storage buildings, driveways, walks, or pools might also be prohibited.

In addition to these common deed restrictions, there are often city ordinances that can restrict your use of a property. Simply because the previous owner parked his 18-wheel tractor trailer in front of his house doesn't mean you'll be allowed to do the same. If you plan to keep or do anything unusual with the property, check with the city to make sure you'll not be in violation of zoning ordinances.

Probably the best indication of compliance with deed and city restrictions is the neighborhood. If your house fits in and is similar in design and use of building materials with the rest of the houses in the neighborhood, you'll not have problems. If there is anything radically different, do some checking before you buy.

13

Buying Attached Housing, Condos, and Co-Ops

THE PREDOMINANT REASON MOST PEOPLE CONSIDER MULTIFAMILY UNITS IS money. It's simply cheaper to build, sell, buy, maintain, heat, and cool a house that is attached to another house. Money savings is certainly not the only reason, but it's the main reason. You'll pay less for a condo than you will for a single family house of the same size and location. Before considering a multifamily structure, however, you need to ask yourself if this type of living arrangement will be right for you.

DETERMINING WHETHER A CONDO IS RIGHT FOR YOU

There are certain groups of people who are more likely to buy condos than others. If you fall within one of these groups, you would have a good reason—besides monetary—to consider a condo:

- Retirement-age people with moderate to above-average wealth. This group has a much higher preference for condominiums compared with any other group. They are attracted to the convenience and amenities of condominiums.
- New or young households with higher-than-average incomes who either don't expect to have children, or who will wait several years to have them.

117

- Childless, middle-aged households with higher-than-average income and/ or wealth who:
  1. Would like to move out of rental units in order to build up equity and get the tax advantages of home ownership;
  2. Hope for property appreciation while retaining the conveniences of rental units; or
  3. Would like to move out of single-family housing to enjoy the convenience of condominiums.
- Young, single, or divorced people, especially single women, who have a reasonably good income and are tired of renting apartments but like the conveniences of apartment living.
- Small families who want a nice home but can't afford one because single-family and town house units are beyond their means.

The biggest disadvantage to condos is their lack of a private yard. If that doesn't bother you, then there are a lot of advantages. Here are some of them:

1. Freedom from the responsibility of upkeep.
2. Property management by professionals.
3. Low cost through group sharing.
4. Neighborhood consistency.
5. Security.
6. Cheaper utilities because less walls and ceilings are exposed to the elements.

When buying a condo or co-op, it's important to have an understanding of all the provisions of ownership. This is especially true of co-ops. For example, the board of directors in a co-op normally has the right to approve or reject prospective buyers of shares. They also have the right to approve or reject prospective sublessees. You have to know what your game plan will be when it comes time to sell or lease.

Most states require a prospectus from developers. Take a look at it before you buy, and study the following:

- Names, addresses, and phone numbers of the members of the board of directors.
- If available, the engineer's or inspector's report on the general physical condition of the building or buildings.
- A current report on the financial background of the building (the underlying mortgage, reserve funds, recent taxes, and assessments).

- The proprietary lease.
- A copy of your subscription agreement.
- A breakdown of your monthly maintenance charges.
- The board of directors' financial restrictions for buyers.

FINANCING

We'll look at financing in detail in later chapters, but at this point I'd like to make some remarks about financing co-ops. Co-ops are treated much differently than other real estate because of the type of ownership they afford.

Banks normally loan 60 to 85 percent of the purchase price of new co-op units. The prospective buyer of a co-op cannot obtain new financing for the unit itself, but must adhere to the provisions of the sole mortgage of the entire building. If the original mortgage on the building is 50 percent paid off, meaning that 50 percent of the mortgage of the unit to be bought is paid off, then the buyer has to come up with 50 percent of the purchase price as a down payment. In other words, you can't go out and get a second mortgage for, say, 30 percent of the purchase price and put down 20 percent in cash. Some co-op owners might be more inclined to owner finance the sale. The smart seller would then go through all of the motions an institutional lender does when qualifying the borrower. He'll run credit checks on the buyer and verify employment. Many sellers might not bother if the buyer's down payment is considerable.

UNDERSTANDING THE LEGAL FRAMEWORK

Buying a condo or co-op involves looking at a lot of details. Not only is it important to consider some of the points I mentioned in Chapter 12 on single family homes, but you have to look at other details you wouldn't consider with a single-family home.

With condos, you must understand the underlying legal structure of the development. Once you've decided on a particular project, get a copy of the documents and familiarize yourself with them. Have the owner, manager, or a lawyer explain any details in them that you don't fully understand. Use the checklist in Fig. 13-1 to help you. This is especially critical of co-ops because there are more limitations. You really aren't buying a unit, but merely a share in the entire project.

INSPECTING WITH A CRITICAL EYE

You can't change many things when you move to a condo or co- op. If you don't like the way you see the grass is being cut, the way the walks are maintained, or

Condo/Co-op Information Checklist

Owner_____

Address_____

Price_____ Phone (w)_____ Phone (h)_____

Schools_____

Shops_____

Heating_____ Air_____ Square feet_____

Garage_____ Storage_____ Roof_____

Foundation_____ Fence_____ Exterior_____

L.R._____ D.R._____ Kit._____

Brkfst._____ Den_____ Util._____

BR 1_____ BR 2_____ BR 3_____

BR 4_____ BR 5_____ Baths_____

Other rooms_____

Pools_____ Community areas_____

Exterior amenities_____

Interior amenities_____

1st mortgage_____ Bal._____

% Int._____ Years_____ Date_____ Payment_____

2nd mortgage_____ Bal._____

% Int._____ Years_____ Date_____ Payment_____

Lot_____ Block_____ Addition_____

Taxes_____ Home owners assn._____

Remarks_____

_____

_____

_____

Fig. 13-1.

how the inside halls are cleaned and decorated, move on to the next project. A condo isn't like a single-family home where you can put money and effort into transforming an ugly duckling into a graceful swan. If you see an ugly duckling now, that's what you'll have to live with, because that's what the current owners and residents are comfortable with.

If you're looking at a town house, it might be a bit different. If everybody maintains his or her own property, then you can look at the project as you do a neighborhood of single-family homes. If most of the units look great except for the one you're looking at, then you can get it in the same shape as the rest of the units. If you are considering buying a town house, you'll want to read Chapters 10, 11, and 12 because many of the critical factors in choosing a single-family home will also apply to town houses.

Find out if there are major upcoming repairs or replacements that'll require large assessments to the owners. Management might be considering adding another pool, or replacing the existing one, or remodeling hallways and common areas and paying for the improvements not from funds already available, but from a one time assessment for the improvements. That can be a shock after plunking down a lot of cash to purchase a unit.

TAXES

You might wonder how the resale of your condo or co-op will be treated. Your profit will be the difference between the original purchase price and the sales price minus: all closing costs from the purchase and sale; the cost of any improvements you have previously made on the property; and the cost of improvements and repairs made specifically to strengthen the sale of the property within 90 days after signing the sales contract.

The seller can also subtract the portion of his monthly maintenance fees that went toward reducing the principal of the cooperative's underlying mortgage.

Condos don't have an underlying mortgage—each unit has its own mortgage—but you can subtract the cost of any additional assessments that you've paid for improvements to the common areas, such as fixing up the swimming pool or club house.

A MATTER OF TASTE, CUSTOM, AND NECESSITY

You might have a hard time answering the question of whether a condo is the answer to your housing needs. Basically, it's a matter of taste, custom, and necessity. If you like the life-style a condo affords, which in some cases is far better than what you can get for comparably-priced single-family units, then you'll lean towards condo ownership. But if you've lived in single-family homes all your life, your decision might be hampered by fears of living so close to other people, that you'll miss your own little yard to poke around in, etc. If economics forces you to go the condo route, your decision will be tough.

If you have doubts or reservations, then lease a condo that's in your price range. You might be able to lease/purchase one, with provisions to cancel the deal after six or twelve months if you find that condo living just doesn't live up to your expectations. Remember: unless it's a hot sellers market, it's easy to buy and hard to sell.

If you've lived in condos all your life, then the decision is simple. You'll be used to the life-style. The hardest part will be finding the right deal.

14

Buying
Investment Property

IF YOU'RE ONE OF THOSE MILLIONS WHO YEARN TO BE A REAL ESTATE INVESTOR, you might have heard about the tremendous profit potential to be had in real estate. You might have even gone to a seminar that extols the benefits of investment property by "professionals" who claim to have made millions of dollars in real estate. Some of these teachers and self-proclaimed experts might have made a bundle in real estate, but you need to ask yourself one question: If there's so much money to be made in real estate, why are they wasting their time teaching and not furthering a real estate business? The answer is simple. There's more money and less risk in teaching and selling real estate books and tapes than there is in real estate.

If you feel the only way you'll ever get rich is through real estate, I hope I don't deflate your balloon with this chapter. There's certainly a lot of money to be made in real estate and a lot of people have made a lot of money in it, but you have to know how the numbers work, and you *must be conservative*, which is something few of these circuit prophets preach.

GAMBLING IS GAMBLING

For most people, the biggest draw to Las Vegas, Atlantic City, Reno, and other gambling spots is the news of someone hitting it big in a jackpot or at an all-night session at blackjack. It's so tempting to want to duplicate the lucky person's winnings, but the odds are stacked against the player. The fact is, most people lose money when they gamble.

Real estate investing involves some gambling, and not most, but a great many people lose money, their credit, or their sanity with investment property.

If you're going to invest in real estate, you have to limit your losses. You have to be careful of the debts you take on. Property can be bought for zero money down, for example, and the very shrewd investor can make money with it, but new real estate investors aren't so shrewd. They have no buying, selling, or landlording experience, so they almost always have some losses.

The more money you put down to purchase an investment property, the less you can leverage your money. For example, if you buy a $50,000 house with a 10 percent total investment, you've spent $5,000. You're highly leveraged. You'll owe at least $45,000, depending on the closing costs. Now, if the house goes up in value 20 percent in two years, and you sell, you'll realize a gain of $10,000, which is a 200 percent profit. That's about 100 percent per year, and your local bank or mutual fund will hardly come close to such a juicy profit margin. Unfortunately, the downsides to this picture can be many, and I'll paint those for you in this chapter.

Don't think that I'm against real estate investing. I'm just against foolish real estate investing, and way too many people practice that game. So to keep you from doing some foolish investing, I'll give you the downside as much as the upside.

WHO SHOULD INVEST

There are only two types of people who should invest in real estate for profit:

1. A homeowner with a lot of equity in a buyers market who is forced to move.
2. The person with money to spare.

The Homeowner Forced to Move

There are times when a homeowner either wants to move, or is forced to move to a different location and finds he must leave his house rented. Let's say you have a $70,000 house, and you owe $30,000. Your total monthly payments on the property are $350. The house will rent easily for $650 in a depressed market. It's a buyers' market, and if the house sells, it might only bring $55,000 if you're lucky. Then, if you can find someone who'll manage it professionally, you're ahead leasing the house for a while until the market brightens and you can get at least $70,000. If you manage the property yourself, that's the best approach. Few people will manage your property with complete devotion.

Sometimes, this type of investor has no choice. He must move, nobody will buy his house except at fire sale prices, and he wants to not only hold on to his investment, but keep his good credit intact. More than likely though, you're reading this book because you want to be an investor by choice.

The Person with Money to Spare

Only if you have money to spare should you purchase investment real estate, even if you can buy with zero money down. By money to spare, I mean enough money to lose your investment entirely and still have savings for a rainy day. Here's an example. Suppose you make $80,000 per year. You have in savings a half year's salary. That's $40,000. Plus, you have another $20,000 that you want to use for investing in real estate. These aren't set figures. You might make $20,000 per year, and have only $2,000 to spare for real estate investing, excluding your reserve for a rainy day. You'll just be more limited in the type of property you can buy.

Be patient, even if the market looks great right now. Don't invest until you have the holding power it takes to be a good investor. The truly good investor is the prudent investor.

THE PRUDENT INVESTOR

Those seminar folks trying to sell you their books and tapes brag on their sojourns to the title or escrow company to close those marvelous deals with fat profits—$100,000, $300,000, a million bucks. One of the fellows I heard in Dallas a while back showed a copy of a six-figure check, payable to him, blown up on a projection screen. I could see all in the room licking their lips. Here was a plain fellow showing other plain fellows how to make great profits. Well, it's not that easy, and he's not such a plain fellow. Deals like that are not uncommon for the knowledgeable, prudent, and patient investor, but they're uncommon for the beginner.

The prudent investor realizes that first and foremost, are his savings that can keep him going should anything happen to his income or he finds himself in the midst of a family disaster. He realizes that, when he invests in real estate, he is taking on a large debt. The really prudent investor borrows no money—he pays cash. Those who sell real estate investing courses rarely mention the prudent investor.

INVESTMENT DEBT

When you buy a rental house for $50,000 with zero down, the best of all situations many say, are you really getting it for zero down? Probably not. Here's why. First of all, if you made a straight assumption of the seller's debt, and he had no equity, you took on the obligation to pay his mortgage, which will take cash sooner or later. Even if you simply took title to the property subject to the mortgage—with no obligation on your part to make the payments—you'd still have to make the payments if you wanted to keep the property. This is how costs mount up.

A ZERO-MONEY DOWN DEAL

Let's assume the payments on a "zero-money down" house are $550 per month, including servicing the mortgage and taxes and insurance reserve. It's June 15, the house needs a little work, and the next payment is due July 1. You work hard at fixing and decorating, spending $400 in materials and 40 hours of your labor which, at this point, we'll assume is worth zero cents per hour since you can't yet collect anything for it. You place a couple of ads in the paper, which cost a total of $50. You show the house several times, and finally, on July 15, it is rented. Occupancy is for the first of August. You take a $500 deposit and the first month's rent of $575. How much has the house cost you so far? Here it is:

July 1 payment	– $550
August 1 payment	– 550
Fixup materials	– 400
Deposit (keep separate, it's not profit yet) $500	
August rent	+ 575
Total	– $925

If you want to consider the deposit, which you must refund if the people live up to their part of the bargain, then you're only out $425. Your zero down deal just cost you a few hundred dollars and some work. Still, that's not too bad.

Now for a bad scenario. You've rented the house to folks who seem real nice—Mr. and Mrs. Nice Guy. They have two lovely children and a cute little pooch who never comes into the house. He's a "yard dog." Everything's going along fine until December 10 when you haven't received your rent. You call Mr. Nice Guy and he tells you that, because of Christmas coming up, he'll be a little late with his rent this month. You ask how long, and he says he'll have it by the 20th. You tell him you can live with that as long as you receive it no later than the 20th. The 20th comes and goes and you hear nothing from Mr. Nice Guy. On the

21st you call him and he gives you another excuse. He promises to give you the rent no later than the 30th. You're angry, but feel you have no choice, so you wait.

On the 30th, he tells you what really happened. He lost his job back in the middle of November, he's now looking for one diligently, he had an offer just yesterday and should be back on his feet within the next week or so. You're really angry now and decide you can't wait for your rent. In Texas, where the cards are somewhat stacked in favor of the landlord, you mail him a 3 Day Notice to Vacate. After three days, you go down to the appropriate JP court and file a suit for Forcible Entry and Detainer. That costs $50. The court date is set for January 10th. You show up at the trial and he doesn't. You win and he loses. You hurry to your rental house to see what's happening. You drive up and notice the blinds are all closed, but the yard's a mess. There are truck tire ruts in the front yard leading to the front door.

You try to look inside, but all of the windows are covered. You have a key, but don't dare go in. The law says you can't forcibly move him out for five days after the court date, and for that you'll have to bring along a peace officer. Just then, the next-door neighbor comes out. He informs you the tenants moved out yesterday afternoon. You sigh with relief. They're out. You open the house, walk in, and want to scream. It's not that bad, but it's so frustrating to see the mess. The walls are dirty, a couple of doors are broken, the carpet's filthy, there are roaches all over the kitchen, the door to the dishwasher is broken, and there's a horrible stench all over the house.

You chalk it up to experience. Next time, you'll give them the three-day notice on the 4th of the month and kick them out a month sooner. You work yourself to the bone again, spend another $400, and get the house to stand tall for new tenants. It's the end of January, and not many people are looking to move that month. A call comes in from someone who's lease expires at the end of February. She asks if you'll hold the house till March 1 if she gives you the deposit. She only wants to give you $525 per month, and a $400 deposit. You're desperate so you accept her offer. Here's how you stand March 1:

Original cost (you kept the deposit)	– $425
September through March payments	– 3,850
September, October, November rent	1,725
New tenant's deposit (not yours yet) $400	
March rent	525
Total	– $2,025

Your zero-money down deal has now cost $2,025 in less than a year and you're going further in the hole every month, not including the costs if the tenants call to tell you the air conditioner's quit working, the stove and dishwasher have died, or any of a million other things that break all of the time in houses.

This is really a typical situation. While the story could be much happier, it too often is this unhappy, and at times, much worse. It has happened to me at times and I hear about it all the time from other investors. So what's the answer? Can you make money on rental property? Of course you can. Here's how.

Take the $2,025 loss above and divide it by the number of months you made payments on the house. That's $2,025 divided by 8. That's $253 per month. You would *break even* if your payments were $253 less per month, or a total monthly house payment of $297. That means you'd need a mortgage balance of about $28,000 for that kind of payment. You would still not have a monthly cash flow on this deal though. The fact is that if you *really* want to make money in real estate, you almost have to own property outright.

Once you get your feet wet, you might not experience a negative cash flow picture as drastic as what I've painted above. You can make money when you sell the property in an appreciating market, even if you've had a negative cash flow for many years. You can deduct your losses from your income taxes as long as you don't make over $100,000 per year on your job. You can also deduct your losses in a limited manner until you hit the $150,000 per year mark. It takes a lot of work and holding power, and holding power is what many new investors don't have.

When things are going great guns, when there is good positive cash flow on one or several properties, you must save some money for the slow times. They always come, and if you've left yourself no cushion, the slow times can bring you down.

CASH FLOW VS. PROFIT

Cash flow is the amount of money you have left every month after you've paid all the expenses on a property. If one month you have a loan payment of $400 plus a $50 repair bill, and the rent is $600, then the cash flow is the difference between the $450 expenses and the $600 rent. That's a $150 cash flow. The deposit tenants give you should go into a separate account so you don't fool yourself into believing you made more than you actually did. If you keep a deposit for some reason later on, then at that time you take it out of the deposit account and put it into your working account. Some investors view the deposit as part of the cash flow as soon as they get it, and when they refund a deposit, they look at it as an expense.

Cash flow, of course, is a form of profit. One year you might make $1,200 and the next lose $1,000. You only know true profit when the house is sold. If you bought the house for $50,000 and sold it for $100,000, then your profit was $50,000. If you made $1,200 cash flow the first year, lost $1,000 the second, and made $800 the last year you owned the property, your cash flow profit was $1,000. So each house will have two types of profit: monthly cash flow and selling profit.

TYPE OF PROPERTY TO BUY

There is a big difference between buying a house to live in and buying one to rent out. That might seem obvious to you, but too often people let their own needs and desires dictate what type of property to buy for investment purposes. They put themselves in the tenants' place and forget the real reason for investing.

The *only* reason to buy a house as an investment is to make a profit. If you make money on a property, then it's worth purchasing. You might live in a $250,000 house and desire to own investment property in that price range. But if the only type of property that will give you a positive cash flow and have the possibility for increase in future value is $30,000 houses, then that's what you must invest in.

Certainly there are other considerations. If you'll be the one personally collecting the rent, you might not want to purchase property where just walking down the street in your rental neighborhood will jeopardize your health. If you have a couple of six-foot-six, 300 hundred pound body builders that collect your rents, then making money is the only consideration in purchasing.

BUYING FROM A HOMEOWNER

The toughest seller is the homeowner. He's emotionally involved in the sale of his property. Simply make an offer that will work for *you*, and don't worry about what he needs. That's his problem. Don't contemplate counteroffers. You have one offer that will absolutely work in your favor. Anything worse just compromises your ability to make the house a viable money maker. People compromise their position all the time. I've been guilty of it myself. For example, there might be a house that if bought for $50,000 with favorable financing will make a great investment. The seller asks $60,000 and counters $54,000 to the buyer's $50,000 offer; he says that's his final figure. Take it or leave it. The buyer takes it because it's still a reasonably good deal and it will still produce cash flow.

That's wrong. Work up your figures, set your maximum, and don't budge an inch. There are plenty of houses out there. If there aren't, then invest in mutual funds, stocks, or CDs. Make your offer and leave it with the seller. Put a clause in your written offer-to-purchase that says, "If this offer is not accepted by seller on or before (date), then this offer will be valid only when signed by seller and approved by buyer within 24 hours after seller accepts it.'' After a certain date, give yourself a way out. Naturally, even if the seller were to sign, you have no obligation to buy if you've not given him earnest money. There's no contract without some consideration in the form of cash or something of value.

BUYING REPOSSESSED HOUSING

There are times when banks and government agencies, such as VA and HUD, have an overwhelming supply of repossessed properties. The properties are usually sold through a bidding process or at an auction. If you want to become involved in this part of the market, you must still decide what figure will work for you, and don't exceed that amount, no matter how tempting the property or how good a sales pitch you receive.

BUYING FIXER-UPPERS

Some of the best investor buys are houses that need to be fixed up. The more fix up they need, the better the deal you should be able to get. Very few people want to take on the responsibility of remodeling a house though. Most people can't see through the grime and disrepair. The only caveat is to be very generous when estimating your fix up costs. If you think the total fix up will be $3,000, then figure $4,500. Give yourself a fudge factor of 50 percent, even if you have building experience. I bought a duplex for $20,000 and figured I could put it back in shape for $22,000. I'd had a lot of experience in new building, remodeling, and real estate. When it was finished, I'd spent almost $29,000 in fix up. That's a 31 percent increase; not good for someone with experience.

Keep in mind what I said earlier. When McDonald's opens a new restaurant, it does so to make money *now*. Look at investment real estate *only* in that light. You *must* make money right away. Always increase your expectations for losses by 50 percent, and decrease your expectations for profits by 50 percent, and you'll be a happy investor.

15

Understanding
Real Estate Financing

THE TYPICAL HOME BUYER BORROWS A LARGE PERCENTAGE OF THE FUNDS HE
needs to purchase a home. The source of the funds can vary: relatives, friends,
mortgage companies, banks and other such institutions, or the seller himself.

WHAT IS A DOWN PAYMENT?

The down payment is the difference between the amount borrowed and the contract price. It's usually stated as a percentage. If you buy a house for $80,000
with a 10 percent down payment, you'll borrow $72,000 and provide $8,000 of
your own money to buy.

There is no typical down payment. There is no law, in other words, that
states you have to put down a certain amount of money for a house loan. I've
closed many VA loans, which require no money down.

There are only two sensible ways to buy real estate. You either put down the
least amount of money and keep as much of your cash as a reserve as you can, or
you pay all cash if that will still leave you a comfortable cash reserve. Here's why
I feel this way. If you bought a house for $100,000 and put down 50 percent,
you'd still owe $50,000. If you qualify for a $100,000 mortgage, then a minor
setback in your income might not affect your ability to make the payments on the

$50,000 mortgage. On the other hand, if you just qualify for the $50,000 mortgage, then a minor interruption in your income could hurt your ability to keep up with your mortgage payments. A prolonged interruption in your income could cause you to lose your home and all of your equity. This would leave you needlessly broke.

If the purchase had been different, the outcome would be more palatable to the homeowner. If you'd paid cash, the only obligations you'd have would be property taxes and homeowners insurance. These are minor expenses compared to making the payments on a mortgage.

Another scenario could be if you'd paid 10 percent down—$10,000—and borrowed $90,000, you would have qualified for a $90,000 mortgage. If things get tough temporarily, you can tap into your $40,000 remaining reserve until your income is back to normal. If your economic condition doesn't improve soon enough, you let the lender have the house back. By the time he gets around to foreclosing, you'd be several months behind on your payments. That's called free rent, which you'd need. You'd still have a large amount of your cash with which to make alternative living arrangements and not have to move into a rat's nest until your income comes back to normal.

You can't make a rational sale if you're about to lose a house through foreclosure with a $50,000 equity in jeopardy. I'm not advocating that you take your responsibilities lightly and give up without trying to make the mortgage payments, but you have to look out for yourself, and it's silly to end up penniless over a hopeless cause.

I'll go into specific details on down payments for the most popular types of loans later. At this point, I'll simply tell you that most down payments range from about 3 percent to 10 percent in the standard home buying market. To that you have to add another two or three percent for closing costs.

UNDERSTANDING THE TIME VALUE OF MONEY

Money has one value today, it will have a different value tomorrow, and it had a different value yesterday. $1,000 yesterday might be worth $1,001 today and $1,002 tomorrow. That's a simplification, but it gives you an idea of the time value of money, and you'll understand the concept a little better after you finish this chapter.

When you borrow money to purchase a house, you borrow today's dollars to be paid back with tomorrow's dollars. Almost all lenders work on a monthly basis. They charge interest each month, and they get paid back some of their principal each month. For example, if you borrow $100,000 at 10% interest, at the end of the first month you'll owe $100,000 + 10% / 12. At the end of one month the balance due is not only the $100,000, but one twelfth of the interest due in one year, which is $833. Consequently, the value of today's $100,000 is $100,833 one month from today. Naturally, most folks don't opt to pay off their mortgage after one month. The loan is amortized over a set number of months instead—360 in the case of a 30-year loan. The above loan would have a payment of $877.57 per month to fully amortize over a period of 30 years. At the end of the first month after the first payment has been made, the loan balance would be thus:

Original principal	$100,000.00
First month principal reduction	− 44.57
Balance after first month	$99,955.43

As you can see, there's very little principal reduction during the first month. As a matter of fact, there's very little principal reduction during the first 10 years. After making the $877.57 payment on this loan every month for 10 years, the principal balance would still be $90,938.02.

Most real estate loans have no prepayment penalty, and you could take this 30-year loan and pay it off early. Not in one big chunk, but in a lot of little chunks. If you only paid an additional $197.04 more per month, you could cut this loan down to a 15-year loan. You'd save $122,496.28 in total interest. Of course, if you're a very disciplined saver, you could put that $197.04 per month away in a savings account paying you 5$^{1/2}$ percent interest, compounded monthly, and at the end of 15 years you'd owe $81,664.56 on your mortgage, and you'd have a savings account worth $55,372.70. In the long run, you're better off paying the mortgage early and foregoing the savings account. Some people feel better with money in the bank, however. You have to realize that the interest payable on a mortgage is tax deductible, so you're not saving as much as it seems by paying off early. If you're not a disciplined saver, you're better off to let your house do your savings and pay off the mortgage early. Just remember my earlier example. A lot of equity won't save you if economic hard times come. You can't buy a hamburger with tied up equity.

If you like the idea that for only $197.04 per month you can pay off your home early, don't be tempted to simply take a 15-year mortgage, even though it's at a slightly lower interest rate, rather than the 30-year mortgage. If you have a 30-year mortgage, but are making payments to amortize in 15 years, you always have the option of going back to the smaller payments if you encounter tight economic times. You don't have that luxury with the shorter term note.

EFFECTS OF INTEREST RATES
ON THE COST OF HOUSING

Generally, there is a difference between the price of a house that's sold for cash—meaning cash on hand—and one sold with financing. That's because more often than not, lenders require the seller, the buyer, or both to pay points—one point is 1 percent of the loan amount—for the use of their money. If the best dealing will buy that $100,000 house for $100,000 cash out-of-pocket, you might still pay $108,100—excluding interest—by the time you get done with your loan closing if you borrow the money to purchase it.

Here's the reason why. Assume the current interest rate without any points is 10 percent. You think that's too high and tell the seller that you'll buy if he can help you get a loan at 9 percent. He calls a lender and learns that a 90 percent loan at 9 percent interest requires 1-point origination fee and 8 discount points. Basically, the lender's *discounting* the loan; charging a fee for not getting the going rate for the use of his money. That's a total of 9 percent on $90,000—the loan being requested. Let's clarify what the lender is offering:

1. A $90,000 loan at 10 percent interest, or;
2. a $90,000 loan at 9 percent interest, but you'll only receive $81,900 from the lender.

If the seller's going to pay all of the points, and you're only going to give him $81,900 (loan proceeds), plus the 10 percent down payment of $10,000, that's only $91,900. Where are you going to get the additional $8,100? Unless you have additional cash, you simply raise the price of the home by the $8,100 plus a few hundred dollars to make things come out even. So there you have $108,100.

Builders "buy down" the loan rate all the time to entice buyers to purchase. That's because people don't pay that much attention to price. They only look closely at down payment, interest rate, and monthly payment. You can lower the last two by the use of points even if it means raising the price of the home.

So which is the better deal? To pay more for a house with a lower interest rate loan and lower monthly payments or to pay less for the house with a higher interest rate and payments.

You can only answer intelligently by knowing how long you'll own the property and how long you'll make payments. If it will cost you $8,100 to save $100 off your monthly mortgage payment, then divide $8,100 by 100 to see how long it will take to break even: 81 months. That's almost seven years. If you're certain of a job transfer in six years (72 months), then you'll save money by taking the higher payments at a cost of $7,200 to save the $8,100. If you're sure you'll be in the house for the next 12 years or more, then the lower payments make sense.

Always work your figures, especially with new homes, before you make a decision on financing options. You could save thousands of dollars over the life of the loan.

TYPES OF LOANS

The most widely used loans are FHA insured, VA guaranteed, and conventional loans—insured and noninsured. Here's just an overview of loan types. Chapter 17 covers what I call Standard Loans in more detail. In Chapter 18, I'll explain some of the many other types of loans and techniques for purchasing a home.

FHA Insured Loans

The Department of Housing and Urban Development (HUD) insures to a lender that you'll make payments on your mortgage. The loans are insured through its Federal Housing Administration (FHA). If you fail to make your payments, the lender will foreclose on the mortgage, take over the house, and either sell the house to HUD—usually for close to the amount the lender has in it—or receive a percentage of the insured amount and keep the house to dispose of it in the best way possible.

VA Guaranteed Loans

The Department of Veterans Affairs (VA) guarantees loans made to veterans. In case of foreclosure, the VA works its program similar to FHA. It generally opts to purchase the house from the foreclosing lender rather than give the lender a cash settlement and allow him to keep a problem property.

Conventional Loans

Almost all other loans can be categorized as conventional loans. Some are insured by a mortgage insurance company. This way, if the lender has to foreclose, he's guaranteed a certain dollar amount to cover losses. Other conventional loans are simply made by banks, mortgage bankers, or savings and loan association without insurance to cover losses from foreclosure. The latter type of lender requires enough down payment from the borrower so that foreclosures are more rare and less costly.

FINANCING CONDOS AND CO-OPS

Financing condos and co-ops can be just as simple and straightforward as it is for single family houses, but it can seem a lot more complicated. This is especially true with co-ops, because these don't give the lender the lien rights that are available with single family homes, town houses, or condos. The information in Chapter 18 on creative financing can be very useful for the co-op buyer.

Ask a lot of questions of the condo or co-op seller. Make sure you're aware of all the local financing alternatives. There might be special funds or programs available that are different from anything I've covered in this book.

Keep in mind that no matter what type of real estate you're attempting to finance, and no matter what the seller might say, there is always more than one way to skin a cat. In the home buying process there are dozens of ways, limited only by your imagination. If you think something will work, propose it to the seller. You might be pleasantly surprised when it works. More on that in the Creative Financing chapter though.

BUYING WITH CASH

If you're using cash out-of-pocket, you might think there's no sense in understanding loans because you won't need one. That's only partly true. What you need to understand is what the seller's thinking was when he offered the house for sale and set the price. Financing was probably in his mind, and you must ask questions to find out. For example, did he have an FHA loan in mind when he put the house on the market? If so, what interest rate was he expecting the buyer to accept? If it's a below-market rate, how many points was he expecting to pay out of his proceeds? Once you have an answer, you'll have a complete picture of his pricing strategy, or that of his real estate agent.

This means there's almost always a discount in price when paying cash for a house. Appraisers take that into account when they set values using sold comparables. You must do the same thing. Never assume the price of the house is the real price, and never assume the discounted price is the real price. If a real estate agent tells you, "This wonderful home was $100,000, but the buyer needs a fast sale and told me just today that he'll look at a $96,000 offer," the only thing that's changed is the asking price. It's now only worth $96,000 to the buyer needing a loan to purchase. If you have cash, you're due a discount.

16

Qualifying for a Loan

TO QUALIFY FOR A LOAN, YOU MUST MEET A PARTICULAR LENDER'S GUIDELINES for the type of loan you've applied for. Each type of loan carries certain guidelines, but each lender interprets those guidelines just a little different. You'd think an FHA 203b loan would be a 203b loan to everyone, but I've found that that's not always the case. One of my agents might take a buyer to one lender and get him turned down for a loan. We'll transfer the loan package to another lender and he'll be approved.

FHA and VA loans have direct endorsement lenders and direct submittal lenders—lenders who do not directly endorse their loans. This can mean a big difference in whether a particular loan gets approved or rejected. Direct endorsement lenders have been approved to underwrite—directly approve—certain government-backed loans without getting the okay from VA or FHA. Other lenders must prepare a loan package and send it to the government agency's underwriters for approval. Sometimes the government agency will be less strict with qualifying the borrower than the direct endorsement lender's underwriters.

LENDER REQUIREMENTS

Lenders qualify you according to your:

- Creditworthiness
- Income
- Job longevity
- Job stability
- Future income prospects

Creditworthiness

If an applicant has bad credit, a lender will automatically disqualify him. Bad credit means different things to different lenders, however. One might assume that if you had a Chapter 7 bankruptcy—where you throw in the towel and not pay anyone you owe—three years ago, that you have bad credit. Not necessarily. A lot depends on the circumstances, and what the whole credit picture looks like.

If the bankruptcy was caused by a sudden illness, a job layoff that was part of a major local economic downturn, or even a business venture that didn't pan out, and if you had good credit before the bankruptcy and have established some good credit since the bankruptcy, then you'll probably have good credit in the eyes of many lenders. If you went bankrupt six years ago because you abused a string of credit card companies, and you had a track record of slow pay for years before the bankruptcy, and have not reestablished good credit since the bankruptcy, then you have bad credit according to most lenders.

Lenders loan money on their perceived idea of a borrower's ability and *intention* to pay back. An applicant might have a great ability to pay, but his track record will show his intentions for repaying the debt. The second case above says, "I don't like to repay my debts. When I do so, I pay back late, and at some point, I'll completely refuse to pay." Under the law, a person can ask for a voluntary Chapter 7 bankruptcy every six years and a day.

Bankruptcies

Here's some information on bankruptcies. There are three types of bankruptcies, all of which are controlled by federal law:

1. Chapter 7 discharge
2. Chapter 13 wage-earner pay back
3. Chapter 11 reorganization.

In Chapter 7, the debtor gives up, hands over all his nonexempt assets to the court, the court divides the assets among the creditors, and all debts are wiped out.

Chapter 13 is for the small wage earner who doesn't want to just give up. The debtor's accounts are set up so they can be paid back in manageable payments, and most creditors receive a small percentage of what they were owed. Chapter 11 is somewhat the same but applies to more complicated cases, often cases with considerable real estate debt.

Often, it's more difficult to obtain a home loan if a person is under a Chapter 11 or a Chapter 13 bankruptcy even though an effort is being made to pay back obligations, if only partially, than under a Chapter 7, where all debts have been written off. Under Chapter 7, the debtor has been discharged and will have put the whole affair behind him. Naturally, if a Chapter 7 has not been discharged, there is no hope of getting a home loan. The bankruptcy hasn't been finalized. That's why Chapters 11 and 13 are a problem. Payments are being made and the debtor is technically still in the bankruptcy. No lender wants to get involved in a bankruptcy. Someone in a Chapter 11 or 13 could suffer setbacks, or he could convert to Chapter 7.

Also, under Chapter 11 and 13, the petitioner—the one in the bankruptcy—must get court approval for major purchases such as those involving a home. Remember, under Chapter 7, you're done with the bankruptcy once it is discharged. With Chapters 11 and 13, a petitioner is in the bankruptcy until he has paid off all the obligations required in the reorganization hearings.

Credit Reports

Most lenders rely on one or more credit reporting companies, or credit bureaus, to show an applicant's paying ability. There are large, national credit companies, such as the TRW system. A lender will pull a credit report immediately after receiving a loan application. The credit report shows the paying record as reported by most current and past credit grantors, including credit card companies, banks, mortgage companies, landlords, etc. It also includes information on public record, such as bankruptcies, judgments, and tax liens.

If you plan to get a regular loan for your home purchase, talk with a lender and have him tell you which credit bureau his company uses. Then go to that credit bureau and request a copy of your credit record. That's normally the only place you'll get a copy of the report. Go over it carefully. If there are no apparent glitches in your record, then you'll have no setbacks when applying for a loan once you go on contract for a home.

Don't assume that just because you've always been punctual with credit obligations that this will be correctly reflected on your report. I've seen cases of fraud against an innocent individual's credit record, faulty credit reporting, name and social security number mixups, and other difficulties that placed erroneous, derogatory information on an otherwise good credit report. Some of these problems can take one or two months to correct. It doesn't make much sense to try and correct a faulty credit report after you're on contract for a house. Do your credit research first.

Correcting Credit Reports

Even if there are problem areas that are your fault in your report, that doesn't mean you'll be denied credit for a home loan. A large majority of bad credit reports can be converted to completely acceptable ones, and you don't have to pay a credit correction agency to do that for you. You can do it yourself with a small amount of effort. Some detrimental items can be removed from a report, and others cannot. Here are some of the items that can be removed:

- Erroneous information
- Tax liens when paid off
- Judgments when paid off

Here are some of the items that cannot be removed:

- Bankruptcies
- Slow payment history
- Charge-off information, even if paid

The most troublesome items on a report are tax liens and judgments. They have to be paid off to be removed. If you have a $10,000 federal tax lien, you will need to come up with the entire amount to get it cleared. If you owe someone a money judgment of $6,000, it would be difficult to convince the judgment holder to release it without full payment, but always try. You could offer to settle for, say, $2,000 to take care of the entire debt. If it's acceptable to the lien holder, have him give you a notarized lien release. File the release at the county court-house, and give a copy of it to the credit bureau to make sure it's removed from your file.

Some of the easiest items to clear up are those that are charged off or placed for collection. You can always go back to the lender and either pay your account in full, or make arrangements to pay off the debt. Most creditors will work with you. If they do, make a first payment, get a receipt for it, and get a written copy of the new payment arrangement. You'll need to give copies of those papers to the loan officer when you make loan application. Pay all small derogatory items off as soon as you can and get written receipts. Make copies for the credit bureau and your lender. It sometimes takes the credit bureaus several months to post corrected information, so keep copies of anything you pay off or any arrangements you make.

If you have several slow pays, only time can help you. At the time of loan application, you'll have to be caught up on all payments that were delinquent, and have at least a couple months of on-time payments on the report. Reporting can sometimes lag a month or two behind, so it could take four to six months to correct slow pays.

You can't delete bankruptcies, you can only help your cause by writing down as well-documented and plausible explanation of the causes for the bankruptcy as you can. Don't make it too wordy, give all pertinent facts, and make it neat.

If you're using a real estate agent, he or she might be able to help straighten out problems in your report. Some of the very energetic agents will even make calls and do a little running around for you. Don't ask or expect them to do the work for you though. If you're working with a buyer's agent who's well qualified and will be paid for her time, you'll certainly get more help than with a seller's agent.

If you have one or several charge offs, always try to negotiate a lower figure. If someone's charged off or placed for collection a $600 debt, offer to pay $200 or $300 in full payment of the account. Give the creditor a sad story, if at all possible, do it in person, and do all you can to negotiate a lower figure. Don't pay one creditor off until you've made *written* arrangements with all such creditors. If you have 10 bad credit items and pay off 5 of them, you've only wasted money because you still have a bad credit record.

Income

Someone who works for a large, recognized corporation or business will have the easiest time meeting income verification. Some lenders might only require a copy or two of the latest paycheck stub as well as the previous year's W-2 income tax reporting form, although most lenders need an original, signed Verification of Employment from the employer.

Self-employed individuals and those working for family-owned businesses must verify their income with copies of their last two income tax returns or with profit and loss statements audited and signed by their accountants. People who have good income but take most of it in cash and report just a fraction of it on their tax returns find it difficult to get home loans, short of turning in false reports—which is fraud, punishable with heavy penalties on conviction.

Job Longevity

Lenders want stable borrowers, and those who have been with strong employers for a substantial, continuous time are a shoe-in for home loans.

Most lenders will deny a loan if a person's been on the job just a month or two. A lender might request that an applicant reapply in six or eight months. Check with local lenders to see what they require.

Professionals recently out of school won't have to show job longevity. Other workers out of school at least a year should also get a loan. The same is true for a person who left the work market a while, then returned and has been back at work two or more years.

Job Stability

Lenders don't like to see people who go from one job to another if the moves are lateral. An auto mechanic who's gone from one shop to another within the last two years without a gain in pay or benefits might be refused a loan. If, on the other hand, he was advancing from working on motorcycles, to Chevys, to Lincolns, and finally, to working on Rolls Royces, each time increasing his income and benefits, he'll have no problem.

Future Income Prospects

Many professionals who are straight out of school will qualify with a lender as long as they've accepted a job requiring their professional services. People such as architects, engineers, physicians, dentists, lawyers, and accountants enjoy that privilege. Highly skilled workers are often in the same league. Some of these include aircraft and complex-equipment mechanics, computer technicians and programmers, and others whose skills are in high demand.

QUALIFYING PROCEDURES

Lenders will allow you to borrow only what they feel you can pay back in comfortable monthly installments. More often than not, the lender himself doesn't make the rules. He simply follows the set guidelines of the loan insuring agency or company, or he follows the requirements of the secondary mortgage company—the company that will eventually buy the loan from the lender.

As I mentioned earlier in this chapter, when loans are made with moderate to low down payments, the lender requires, or is required, to be protected from losses by having the loan insured or guaranteed by a federal agency or a mortgage insurance company. Because the insurer or guarantor is ultimately responsible for the loan, it only makes sense that the insurer or guarantor make the rules. He's the one at risk. Consequently, you'll encounter varying income and credit requirements depending on what type of loan you're applying for.

You might find that a VA loan is quite easy to get or a conventional one might be just as easy because of your income and credit standing. It's also possible that you can be approved for one type of loan and not for another. If you fail on your first attempt, don't give up. Ask your lender if you can try for a different type of loan. You might have to come up with more down payment or you might not get as favorable terms, but you'll probably get the loan.

Ratios

Most lenders work under the 28/36 rule. It says a buyer's payments for principal, interest, taxes, and insurance (PITI) can be no more than 28 percent of gross monthly income, and that all loan payments—house PITI, car payments, furniture payments, credit card payments—can be no more than 36 percent of the gross monthly income.

Computing Principal and Interest (PI). We'll use a $54,000 loan as an example. Assume a new loan at 13 percent interest, payable over 30 years. If you look at Table A in the back of the book, you'll find the factor for 13 percent is 11.0620. Multiply 54 by 11.0620 to determine the payment, $597.35. At 9 percent interest, you would multiply 54 × 8.0462 and have a payment, for principal and interest, of $434.49.

Adding Taxes and Insurance (TI). You must now add taxes and insurance, which are always paid with the monthly payment. Assume that annual taxes and insurance total $1,519.20. Divide by 12, and the monthly payment for taxes and insurance is $126.60. Add this amount to the principal and interest. You'll come up with the total monthly payment for PITI. On the 13 percent loan it is $723.95.

The 28 Percent Rule. PITI should be no more than 28 percent of the gross monthly income of the buyer (or the buyer and his or her spouse). To see if you qualify, divide the payment by 0.28 (28 percent):

Payment/0.28 = minimum gross monthly income
$723.95/0.28 = $2,585.54

Now multiply $2,585.54 × 12. That's approximately $31,000, the minimum annual income needed to qualify for this loan.

To show you the effects of interest rates on what you can afford to buy, here's what you would need to earn with the 9 percent loan:

$561.09/.28 = $2,003.89

Now multiply the total × 12. That's approximately $24,000, the annual income needed to qualify. It's a big difference.

The 36 Percent Rule. You might have other payments, for cars, boats, student loans, credit cards. These payments come under the 36 percent guideline. In the previous example, if your income was $31,000 per year, then total monthly payments—for house, cars, boats, credit cards, and other fixed loans—could be no more than $31,000 × 0.36/12, which is $930 per month. Now subtract the house payment from this total:

$$\$930 - \$723.95 = \$206.05.$$

This means total fixed monthly obligations, *other than the house payment*, must not be more than $206.05. If you made the same income, but the loan was at 9 percent interest, then the calculation would be:

$$\$930 - \$561.09 = \$368.91.$$

Now your total, fixed monthly payments for everything other than the house payment can be as high as $368.91.

Some lenders allow a little leeway; they have less strict guidelines. The VA and the FHA have slightly different guidelines, but if you use the above method you'll be in the ballpark when setting a goal.

Of course, if you don't have to qualify for the loan—let's say you assume a loan and take a second lien from the seller for the entire balance of his equity—then you must use your own good judgment to purchase. This will make more sense when you read the chapters on financing. Don't deviate far from the 28/36 rule though. It makes very good sense.

Some lenders might use a 25/33 ratio. This is especially true with conventional loans requiring only 5 percent down payment. The less the down payment, the more stringent are many lenders' qualifying guidelines. Use the qualifying sheet in Fig. 16-1 to do your calculations.

PREPARING FOR THE LOAN APPLICATION

You'll save yourself and the loan officer time if you go to the loan application well prepared. Take along copies of your and your spouse's recent paycheck stubs and the past year's W-2 forms. It would help to have along the last two years' income tax returns as well. The latter you'll need if you are self employed, or have income in addition to a normal job.

Take along information regarding your financial obligations, and if you've obtained a copy of your credit report, take that along also. If you have credit problems that need to be explained, take along letters of explanation. If you're self-employed and will need audited financial statements, get them prepared beforehand. Anything you can do ahead of time, do it, because once you apply you might want to lock in points, and the lock-in period is only 45 to 60 days. You don't want to give the lender an excuse for letting a point lock expire. Interest rates might have climbed and you'll be the one that loses.

144

QUALIFYING SHEET

BORROWER _____ SALES PRICE _____ LOAN AMOUNT _____ LTV _____

CLOSING COSTS

	Conventional		FHA		VA	
	Buyer	Seller	Buyer	Seller	Buyer	Seller
Origination Fee	___	___	___	___	___	___
Discount Points	___	___	...	___	___	___
Appraisal	___	___	___	___	___	___
Credit Report	___	___	___	___	___	___
Title Policy	___	___	...	___	___	___
Survey	___	___	___	___	___	___
Attorney Fees	___	___	___	___	**	___
Restrictions	___	___	___	___	**	___
Underwriting Fee	___	___	-0-	___	-0-	___
Tax Service	___	___	-0-	___	-0-	___
Escrow Fee	___	___	___	___	**	___
Recording Fee	___	___	___	___	___	___
Mortgagee Title Policy	___	___	___	___	___	___
VA Funding Fee/PMI/FHA MIP	___	___	...	___	___	___
Subsidy Fee	___	___	___	___	___	___
Processing Fee	___	___	___	___	___	___
Other	___	___	___	___	___	___
Total Estimated Closing Costs	___	___	*	___	___	___

ESTIMATED TOTAL MONTHLY PAYMENT

P&I _____

Hazard Insurance _____

Taxes _____

PMI _____

Other _____

TOTAL _____

LIABILITIES _____

ESTIMATED PREPAIDS

15 Days prepaid interest _____

14 mo. hazard insurance _____

2 mo. taxes _____

2 mo. PMI _____

TOTAL PREPAIDS _____

INCOME _____

QUALIFYING

CONVENTIONAL

Payment/Income Ratio _____
Obligations/Income Ratio _____

ESTIMATED CASH FOR CLOSING

Downpayment _____

Closing Costs _____

Prepaids _____

Total _____

Earnest Money _____

Cash For Closing _____

FHA/VA

Total monthly payment _____
Maintenance _____ +
Utilities _____ +
Total housing payment _____ =
Social Security* _____ +
Liabilities _____ +
Total fixed payment _____ =
Income _____
Income taxes _____ −
Net effective income _____ =

Expendable income _____
(Net Effective Income less Total Fixed Payment)
*Max. SS $250.25/person (430.50—self-employed)

EXPENDABLE INCOME (FHA/VA)
FHA/VA

1 person	$400	3 people	$670	5 people	$850	7 people	$1030	9 people	$1210
2 people	$570	4 people	$760	6 people	$940	8 people	$1120	10 people	$1300

*Use for FHA submission application for estimated closing costs.
**Veteran may not pay if he pays the loan origination fee.
***Do not include in acquisition costs.

Fig. 16-1.

17

Standard Loans

WHAT I CALL STANDARD LOANS CAN ALSO BE REFERRED TO AS TRADITIONAL financing. In this chapter, we'll look at the following types of loans: Department of Veterans Affairs loans (VA), Federal Housing Administration loans (FHA), and conventional loans.

VA LOANS

Unless a buyer can borrow money from a relative under better terms, there is no loan better than a VA loan. Remember, the VA does not loan money. It merely guarantees the lender that you'll make your mortgage payments.

There are well over 20 million veterans who have never used their benefits. If you're one of them, it can be your chance to purchase a home with no money down. The seller can pay all of the closing costs for you, including the prepaids— tax and insurance reserves, the first year's homeowners insurance policy, and any prepaid interest from the day of closing to the end of the closing month. This is truly the loan of choice for the veteran. And not only veterans are eligible for a VA loan, there are other examples of VA benefits:

- Widows of veterans who haven't remarried are eligible for VA mortgage loans.

146

- A common-law spouse is equal to a spouse, so her income can be used as well as his in qualifying for a VA loan.
- Two veterans can purchase a home together to help qualify for a loan. A veteran can also get a cosigner to help him qualify.

You don't have to contact or deal with the Administration of Veterans Affairs unless you don't have your Certificate of Eligibility. If you don't have the Certificate, the VA will help you obtain one. Once you have your certificate, you deal directly with the lender. The lender will make sure it gets its loan guarantee from the VA. As in other forms of traditional financing, the veteran must have the following:

- Excellent credit record.
- Enough income to make the monthly payments.
- Lack of other, excessive payment obligations.
- Stable job.

Interest Rate

The VA sets the maximum interest rate that lenders can charge. If the market rate for loans is 10 percent and the VA has set its rate at 9 percent, then the lender will charge the seller *points* to make up for his loss in income. As I've stated, a point is 1 percent of the loan amount.

Maximum Amount

A veteran can obtain a loan of $144,000 with no down payment required. Loans are available for more than $144,000 with a down payment. If the veteran has full eligibility, then he needs to have a 25 percent down payment of anything over the $144,000.

Some Great Advantages

At first, it might seem like there's no advantage to using the VA loan when the buyer has to come up with a down payment, but look at these great pluses for the buyer:

- Assumability.
- No cost for mortgage insurance.
- Less strict qualifying guidelines.
- Second mortgages can be used in conjunction with new VA loan.

Assumability. Loans made prior to March 1, 1988 are fully assumable with no qualifying and no change in interest rate. That means that if you find a home with an 8 percent VA loan, you can pay the seller's equity and assume the loan under the exact terms he had.

Beginning March 1, 1988 the assumability changed. VA loans are now assumable after qualifying ($500.00 assumption fee + $1/2$ percent funding fee). The new buyer must qualify with the lender, but the terms of the note remain the same. It's still a great type of loan. If you take out a new VA loan and then later sell on an assumption, the fact that the new buyer must qualify means if the house ever goes into foreclosure, you'll not be obligated for the loan as was the case with the old, non-qualifying assumable loans.

No Need for Mortgage Insurance. There is no need for mortgage insurance with a VA loan. Let's suppose the veteran buys a house for $174,000. His total down payment will be 25 percent of the difference between the purchase price and $144,000. That's $7,500. The loan amount would be $166,500. The down payment is just slightly more than 4 percent of the purchase price. *If* you could obtain a conventional loan for this home with only 4 percent down, you would need mortgage insurance. That could add $40 to $60 per month to your payment.

Easier Qualifying Guidelines. The VA's guidelines for qualifying are less strict than those of other programs. The veteran doesn't need to make as much money because of the way the VA looks at income, size of family, other obligations, and size of house.

Use of Junior Mortgages. The VA loan can also be used to buy more expensive housing if the seller will carry a second mortgage on the amounts that are not guaranteed by the VA. For example, let's say you buy a home for $200,000. The deal can be structured this way:

VA first lien	$144,000
Down payment	40,000
Second lien to seller	16,000
Sales price of home	$200,000

Certificate of Eligibility. In order for the veteran to receive the benefits of a VA loan, he must have a Certificate of Eligibility. All veterans are entitled to the full eligibility of $36,000, even if their certificate states less. The $36,000 entitles him to a full $144,000 loan with no down payment. $36,000 is 25 percent of 144,000.

Some Disadvantages

There are some disadvantages to a VA loan. For example, it sometimes happens that a VA appraisal for a particular home will come in lower than a conventional appraisal. This used to be the rule, though it's now more an exception. Also, loan processing time can be two or three weeks longer than with a conventional loan.

If the interest rates on conventional loans are higher than on VA loans, the points required by the lenders for VA loans could cause some grief, so you need to check with lenders to see where interest rates stand. No investment property is allowed. You must live in the property financed with the VA loan, although you could move out after a few months and rent it.

Multifamily Dwelling Units and Acreages

The VA will allow homes, as well as duplexes, triplexes, and fourplexes to be financed under its program with the vet occupying one unit. Any number of acres are also allowed, including farms, if the veteran will be occupying the house on the farm.

Buydowns

You're more likely to hear about buydowns from home builders than from real estate agents. Buydowns are subsidies given to a home buyer by the seller or by anyone else—parents and other relatives. Buydown money goes either to get the payments down for the first few years (temporary buydowns), or to buy the interest rate down for the life of the loan (permanent buydowns).

I'm not sold on buydowns, because the net effect is to raise the price of a home. If someone is selling a house for $60,000, and is willing to pay $3,000 in buydowns, or even if a relative is willing to pay those $3,000 in buydowns, the easiest and most logical thing to do is to deduct the $3,000 directly from the selling price, and get the house for $57,000. But there are a few times when buydowns can make sense. For example, someone with a high earning potential who's just out of school can buy more house now than he can afford without a buydown. If you're certain your income will increase substantially in the near future, then a buydown makes sense.

Temporary Buydowns

Assume the interest rate on a VA loan is 10 percent. You can get a temporary interest rate buydown from the seller up to a maximum of 3 percent during the first three years. Therefore, you would pay 7 percent the first year, 8 percent the second year, and 9 percent the third year. On the 4th through 30th years, the rate would be 10 percent. This example is called a 3-2-1 buydown: 3 percent off during the first year, 2 percent off during the second year, and 1 percent off in the third year.

The buydown is an excellent way to buy a house you don't quite qualify for. The payments are low during the first few years, and as income rises, the higher payments should be affordable. The cost of the buydown is a total of the difference in the payments during those first three years. For example, if you have an $80,000 loan at 10 percent with a 3-2-1 temporary buydown, the payments would be as follows:

Year	Rate	Normal Payment	Actual Payment
1	7%	$702.01	$532.24
2	8%	702.01	587.01
3	9%	702.01	643.70
4-30	10%	702.01	702.01

In this example, you save $169.77 per month the first year, $115.00 per month the second year, and $58.31 per month during the last year of the buydown. If you take all these savings and multiply them by 12 and add them all together, the savings to you as a buyer is $4,116.96. It will cost the seller almost that much for the buydown (he gets a rebate for some interest while the money is not being used). Builders use this in a tough market, or with a marginal buyer, because they'll make the sale if the buyer is qualified on the *first year's* payments.

Before you go this route, ponder if you might not be better off having a $76,000 loan instead of $80,000. It's going to cost the seller the same $4,000 whether he pays it on the buydown, or gives the buyer a price reduction.

Permanent Buydowns

As with a temporary buydown, you can also have the money go towards a permanent buydown. If the rate is 9 percent, the lenders might quote lower rates with points: 8 1/2 percent with four points, 8 percent with six points, for example. The amount of money the payment drops during the first year is not as much as it would with a temporary buydown, but after four years, the payment will be lower than with a temporary buydown.

Graduated Payments

The VA also has *graduated payment mortgages* that can do almost the same thing as the buydown. The payments start out low and increase 7½ percent per year (remember, it is the *payment* that increases, not the interest rate) for five years, then remain level for the remaining 25 years. The disadvantage of this program is that there is some *negative amortization* (an increase of the principal due on the loan) during the first few years, and there is a down payment of as high as 12 percent on some properties.

FHA LOANS

The Federal Housing Administration (FHA) was established in 1934 to help people obtain long-term home financing, which was not available at the time. Today, *FHA loans* account only for about 25 percent of all the home mortgages, but that's still a significant amount. FHA works almost the same as the VA. It does not originate loans, but charges a fee to insure loans to the lenders making them.

As with the Veterans Administration, the borrower will not be dealing directly with FHA. All your dealings are with the lender. The lender complies with all of the FHA loan requirements, then receives the loan insurance from FHA after paying FHA its mortgage insurance premium (explained below).

Unlike VA loans, you do not have to have certain qualifications to apply for an FHA loan. You can be a veteran, a non-veteran, white, black, old, young, male, or female. You don't even have to be a U.S. citizen. As long as you are a legal resident who qualifies economically, you are eligible for an FHA loan. As a matter of fact, I've heard of illegal aliens who were granted new FHA loans.

There is a small down payment, as I'll explain in more detail later, and, in most instances, an FHA loan is easier to obtain than a conventional loan. Borrowers must have the following to be approved for an FHA loan:

- Excellent credit record.
- Enough income to make the monthly payments.
- Lack of other, excessive payment obligations.
- Stable job, generally with a minimum of two years tenure.

Interest Rate

The FHA no longer sets interest rates as it did in the past. Lenders are allowed to charge the going rate on loans. As a rule, FHA loans are made at lower interest rates than conventional loans.

Assumability

All FHA loans made prior to December 1986 are fully assumable, just like old VA loans (no qualifying). For loans made after that date, there is a period of 12 months after the closing of each loan wherein the purchaser will have to be approved by the lender in order to take over an FHA loan (24 months for FHA loans that were made to investors). At this time all FHA loans are assumable only after qualifying.

Mortgage Insurance Premium (MIP)

One of the disadvantages of FHA loans, and any conventional loans that are made with less than a 20 percent down payment is that the buyer has to pay mortgage insurance. On a 30-year FHA loan, the buyer has to pay—or finance into the loan—a 3.8 percent MIP. If the loan is for $90,000, then $3,420 is added to it for MIP. This money goes to FHA to cover operating expenses and losses due to foreclosures. With these fees, the FHA is a money-making arm of the federal government.

FHA 203b Program

The FHA program with level payments is designated 203b. Most of the loans the FHA insures are this type. The 203c program is the same as the 203b, except it's for condominiums. The 203b program can be used not only for single-family homes, but also for properties with up to four living units—duplexes, triplexes, and fourplexes.

FHA loans require a minimum down payment. With the 203b program the buyer pays $750 on the first $25,000 of the loan, then 5 percent on anything up to the maximum loan amount of $90,000. If the sales price is under $50,000, the down payment is only 3 percent of the total purchase price. In some hi-cost areas, the maximum loan amount is higher, so you'll need to check with a lender in your area.

FHA loans are also made to investors. That's a major difference between FHA and VA loans. The down payment is 25 percent, but it's a good route to follow if you're looking at investment property. The down payment requirements have changed over the years, so ask the lender about current requirements before you commit to a property.

The FHA will also allow an owner-occupant to purchase the home along with an investor, as long as the owner-occupant owns at least 55 percent interest in the property. Each party must make a monthly payment equal to his or her ownership share. If an investor owns 45 percent, then his share of the payment is 45 percent. If you are young, this might be a good way to have relatives help you purchase a home. You can own 55 percent of your home and your parents 45 percent of it.

FHA 245 Graduated Payment Programs

FHA 245 graduated payment programs require a down payment of 3 to 12 percent depending on the program and the interest rate. Total amount of the loan is generally the same as with the 203b program.

The FHA comes up with different programs, or variations of existing graduated payment programs, from time to time. That's why it is beneficial to understand what's available before you go on contract for a property.

FHA 245a Program

Table 17-1 will give you an idea of the payments required (for each $1,000 financed) with FHA financing on a 10 percent loan. The left column is for the standard 203b level payment program; the others are the five plans available under the 245a graduated payment programs.

Be aware that the 245a plans do develop some negative amortization. Plan 1 develops 0.61 percent of the original balance after two years. Plan 2 is 2.99 percent after four years, Plan 3 is 5.52 percent after four years, Plan 4 is 1.90 percent after five years, and Plan 5 is 4.7 percent after six years. If you borrowed $60,000 and used Plan 2, at the end of four years you would owe $61,794. At that point, the loan would start amortizing and the principal due at the end of each month would be less than it was the previous month.

The 245a program is good for those who don't quite qualify to purchase a home that completely fits their needs. But it is somewhat discouraging to have made mortgage payments on a home for several years, and each year realize that you owe more than when you made your first payment. During tough times, when home prices plummet, many a homeowner "walks" on his mortgage because of that fact. If a homeowner borrowed $60,000 originally, and four years later owes $61,794, and the house is now only worth $50,000, he can get despondent with the least economic setback and allow the home to go into foreclosure.

FHA 245b Program

FHA also offers a 245b graduated payment mortgage, designed to supplement the 203b and 245a programs. The down payment is similar to, and in some cases less than, that for the 203b program. To be eligible, the borrower must *not* be able to qualify under the 203b program, and must *not* have enough cash assets to

Table 17-1.
_____ **FHA Loan Payments** _____
(per $1,000 financed, 10% interest rate)

	FHA			*FHA 245a*		
Year	203B	Plan 1	Plan 2	Plan 3	Plan 4	Plan 5
1	8.78	8.0057	7.3059	6.6704	7.8003	7.3457
2	8.78	8.2058	7.6712	7.1706	7.9564	7.5661
3	8.78	8.4110	8.0547	7.7084	8.1155	7.7931
4	8.78	8.6213	8.4575	8.2866	8.2778	8.0269
5	8.78	8.8368	8.8804	8.9081	8.4433	8.2677
6	8.78	9.0577	9.3244	9.5762	8.6122	8.5157
7	8.78	9.0577	9.3244	9.5762	8.7845	8.7712
8	8.78	9.0577	9.3244	9.5762	8.9601	9.0343
9	8.78	9.0577	9.3244	9.5762	9.1393	9.3053
10	8.78	9.0577	9.3244	9.5762	9.3221	9.5845
12	8.78	9.0577	9.3244	9.5762	9.5086	9.8720
13	8.78	9.0577	9.3244	9.5762	9.5086	9.8720
14	8.78	9.0577	9.3244	9.5762	9.5086	9.8720
15	8.78	9.0577	9.3244	9.5762	9.5086	9.8720
16	8.78	9.0577	9.3244	9.5762	9.5086	9.8720
17	8.78	9.0577	9.3244	9.5762	9.5086	9.8720
18	8.78	9.0577	9.3244	9.5762	9.5086	9.8720
19	8.78	9.0577	9.3244	9.5762	9.5086	9.8720
20	8.78	9.0577	9.3244	9.5762	9.5086	9.8720
21	8.78	9.0577	9.3244	9.5762	9.5086	9.8720
22	8.78	9.0577	9.3244	9.5762	9.5086	9.8720
23	8.78	9.0577	9.3244	9.5762	9.5086	9.8720
24	8.78	9.0577	9.3244	9.5762	9.5086	9.8720
25	8.78	9.0577	9.3244	9.5762	9.5086	9.8720
26	8.78	9.0577	9.3244	9.5762	9.5086	9.8720
27	8.78	9.0577	9.3244	9.5762	9.5086	9.8720
28	8.78	9.0577	9.3244	9.5762	9.5086	9.8720
29	8.78	9.0577	9.3244	9.5762	9.5086	9.8720
30	8.78	9.0577	9.3244	9.5762	9.5086	9.8720

use the 245a program. It is limited to a fixed number of mortgages each year, so it might be hard to get in your area.

Buydowns

Buydowns will work with FHA loans as well as with VA loans. The buydown money goes either to get the payments down for the first few years (temporary buydowns), or to buy the interest rate down for the life of the loan (permanent buydown).

The FHA program, like the VA program, will work with a temporary or permanent buydown. But with FHA, the buydown must not exceed 5 percent of the sale price of the home. If the 5 percent is exceeded, then the appraiser of the subject property is instructed to reduce any comparable sales on a dollar-for-dollar basis over the 5 percent allowance. That means the home you're interested in might not appraise high enough for the loan you're requesting. Buydowns work best if left at, or below, the 5 percent maximum.

CONVENTIONAL LOANS

A conventional loan is handled the same as a VA or an FHA loan. The borrower—any borrower regardless of race, creed, color or nationality—goes to a lender and takes out a loan to purchase a property. The differences are in the requirements:

- How much down payment is required.
- How much the borrower must earn.
- What is the most the borrower can pay in other monthly obligations.

Conventional loans are made by the same lending institutions that originate FHA and VA loans. The big difference to the lender is that some conventional loans don't have another institution guaranteeing the loan in case the buyer defaults. On any non-insured loan, if the borrower defaults, the lender takes the entire loss. Whereas on VA loans the Administration of Veterans Affairs guarantees to the lender that the borrower will make his payments, and on FHA loans, the Federal Housing Administration insures to the lender that the borrower will make his payments. Insured conventional loans are secured by a private mortgage insurance (PMI) company, such as Mortgage Guaranty Insurance Corp. (MGIC), one of the leaders in the field.

Conventional mortgages are primarily used on homes over $100,000, because that's usually over the FHA limits. There are many types of conventional mortgages, and the maximum amounts can be a million dollars and more.

As in the two government programs I've explained, the borrowers must have the following:

- Excellent credit record.
- Enough income to make the monthly payments.
- Lack of other, excessive payment obligations.
- Stable job, with tenure required varying from lender to lender.

The Secondary Mortgage Market

Some of the rules regarding conventional loans are set up by the secondary mortgage buyers. The secondary market works as follows: A lender uses its funds to originate a series of loans, let's say $5 million worth. He then packages them and sells them to secondary investors such as the Federal National Mortgage Association (FNMA, also called Fannie Mae), the Federal Home Loan Mortgage Corporation (FHLMC, also called Freddie Mac), or the Government National Mortgage Association (GNMA, also called Ginnie Mae). There are several others of lesser importance.

If you find that a lender is particularly careful about lending you money, it's because if the loans are not made according to the secondary lender's guidelines, the primary lender might not be able to sell your loan. This means the lender is stuck with a long-term loan using money that he's borrowed on a short-term basis. Too many of these loans can bankrupt a lender when short-term money rates climb.

Maximum Amount. For mortgages that comply with FNMA and FHLMC guidelines, and which will more than likely be eventually sold to one of those secondary mortgage agencies—the large majority of all mortgages are—the maximums are $168,700 for single-family homes, $215,800 for duplexes, $260,800 for triplexes, and $324,150 for fourplexes. Of course, some lenders will exceed these maximums, and some even offer "jumbo" loans in the million-dollar range.

Conventional Loan Down Payments. The required down payment is 20 percent (80 percent loan). Loans are also available with 5 percent down (95 percent loan) and 10 percent down (90 percent loan). With the latter two types, the buyer has to pay a mortgage insurance premium (MIP), which is generally less than the premium on an FHA loan. The MIP is $2^1/2$ percent of the loan amount on the 95 percent loan, and 2 percent of the loan amount on the 90 percent loan. The MIP is payable at closing, or it might be financed. If it is financed, 1 percent is payable at closing on the 95 percent loan and an additional $^1/4$ percent per year is payable each month as part of the house payment. On the 90 percent loan, $^1/2$

percent is payable at closing and an additional 1/4 percent is payable each month with the house payment.

Assumability. Some conventional loans are assumable at the same interest rate as the original note, but most lenders reserve the right to increase the interest rate when the loan is assumed. Some lenders will negotiate an interest rate that's not quite as high as the prevailing loan rate at the time of the assumption, but higher than the original note.

One of the nicer features of conventional loans is the speed of approval. It normally only takes two or three weeks to process them. That can be a real benefit when time is tight.

If you're thinking of using the 95 percent loan, check with lenders to see who offers that type of loan. Some have pulled away from 95 percent loans because the PMI companies have taken such tremendous losses in recent years. As a matter of fact, more than a few have gone under, leaving lenders holding the bag.

Qualifying Is More Strict. Lenders are typically more strict in granting conventional loans than VA or FHA loans, but there are certain properties that will not be accepted by VA or FHA or won't appraise high enough and conventional loans are the only alternative. Some properties also have to go conventional because of age, condition, or location.

18

Creative Financing

CREATIVE FINANCING IMPLIES ANY TYPE OF LOAN WHERE THE SELLER IS A PARTY to the lending process. There are assumptions, wraparounds, second mortgages (second liens), even third and fourth mortgages, contracts for deed (sale on contract or land contract), and many others. Creative financing also includes, to a certain extent, buydowns.

Creative financing is the financing of choice for the seller in a poor market. He won't use it if he has plenty of time to sell, the market is normal, or his house is either very well priced or in tip-top shape.

If you have credit problems, problems in qualifying because you're self employed, or because you already have a bundle of properties, maybe you're not even a legal alien in the U.S., then creative financing can be a real benefit for you.

ASSUMPTIONS

Under a straight assumption, you pay the seller the difference between what is owed on the first mortgage and the sale price. A $70,000 house with a $50,000 first lien requires a $20,000 down payment. If there's an old FHA or VA loan, then an assumption is easy. If the seller has $20,000 in equity, you simply hand him $20,000 and he transfers his rights and obligations to you. It's that simple.

If there's some qualifying it won't be as easy. The newer FHA and VA loans, as well as most conventional loans, will need qualifying through the note holder. See Chapter 17 for more details.

Be Creative

Sometimes, the process can get a little more creative with a straight assumption. Suppose you don't have the $20,000 cash, but you have a $10,000 car that's paid for, and a lake lot that's worth $10,000, and it's also paid for. Why not offer them in on a trade for the equity in the home. The seller might not need the cash. The car might be just what he needs, and the lake lot he can resell or keep for future use. Builders, especially custom builders, are very much into this type of creativity in the sale of their homes, particularly when they're stuck with a house that's eating their lunch in interest payments.

Suggest to the seller that he might also find another seller who will go along with a trade if the seller's moving up to a bigger house. A majority of lenders will allow a trade for the down payment. The car and lot would qualify, though they might have to be professionally appraised.

CONTRACTS FOR DEED

Early in the 1970s, lenders started using the due-on-sale clause in their conventional mortgages to protect themselves from being locked into 30 years of low interest mortgages in case the interest rates they payed on deposits escalated. Today, almost all conventional mortgages have the due-on-sale clause, and you might have to find ways to get around it. One of the easiest is the contract for deed. As the buyer, you should be aware of the pitfalls.

Under a contract for deed, also known as a sale on contract or a land contract, you make a down payment—oftentimes a very nominal down payment—make payments to the seller, and purchase the home without receiving title at the time of purchase. The seller receives payments on his loan to you, and keeps making payments on his own original loan. This way, the lender is not aware you bought the house. This is the easiest form of creative financing, but it is also the one with the greatest number of pitfalls and risks, especially for the buyer.

Advantages

The major advantages are little or no down payment, no qualifying for the loan (the seller is the lender), perhaps a low interest rate, and immediate possession. For the seller, the advantages are that he has no discount points to pay, the sale can be made rather quickly (normally without a broker), without worry that the property won't appraise for the sale price, and with no closing costs. Under certain conditions, this is a good way to purchase, such as when the buyer has abominable credit, when he has very little money to put down, or when he has judgments against him, or creditors on his tail.

Disadvantages

The one major disadvantage is that you are not the owner of record until all of the terms of the contract are fulfilled. In other words, you don't receive a deed to record at the county courthouse to show you are the rightful owner. Problems could arise if the seller can't deliver a valid title to you after you've met the conditions of the contract.

If the seller has any judgments filed against him, has tax liens, or goes through a bankruptcy, or a devastating divorce, and does not make payments on his loan, then there could be liens on the property that would have to be paid before the seller can give clear title to you (even though you might have promptly made all of your payments to him). If the seller can't clear the liens, you might have paid for a house once and face the prospect of paying for it again. That's a real nasty prospect.

With the serious pitfalls this type of transaction can have, there should be an agreed-upon course of action should any of them arise. The safe course for you is to obtain title to the property as soon as you have enough equity, through appreciation and mortgage principal reduction (usually sometime between the second and fifth years), and that the seller then take back a mortgage or deed of trust to guarantee his remaining loan. You must understand, however, that if the first lienholder (the seller's mortgage company) calls the loan due because he finds out about the contract for deed, you must immediately refinance. While this is very unlikely, it can happen.

In most states, if the contract for deed is recorded, it will protect the buyer sufficiently in case the seller does encounter economic setbacks down the road. If the seller's first lien is with an out-of-town lender, then the contract can be safely recorded. The lender would probably never be aware that you bought the house, and the due-on-sale clause would not be triggered.

One easy way to be protected is to take a second lien from the seller and record it. The second lien would cover the contract for deed and would take precedence over any other liens, judgments, bankruptcies, or divorces that could get in the way of your future right to clear title. In this case, the seller will require a release of lien from you, to be escrowed with an attorney or title company in case you default on the payments. Because the contract for deed would not be recorded in this case, there's no way the lender can become aware of ownership transfer.

SECOND MORTGAGES

A second mortgage is used when you don't have enough money to pay the seller his entire equity, or when rates for new mortgages are so high that it makes sense to borrow only a partial amount of the purchase price at high interest rates. If the seller is asking $60,000 for his home, and he has an assumable VA mortgage that carries an interest rate of 8 percent with a $30,000 balance, then you have to come up with $30,000 equity. Not many people are able to pay 50 percent down for a house, and even if they have it, the smart buyer won't part with that much money.

Let's say you put down 10 percent (most second lien lenders require a 10 percent minimum down payment), or $6,000, and you get a second mortgage (second lien) from a commercial lender for $24,000 to pay the seller the balance of his equity. Usually, that second mortgage will be two to four percentage points higher than the going rate for new first mortgage loans. The second mortgage will also be short-term—shorter than the 25 or 30 years available on first mortgages. Twelve or fifteen years is standard.

In the above example, if the interest rate on the second mortgage is 14 percent, the combined interest rate on the entire amount of the mortgages is still only 10.67 percent. You find the average by multiplying the first lien amount by its interest rate, multiplying the second lien amount by its interest rate, adding the two totals, and dividing that amount by the total of the first and second lien amounts. In this example, it is calculated as follows:

$$\$30,000 \times 8\% = \$2,400 \text{ First lien}$$
$$\$24,000 \times 14\% = \$3,360 \text{ Second lien}$$
$$\$5,760/\$54,000 = 10.67 \text{ percent}$$

If the rate you get by blending the two together is less than the going rate for new loans, considering all costs involved with a new loan, then this is a good way to finance a purchase. There is only one problem: even though this blended interest rate is lower than the prevailing rates for new first liens, the monthly payment might not be any better because the second lien will be payable during a shorter term. This could be an advantage, because you'll have the house paid off sooner.

GETTING MORE CREATIVE

Now let me tell you about situations that are more creative. Assume we have the same circumstances as above, but the seller decides to take back a second mortgage instead of making the buyer go to a commercial lender to get one. If the seller takes $6,000 as a down payment and carries the $24,000 at 9 percent, then the combined interest rate on both mortgages is about 8.45 percent. That's 2.22 percent better. If he doesn't want to wait 15 years to get all of his money, there can be a balloon payment at the end of the third, fifth, seventh, or whatever year seems comfortable to him and to you. Then at the time of the balloon payment, you'd have to refinance that second lien if you didn't have all of the money to pay him off.

Alternately, you could use a commercial second lien, and the seller takes a third lien, each of which would be for $12,000. The seller would end up with more cash than in the above example, but the rate will still be lower than if you had gone the straight commercial, second lien route.

The big disadvantage to the seller taking a third lien position is that if you default on the first or second mortgages, he must foreclose on you and make payments on the first two liens, or else those other lienholders will wipe him out when they foreclose.

WRAPAROUNDS

A wraparound mortgage is an excellent way for a seller to sell his property and for you to get built-in financing without the hassles of stringent qualifying. Let's say the seller has a first lien with a $52,000 balance at 13 percent interest and it's an FHA assumable loan. His payments for principal and interest are $575 and the taxes and insurance are $100; a total payment of $675. The market is slow. The house is worth $80,000, but in this slow market, he'll probably have to discount it by 10 percent to find a buyer. But you're there to suggest a wraparound mortgage.

Now, let's also assume he doesn't need all of his cash right away and he's willing to do owner financing with a wraparound. You can show him how he can get a quick sale this way.

You offer to purchase the house for $79,900. He takes $1,900 down and finances $78,000, acting as the lender. His loan to you is at 9.5 percent interest—in these situations, the higher the price, the lower the interest rate if you don't change the payment—with principal and interest payments of $655, plus tax and insurance reserves of $110, for a total payment of $765. This is $90 per month more than what the seller pays for his FHA loan, and the $90 is all profit to him.

This is a great situation for the seller, and it can be a wonderful opportunity for the buyer who doesn't have the money needed for a normal closing, or the credit necessary to qualify for a normal loan. What you *must* be certain about is your ability to make the payments. You have to make enough money to service the loan comfortably using the qualifying techniques I've explained earlier.

The seller can finance the loan with the above financing and put a balloon payment on the loan in three to six years. The longer you get him to stretch the financing, the better off you'll be. As a matter of fact, do all you can to stretch the time period for a balloon as far into the future as possible. If the seller will go along with a long-term loan, then don't even mention a balloon payment. Use one only if the seller just doesn't want to carry you for the next 30 years. The younger the seller, the more likely that he can see 30 years into the future. With older folks, you might not get them to agree to a wraparound without a balloon in the near future. If you're forced to take a note with a balloon, then understand that a year or two before the loan balloons, you have to be looking for permanent financing. If rates drop, and your credit situation looks good at any time into the wraparound, refinance to avoid coming onto the deadline without a way to pay the balloon.

The beauty of the wraparound is that most closing costs and all points and fees are avoided. The property goes into your name, so you are free from the problems of a contract for deed. There is one obstacle, however, make sure the seller pays his mortgage to the first lien holder. The wraparound is basically a second lien. If the first lien isn't paid, the lender can foreclose, and you're out in the cold. With a wraparound, you'd do well to make sure a lawyer looks at the papers.

DESPERATE SELLERS

Very few sellers are aware of the many opportunities to sell under trying market conditions. If the market is right, and even if the market is quite normal, you're bound to find sellers who are up against a wall and are desperate for a sale. I don't endorse all or any of these methods, but I've been in the business long enough to have seen every trick in the book used by sellers who understood financing and who needed to make a sale. So in all fairness, I believe you should at least understand some of the tricks used in house selling by despairing sellers. If done right, these tricks will work with no danger to seller or buyer.

If you're desperate enough to have your own home, then you might be able to use some of these ideas to get a homeowner to sell to you and stay legal. What I mean to say is, don't get into any fraudulent scheme. A double contract is fraud. Stay away from that situation. A double contract is when you make an agreement with the seller, you give a copy to the lender, then you have another agreement with the seller that doesn't reflect the terms of the original contract, and the lender is not aware of that second agreement.

Have the Buyer Borrow the Down Payment

Suppose you have credit and are able to borrow $3,000 on your signature, or perhaps on a car or boat to which you have clear title. The money from that loan can be used to purchase the $60,000 house with a 5 percent down payment, as long as the seller will pay *all* of the closing costs as well as the *prepays* (that is, any closing costs you would have been responsible for and any amounts to be escrowed by the lender for hazard insurance, taxes, mortgage insurance, as well as the first year's hazard insurance premium—as much as the lender will allow). Don't forget that a 5 percent down payment never really means 5 percent. There are always costs to closing a home loan that can run anywhere from two to ten percent of the loan amount, so the seller would have to pay those other costs for you.

The mortgage company will want to know if the debt is a furniture loan or a car loan, etc. There's nothing wrong with a buyer having a number of debts, as long as you qualify for the house loan. Don't come out and say that you've borrowed the down payment though, that is a real no, no.

ADJUSTABLE OWNER FINANCING

Most sellers have the idea that just because commercial lenders are getting, let's say, 12 percent interest for home loans, that they're due the same interest rate. Lenders have to pay for the use of the money to lend to you, while the seller doesn't have this expense. Try to convince the seller that all he'd get for his money if he had it in a savings account is 5 percent, or whatever the going rate is.

When he understands that all he should expect is savings account rates, then go for as long a term as possible at those rates. The loan might start at 5 percent for the first year, or even the first five years, then go to 6 percent for another period—the longer the better. At some point it can reach a specified limit. Your payments will be easier at first, and, as our economy seems to have a permanent inflation factor, you know your income will increase through the years, even if ever so slightly. The slower the seller's rate goes up, the more secure your position in the future.

NEGATIVE AMORTIZATION OWNER FINANCING

Negative amortization owner financing should be your last-resort tactic. Many people shy away from negative amortization loans, and I think rightly so. If you've found the perfect property but can't seem to get the seller to owner finance at a very low interest rate, then offer him a negative financing situation where you'll owe him more at the end of a few years than at the beginning of the loan. If you think about it, on a normal loan that amortizes over 30 years, only 1 percent of the loan amount is reduced during the first five years. On a negative amortization graduated payment (GPM) loan, the loan amount might increase 7 to 8 percent during the first five years. Therefore, on a $90,000 "standard" loan, the balance at the end of five years might be $89,000. On the GPM, the balance might be $97,000. If you figure the difference in payments during those years, however, you'll generally find that you'll have saved at least the $8,000 difference. This isn't bad if the house is $8,000 to $10,000 below market value. If the house should increase a nominal 5 percent per year in value, the home would be worth $115,000 at the end of five years.

NO INTEREST OWNER FINANCING

No interest owner financing is my all-time favorite. There is no reason not to ask the seller to carry a loan at no interest. I doubt you'll get anyone to give you a 30-year, zero interest loan though. There aren't too many people out there that naive. But how about no interest during the first five years, then the loan could convert to interest bearing, or perhaps there is a balloon at the end of those five years. At that time, you refinance, or better yet, pay the loan off in full. A $50,000 loan can be paid off in five years with $833 P&I monthly payments. That's 25 percent of the gross income for a couple making $40,000 per year, and 20 percent for those making $50,000. Tough proposition? You bet. But impossible? Not at all. Just think, five years of struggle and you're forever through with house payments.

This won't work with a seller who still has debt on the property, unless you make sure your extra-steep payments are used to reduce the seller's existing first lien so that when you finish paying off your loan, he's finished paying off the original first lien and you end up with a free and clear property. Naturally, there are folks out there who have paid off their property and who won't worry about selling with owner financing at no interest as long as the payments are hefty and they get their money back in a reasonable time. You can convince a seller to this plan by showing him that every month he'll be making interest on an additional $833 in his savings account.

19

Working with the Loan Company

FOR MOST BUYERS, THERE'S NO PURCHASE IF THERE'S NO FINANCING, AND MOST buyers will have to work with a lender for the financing. Only a few bold, and/or lucky ones will get the financing from the seller.

Some lenders make it very easy to go through the loan process. Others make it difficult. Sometimes it's the borrower that makes it difficult for the lender, and so it seems that the lender is the one dragging his feet or being uncooperative. To speed things along, and to make life easier for you and the lender, you should understand the steps necessary for loan qualifying and approval.

THE LOAN APPLICATION

The first time you meet with the loan officer might be just to get a very good idea of what you qualify for, and what type of loan you should go after. You might want the lender to prequalify you so that you understand your purchasing limitations and don't waste your time or that of agents and sellers. Whether you're attempting to prequalify, or are already on contract for a house, the loan officer will ask you to fill out a loan application.

Loan applications take different forms. Most of them ask the same basic information that's included in the loan application at the end of this chapter. To be prepared to answer all of the questions in the lender's application, fill out a copy of your application in this book. Make a list of the account numbers for all of your debts. Many lenders require those numbers to compare against those that show up on a credit report.

Don't lie on the application, but don't put down anything not requested. For example, if you owe your cousin $5,000, and are paying her $100 per month, leave that out, as the loan will only count against you in qualifying, and cause more paperwork if the lender tries to verify the loan with your cousin. If your father bought a car that you drive and make the payments on, mention nothing about the car or your father's loan. It's not in your name, and it's better to not receive credit for prompt payments than to have the loan payments counting against you.

The loan application can be done anywhere. If you're borrowing from a bank or savings and loan, then you'll apply at the lender's office. Mortgage companies strive to make things easy for the buyer as well as the real estate agent involved. Loan officers will take applications anywhere, including a real estate agent's office and even your home. Rarely is a loan application not done in person through a loan officer.

OWNER FINANCING

If you want to have the owner do the financing on the home, you might want to be prepared to show him that you're a creditworthy individual. The owner might ask for financial information, although many won't. The best situation is to have the information and offer it to the owner so he can see it at the time you're in the process of negotiating the contract that calls for owner financing. If you have a good financial statement, or very good credit, proof of it can be what convinces the seller to carry the financing.

Many owners don't want to fool with owner financing because of the hassle involved in repossessing a house if a buyer doesn't make payments, or even because of the nuisance caused by a seller who must be constantly reminded to make payments on time. If your credit report shows a long stream of timely payments, it can sway the seller to your request for a buyer's easiest form of financing: directly from the seller.

EXPEDITING THE LOAN

I've seen loans take months to be approved. Anything longer than three or four weeks is too long. It's rarely the fault of any one individual. What often happens is that the lender drags his feet, real estate agents involved don't keep up with the loan process, employers are slow at returning verifications of employment, creditors and banks linger in returning requested information about loans and bank balances. To top it off, the buyer assumes the other individuals are doing their part.

It's important that a loan application move along rapidly because point locks can expire and rates could change drastically as a result. I'll explain about that in a moment. You can do a lot to expedite the approval of a loan if you stay on top of the process.

Find out who is processing your loan with the lender. Ask the loan officer when you make application the name of her processor. Then you can call the processor a couple of times a week to make sure she's getting the paperwork she needs to complete the loan package. Ask if you can hand carry the verification of employment to your employer, any verifications of accounts to your creditors, and verifications of deposit to your banks. Many lenders will let you do so. In that case, if the verifications are not prepared on time by the processor, you'll know to push the lender; if the verifications are not returned by employers, creditors or banks, then you can push to get them to the lender. You won't usually be allowed to pick up a verification and hand carry it back—the lender doesn't trust the borrower to not alter a paper. So verifications will have to be returned to the lender by mail.

Make a list of all the items the lender has requested and call the people responsible for returning them. Once you know a paper's been sent out, when you check with the processor on the loan's status you can find out if something got sidetracked in the mail and push for a duplicate. There is no reason not to have all verifications back to the lender within two weeks of loan application. Once all of the paperwork's in, it's only a matter of a week or so before loan approval. If everything runs smoothly, a loan can be approved three to four weeks after you applied, and it can close four to five weeks after loan application.

A delay in getting a loan approved promptly can cost you headaches and money, so stay behind it and don't worry that you might inconvenience the lender. You're the customer, the lender will make money from your business, and he should be glad to have you help expedite the loan application.

LOCKING IN THE POINTS

Lenders will lock in points for 45 to 60 days. So if the going market is three and one half plus one for a 10 percent loan, it means the lender expects to receive $3^1/2$ percent of the loan amount, plus 1 percent of the loan amount, for a loan made at a 10 percent interest rate. On a $150,000 loan, the lender will receive:

$$\$150,000 \times .035 = \$5,250 \text{ plus}$$
$$\$150,000 \times .01 = \$1,500$$

Total $6,750

It could be that your contract calls for the seller to pay the discount points—$5,250, and you would pay the one percent origination fee of $1,500.

Let's say you're on contract for a home and have a 45-day lock on the points. That means the lender will give you that loan at 10 percent as long as you close the loan within 45 days of the point lock. Home loan markets change constantly. At the end of the 45 days, the going rate for a 10 percent loan could be six plus one. On a $150,000 loan the picture changes to:

$$\$150,000 \times .06 = \$9,000$$
$$\$150,000 \times .01 = \$1,500$$

Total $10,500

The difference is $3,750. The seller has already agreed to pay $5,250. Who will pay the difference? The seller might if he's desperate. On the other hand, the seller might have received a back-up contract to yours at $160,000 with no points. The seller would stand to gain $15,250 and would be itching for your loan to fall through and for you to back out of the deal. In that case, you'd be the one to pay the extra $3,750. If a lender drags his feet in getting the paperwork together, the point lock period will expire. Many lenders love to be in that situation, because they'll often stick you with the extra points and perhaps still have money committed at the old rate. The lender then would be the one who makes the additional $3,750.

I've worked with lenders who all too often drag the loan process out and force the seller, the buyer, and even the real estate agent to pay for extra points after the point-lock expires. Their policy is to work this trick as often as possible. Ask the lender straight out just how often he closes his loans on time. Pose the question to your real estate agent if you have one.

You see now why you need to stay behind the loan process and move it along at a rapid pace. Of course, there are times when rates are coming down. In this case, you may not need to do any pushing. The lender will want to close the loan as soon as possible. Most lenders won't let you close the loan at a lower rate than that at point lock. If rates have come down drastically, you might have to change lenders and start the process all over again. Or, if at loan application, you see that rates are coming down, and it looks like the trend will continue for the next month or two, gamble a bit and don't lock in the points until it looks like rates are at their lowest. You can even wait until a day or two before closing. The points can be locked in at any time before closing.

After you lock in the points, ask the lender to give you a written confirmation of your point lock. Most often it's done verbally. But I've seen confusion and false assumptions too often to trust a verbal point lock. Recently, one of my agents thought the points had been locked on the loans for a couple of duplexes her investor was purchasing. Thirty days into the loan process, the loan was approved and she found out the points had been allowed to float. Rates had gone up considerably. The buyer refused to pay the additional points, or close at a higher rate. The seller was a government agency—it doesn't negotiate. It cost us half of our commission for the additional points. The agent learned never to take a verbal point lock again.

CHANGING LENDERS

For one reason or another, you might want to change lenders after loan application. You can simply go to another lender and make application. Explain that you've applied with another lender, and give the reason for your change. The cost to change will be nominal. Often times, if your loan has been denied, or if the point lock has expired, the first lender will transfer much of the paperwork to the next lender, rather than cause bad feelings and have you go through the entire process all over again. If at all possible, have the paperwork transferred from the first lender to the second one. It can save several weeks of time.

CLOSING COSTS

Some lenders are very reasonable with the closing costs required to close their loans. Others will tack on every little charge imaginable. Some costs will go on the seller's side of the closing statement, and others on the buyer's side. I've seen some ridiculous charges, so if at all possible, at loan application have the lender prepare an estimated "HUD-1" settlement statement, which is used by literally every lender in the country. Figures 19-1 and 19-2 are examples of a HUD-1. Have the loan officer explain every charge, and if you see a multitude of unusual charges for every service imaginable, try another lender.

Every part of the country has "standard" closing costs. Some areas might have transfer stamps or transfer taxes, other areas will have title insurance or abstracting fees. Once you have the estimated settlement statement, call a title company or escrow company and inquire about the figures on it. They'll normally verify everything as being correct, but once in a while, you'll find that some charges are unusual and unnecessary.

Form Approved
OMB NO. 63-R-1501

A.	U.S. DEPARTMENT OF HOUSING AND URBAN DEVELOPMENT	B. TYPE OF LOAN

SETTLEMENT STATEMENT

B. TYPE OF LOAN
1. ☒ FHA   2. ☐ FmHA   3. ☐ CONV. UNINS.
4. ☐ VA   5. ☐ CONV. INS.

6. File Number

7. Loan Number

8. Mortgage Insurance Case Number:

C. NOTE: This form is furnished to give you a statement of actual settlement costs. Amounts paid to and by the settlement agent are shown. Items marked "(p.o.c.)" were paid outside the closing; they are shown here for informational purposes and are not included in the totals.

D. NAME OF BORROWER:	E. NAME OF SELLER:
John and Jane Dough	Richard and Ruth Rowe

F. NAME OF LENDER:	G. PROPERTY LOCATION:
Points Galore Mortgage Co.	39 Wistful Vista, Anytown, TX

H. SETTLEMENT AGENT:	PLACE OF SETTLEMENT:	I. SETTLEMENT DATE:
Cloud 9 Title Co.	345 Mechanic's Lane, Anytown, TX	2-4-85

J. SUMMARY OF BORROWER'S TRANSACTION		K. SUMMARY OF SELLER'S TRANSACTION	
100. GROSS AMOUNT DUE FROM BORROWER:		**400. GROSS AMOUNT DUE TO SELLER:**	
101. Contract sales price	87,000.00	401. Contract sales price	87,000.00
102. Personal property		402. Personal property	
103. Settlement charges to borrower (line 1400)	4207.89	403.	
104.		404.	
105.		405.	
Adjustments for items paid by seller in advance		*Adjustments for items paid by seller in advance*	
106. City/town taxes to		406. City/town taxes to	
107. County taxes to		407. County taxes to	
108. Assessments to		408. Assessments to	
109.		409.	
110.		410.	
111.		411.	
112.		412.	
120. GROSS AMOUNT DUE FROM BORROWER	91,207.89	**420. GROSS AMOUNT DUE TO SELLER**	87,000.00
200. AMOUNTS PAID BY OR IN BEHALF OF BORROWER:		**500. REDUCTIONS IN AMOUNT DUE TO SELLER:**	
201. Deposit or earnest money	500.00	501. Excess deposit (see instructions)	
202. Principal amount of new loan(s)	72,200.00	502. Settlement charges to seller (line 1400)	2954.00
203. Existing loan(s) taken subject to		503. Existing loan(s) taken subject to	
204. Refund due on Credit Report	7.00	504. Payoff of first mortgage loan thru 2/4 Heritage Banc Savings	62,882.08
" " " Appraisal	25.00		
Rent Deposit Credit	900.00	Earnest Money from Buyers	500.00
205.		Rent deposits to Buyers	900.00
		505. Payoff of second mortgage loan	
206.		506.	
207.		507.	
208.		508.	
209.		509.	
Adjustments for items unpaid by seller		*Adjustments for items unpaid by seller*	
210. City/town taxes 1985 to TAXES		510. City/town taxes 1985 to TAXES	
211. County taxes 1-1-85 to 2-4-85	115.15	511. County taxes 1-1-85 to 2-4-85	115.15
212. Assessments to		512. Assessments to	
213.		513.	
214.		514.	
215.		515.	
216.		516.	
217.		517.	
218.		518.	
219.		519.	
220. TOTAL PAID BY/FOR BORROWER	73,747.15	**520. TOTAL REDUCTION AMOUNT DUE SELLER**	67,351.23
300. CASH AT SETTLEMENT FROM/TO BORROWER		**600. CASH AT SETTLEMENT TO/FROM SELLER**	
301. Gross amount due from borrower (line 120)	91,207.89	601. Gross amount due to seller (line 420)	87,000.00
302. Less amounts paid by/for borrower (line 220)	(73,747.15)	602. Less reductions in amount due seller (line 520)	(67,351.23)
303. CASH (☐ FROM)(☒ TO) BORROWER	17,460.74	603. CASH (☐ TO)(☐ FROM) SELLER	19,648.77

Fig. 19-1.

L. SETTLEMENT CHARGES

		PAID FROM BORROWER'S FUNDS AT SETTLEMENT	PAID FROM SELLER'S FUNDS AT SETTLEMENT
700. TOTAL SALES/BROKER'S COMMISSION based on price $ @ % =			
Division of Commission (line 700) as follows:			
701. $ N/A to			
702. $ to			
703. Commission paid at Settlement			
704.			
800. ITEMS PAYABLE IN CONNECTION WITH LOAN			
801. Loan Origination Fee %			696.00
802. Loan Discount 1.50 % POINTS GALORE MORTGAGE CO.			1,083.00
803. Appraisal Fee P.O.C. $200 00			
804. Credit Report P.O.C. $50 00 to			
805. Lender's Inspection Fee			
806. Mortgage Insurance Application Fee to			
807. Assumption Fee			
808. Messenger Fees			25.00
809. Tax Service Fee			42.00
810. Processing Fee			100.00
811. Recording Fee			5.00
900. ITEMS REQUIRED BY LENDER TO BE PAID IN ADVANCE			
901. Interest from 2-4 to 3-1-85 @ $ 25.07 /day		626.75	
902. Mortgage Insurance Premium for FHA MIP months to		2,644.80	
903. Hazard Insurance Premium for 1 years to Tom Jones Ins.		374.00	
904. years to			
905.			
1000. RESERVES DEPOSITED WITH LENDER			
1001. Hazard Insurance 2 months @ $ 31.17 per month		62.34	
1002. Mortgage Insurance months @ $ per month			
1003. City property taxes months @ $ per month			
1004. County property taxes months @ $ per month			
1005. Annual assessments months @ $ per month			
1006. 1985 TAXES 5 months @ $ 100 00 per month		500.00	
1007. months @ $ per month			
1008. months @ $ per month			
1100. TITLE CHARGES			
1101. Settlement or closing fee to			
1102. Abstract or title search to			
1103. Title examination to			
1104. Title insurance binder to			
1105. Document preparation to POINTS GALORE MORTGAGE CO./CLOUD 9			60.00
1106. Notary fees to			
1107. Attorney's fees to CLOUD 9 TITLE			
(includes above items numbers:			
1108. Title insurance to CLOUD 9 TITLE			697.00
(includes above items numbers:			
1109. Lender's coverage $ 64,600.00			
1110. Owner's coverage $ 87,000.00			
1111. Escrow Fees			50.00
1112. Restrictions			5.00
1113. Tax Certificates			15.00
1200. GOVERNMENT RECORDING AND TRANSFER CHARGES			
1201. Recording fees: Deed $ 5 00 : Mortgage $ 11 00 : Release $ 5.00			21.00
1202. City/county tax/stamps: Deed $: Mortgage $			
1203. State tax/stamps: Deed $: Mortgage $			
1204.			
1205.			
1300. ADDITIONAL SETTLEMENT CHARGES			
1301. Survey to BIG STATE Land Surveyors			155.00
1302. Pest inspection to			
1303.			
1304.			
1305.			
1400. TOTAL SETTLEMENT CHARGES (enter on lines 103. Section J and 502, Section K)		4,207.89	2,954.00

Attached to and made part of Disclosure/Statement File # _____

HUD-1 Rev. 5/76

I (we) acknowledge receipt of a copy of the Disclosure/Settlement Statememt and confirm same as correct. Buyer's/Seller's signature hereunder acknowledges his approval of tax prorations, and signifies his understanding that prorations were based on figures for preceding year, or estimates for current year, and in the event of any change for current year, all necessary adjustments must be made between Buyer and Seller direct.

Seller _____ Buyer _____

Seller _____ Buyer _____

By: _____
closer

Fig. 19-1. Cont.

NOTE

LOAN # 1234567

US $ 90,000.00

City Dallas, State Texas

Nov. 12, 19 87

FOR VALUE RECEIVED, the undersigned ("Borrower") promise(s) to pay Olive Oil's Investment Corporation on order, the principal sum of Ninety thousand and 00/100 ($90,000.00)------------------ Dollars, with interest on the unpaid principal balance from the date of this Note, until paid, at the rate of 12 percent per annum. Principal and interest shall be payable at 323 Brick Rd., Dallas Texas, or such other place as the Note holder may designate, in consecutive monthly installments of one thousand twenty eight and 62/100--------------------------Dollars (US$ 1028.62), on the 1st day of each month beginning January 1, 19 88. Such monthly installments shall continue until entire indebtedness evidenced by this Note is fully paid, except that any remaining indebtedness, if not sooner paid, shall be due and payable on Dec. 1, 2017.

If any monthly installment under this Note is not paid when due and remains unpaid after a date specified by a notice to Borrower, the entire principal amount outstanding and accrued interest thereon shall at once become due and payable at the option of the Note holder. The date specified shall not be less than thirty days from the date such notice is mailed. The Note holder may exercise this option to accelerate during any default by Borrower regardless of any prior forebearance. If suit is brought to collect this Note, the Note holder shall be entitled to collect all reasonable costs and expenses of suit, including, but not limited to, reasonable attorney's fees.

Borrower shall pay to the Note holder a late charge of four (4) percent of any monthly installment not received by the Note holder within fifteen (15) days after the installment is due.

Borrower may prepay the principal amount outstanding in whole or in part. The Note holder may require that any partial payments (i) be made on the date monthly installments are due and (ii) be in the amount of that part of one or more monthly installments which would be applicable to principal. Any partial prepayment shall be applied against the principal amount outstanding and shall not postpone the due date of any subsequent monthly installments or change the amount of such installments, unless the Note holder shall otherwise agree in writing. If, within five years from the date of this Note, Borrower make(s) any prepayments in any twelve month period beginning with the date of this Note or anniversary dates thereof ("loan year") with money lent to Borrower by a lender other than the Note holder, Borrower shall pay the Note holder (a) during each of the first three loan years -0- percent of the amount by which the sum of prepayments made in any such loan year exceeds twenty percent of the original principal amount of this Note and (b) during the fourth and fifth loan years -0- percent of the amount by which the sum of prepayments made in any such loan year exceeds twenty percent of the original principal amount of this Note.

Presentment, notice of dishonor, and protest are hereby waived by all makers, sureties, guarantors and endorsers hereof. This Note shall be the joint and several obligation of all makers, sureties, guarantors and endorsers, and shall be binding upon them and their successors and assigns.

Any notice to Borrower provided for in this Note shall be given by mailing such notice by certified mail addressed to Borrower at the Property Address stated below, or to such other address as Borrower may designate by notice to the Note holder. Any notice to the Note holder shall be given by mailing such notice by certified mail, return receipt requested, to the Note holder at the address stated in the first paragraph of this Note, or at such other address as may have been designated by notice to Borrower.

This indebtedness evidenced by this Note is secured by a Deed of Trust dated Nov. 12, 1987, and reference is made to the Deed of Trust for rights as to acceleration of the indebtedness evidenced by this Note.

Lady N. Shoe

123 Candlestick Lane
Dallas, Texas 77777

Property Address

(Execute Original Only)

Fig. 19-2.

DEED OF TRUST

THIS DEED OR TRUST is made this __12th__ day of __November__ 19 __87__, among the Grantor, __Lady N. Shoe, a single woman__ _____ (herein "Borrower"), __John Smith__ _____ (herein "Trustee"), and the Beneficiary, __Olive Oil's Investment Corporation__ _____, whose address is _____ __323 Brick Road, Dallas, Texas__ _____ (herein "Lender").

BORROWER, in consideration of the indebtedness herein recited and the trust herein created, irrevocably grant and conveys to Trustee, in trust, with power of sale, the following described property located in the County of __Dallas__, State of __Texas__:

Being Lot 5, in Block 9 of Forest Park, an Addition to the City of Dallas, Texas, according to the Map thereof recorded in Volume 188, Page 2179, Map Records of Dallas County, Texas

which has the address of __123 Candlestick Lane, Dallas, Texas 77777__ _____ (herein "Property Address");

TOGETHER with all the improvements now or hereafter erected on the property, and all easements, rights, appurtenances, rents (subject however to the rights and authorities given herein to Lender to collect and apply such rents), royalties, mineral, oil and gas rights and profits, water, water rights, and water stock, and all fixtures now or hereafter attached to the property, all of which, including replacements and additions thereto, shall be deemed to be and remain a part of the property covered by this Deed of Trust; and all of the foregoing, together with said property (or the leasehold estate if this Deed of Trust is on a leasehold) are herein referred to as the "Property";

TO SECURE to Lender (a) the repayment of the indebtedness evidenced by Borrower's note dated __November 12, 1987__ (herein "Note"), in the principal sum of __ninety thousand and 00/100 ($90,000.00)__ Dollars, with interest thereon, providing for monthly installments of principal and interest, with the balance of the indebtedness, if not sooner paid, due and payable on __December 1, 2017__; the payment of all other sums, with interest thereon, advanced in accordance herewith to protect the security of this Deed of Trust; and the performance of the covenants and agreements of Borrower herein contained; and (b) the repayment of any future advances, with interest thereon, made to Borrower by Lender pursuant to paragraph 21 hereof (herein "Future Advances").

Borrower covenants that Borrower is lawfully seized of the estate hereby conveyed and has the right to grant and convey the Property, that the Property is unencumbered, and that Borrower will warrant and defend generally the title to the Property against all claims and demands, subject to any declarations, easements or restrictions listed in a schedule of exceptions to coverage in any title insurance policy insuring Lender's interest in the Property.

UNIFORM COVENANTS. Borrower and Lender covenant and agree as follows:

1. Payment of Principal and Interest. Borrower shall promptly pay when due the principal of and interest on the indebtedness evidenced by the Note, prepayment and late charges as provided in the Note, and the principal of and interest on any Future Advances secured by this Deed of Trust.

2. Funds for Taxes and Insurance. Subject to applicable law or to a written waiver by Lender, Borrower shall pay to Lender on the day monthly installments of principal and interest are payable under the Note, until the Note is paid in full, a sum (herein "Funds") equal to one-twelfth of the yearly taxes and assessments which may attain priority over this Deed of Trust, and ground rents on the Property, if any, plus one-twelfth of yearly premium installments for hazard insurance, plus one-twelfth of yearly premium installments for mortgage insurance, if any, all as reasonably estimated initially and from time to time by Lender on the basis of assessments and bills and reasonable estimates thereof.

The Funds shall be held in an institution the deposits or accounts of which are insured or guaranteed by a Federal or state agency (including Lender if Lender is such an institution). Lender shall apply the Funds to pay said taxes, assessments, insurance premiums and ground rents. Lender may not charge for so holding and applying the Funds, analyzing said account or verifying and compiling said assessments and bills, unless Lender pays Borrower interest on the Funds and applicable law permits Lender to make such a charge. Borrower and Lender may agree in writing at the time of execution of this Deed of Trust that interest on the Funds shall be paid to Borrower, and unless such agreement is made or applicable law requires such interest to be paid, Lender shall not be required to pay Borrower any interest or earnings on the Funds. Lender shall give to Borrower, without charge, an annual accounting of the Funds showing credits and debits to the Funds and the purpose for which each debit to the Funds was made. The Funds are pledged as additional security for the sums secured by this Deed of Trust.

If the amount of the Funds held by Lender, together with the future monthly installments of Funds payable prior to the due dates of taxes, assessments, insurance premiums and ground rents, shall exceed the amount required to pay said taxes, assessments, insurance premiums and ground rents as they fall due, such excess shall be, at Borrower's option,

1 to 4 Family—6/75—FNMA/FHLMC UNIFORM INSTRUMENT

Fig. 19-3.

either promptly repaid to Borrower or credited to Borrower on monthly installments of Funds. If the amount of the Funds held by Lender shall not be sufficient to pay taxes, assessments, insurance premiums and ground rents as they fall due, Borrower shall pay to Lender any amount necessary to make up the deficiency within 30 days from the date notice is mailed by Lender to Borrower requesting payment thereof.

Upon payment in full of all sums secured by this Deed of Trust, Lender shall promptly refund to Borrower any Funds held by Lender. If under paragraph 18 hereof the Property is sold or the Property is otherwise acquired by Lender, Lender shall apply, no later than immediately prior to the sale of the Property or its acquisition by Lender, any Funds held by Lender at the time of application as a credit against the sums secured by this Deed of Trust.

3. Application of Payments. Unless applicable law provides otherwise, all payments received by Lender under the Note and paragraphs 1 and 2 hereof shall be applied by Lender first in payment of amounts payable to Lender by Borrower under paragraph 2 hereof, then to interest payable on the Note, then to the principal of the Note, and then to interest and principal on any Future Advances.

4. Charges; Liens. Borrower shall pay all taxes, assessments and other charges, fines and impositions attributable to the Property which may attain a priority over this Deed of Trust, and leasehold payments or ground rents, if any, in the manner provided under paragraph 2 hereof or, if not paid in such manner, by Borrower making payment, when due, directly to the payee thereof. Borrower shall promptly furnish to Lender all notices of amounts due under this paragraph, and in the event Borrower shall make payment directly, Borrower shall promptly furnish to Lender receipts evidencing such payments. Borrower shall promptly discharge any lien which has priority over this Deed of Trust; provided, that Borrower shall not be required to discharge any such lien so long as Borrower shall agree in writing to the payment of the obligation secured by such lien in a manner acceptable to Lender, or shall in good faith contest such lien by, or defend enforcement of such lien in, legal proceedings which operate to prevent the enforcement of the lien or forfeiture of the Property or any part thereof.

5. Hazard Insurance. Borrower shall keep the improvements now existing or hereafter erected on the Property insured against loss by fire, hazards included within the term "extended coverage", and such other hazards as Lender may require and in such amounts and for such periods as Lender may require; provided, that Lender shall not require that the amount of such coverage exceed that amount of coverage required to pay the sums secured by this Deed of Trust.

The insurance carrier providing the insurance shall be chosen by Borrower subject to approval by Lender; provided, that such approval shall not be unreasonably withheld. All premiums on insurance policies shall be paid in the manner provided under paragraph 2 hereof or, if not paid in such manner, by Borrower making payment, when due, directly to the insurance carrier.

All insurance policies and renewals thereof shall be in form acceptable to Lender and shall include a standard mortgage clause in favor of and in form acceptable to Lender. Lender shall have the right to hold the policies and renewals thereof, and Borrower shall promptly furnish to Lender all renewal notices and all receipts of paid premiums. In the event of loss, Borrower shall give prompt notice to the insurance carrier and Lender. Lender may make proof of loss if not made promptly by Borrower.

Unless Lender and Borrower otherwise agree in writing, insurance proceeds shall be applied to restoration or repair of the Property damaged, provided such restoration or repair is economically feasible and the security of this Deed of Trust is not thereby impaired. If such restoration or repair is not economically feasible or if the security of this Deed of Trust would be impaired, the insurance proceeds shall be applied to the sums secured by this Deed of Trust, with the excess, if any, paid to Borrower. If the Property is abandoned by Borrower, or if Borrower fails to respond to Lender within 30 days from the date notice is mailed by Lender to Borrower that the insurance carrier offers to settle a claim for insurance benefits, Lender is authorized to collect and apply the insurance proceeds at Lender's option either to restoration or repair of the Property or to the sums secured by this Deed of Trust.

Unless Lender and Borrower otherwise agree in writing, any such application of proceeds to principal shall not extend or postpone the due date of the monthly installments referred to in paragraphs 1 and 2 hereof or change the amount of such installments. If under paragraph 18 hereof the Property is acquired by Lender, all right, title and interest of Borrower in and to any insurance policies and in and to the proceeds thereof resulting from damage to the Property prior to the sale or acquisition shall pass to Lender to the extent of the sums secured by this Deed of Trust immediately prior to such sale or acquisition.

6. Preservation and Maintenance of Property; Leaseholds; Condominiums; Planned Unit Developments. Borrower shall keep the Property in good repair and shall not commit waste or permit impairment or deterioration of the Property and shall comply with the provisions of any lease if this Deed of Trust is on a leasehold. If this Deed of Trust is on a unit in a condominium or a planned unit development, Borrower shall perform all of Borrower's obligations under the declaration or covenants creating or governing the condominium or planned unit development, the by-laws and regulations of the condominium or planned unit development, and constituent documents. If a condominium or planned unit development rider is executed by Borrower and recorded together with this Deed of Trust, the covenants and agreements of such rider shall be incorporated into and shall amend and supplement the covenants and agreements of this Deed of Trust as if the rider were a part hereof.

7. Protection of Lender's Security. If Borrower fails to perform the covenants and agreements contained in this Deed of Trust, or if any action or proceeding is commenced which materially affects Lender's interest in the Property, including, but not limited to, eminent domain, insolvency, code enforcement, or arrangements or proceedings involving a bankrupt or decedent, then Lender at Lender's option, upon notice to Borrower, may make such appearances, disburse such sums and take such action as is necessary to protect Lender's interest, including, but not limited to, disbursement of reasonable attorney's fees and entry upon the Property to make repairs. If Lender required mortgage insurance as a condition of making the loan secured by this Deed of Trust, Borrower shall pay the premiums required to maintain such insurance in effect until such time as the requirement for such insurance terminates in accordance with Borrower's and Lender's written agreement or applicable law. Borrower shall pay the amount of all mortgage insurance premiums in the manner provided under paragraph 2 hereof.

Any amounts disbursed by Lender pursuant to this paragraph 7, with interest thereon, shall become additional indebtedness of Borrower secured by this Deed of Trust. Unless Borrower and Lender agree to other terms of payment, such amounts shall be payable upon notice from Lender to Borrower requesting payment thereof, and shall bear interest from the date of disbursement at the rate payable from time to time on outstanding principal under the Note unless payment of interest at such rate would be contrary to applicable law, in which event such amounts shall bear interest at the highest rate permissible under applicable law. Nothing contained in this paragraph 7 shall require Lender to incur any expense or take any action hereunder.

8. Inspection. Lender may make or cause to be made reasonable entries upon and inspections of the Property, provided that Lender shall give Borrower notice prior to any such inspection specifying reasonable cause therefor related to Lender's interest in the Property.

9. Condemnation. The proceeds of any award or claim for damages, direct or consequential, in connection with any condemnation or other taking of the Property, or part thereof, or for conveyance in lieu of condemnation, are hereby assigned and shall be paid to Lender.

Fig. 19-3. Cont.

In the event of a total taking of the Property, the proceeds shall be applied to the sums secured by this Deed of Trust, with the excess, if any, paid to Borrower. In the event of a partial taking of the Property, unless Borrower and Lender otherwise agree in writing, there shall be applied to the sums secured by this Deed of Trust such proportion of the proceeds as is equal to that proportion which the amount of the sums secured by this Deed of Trust immediately prior to the date of taking bears to the fair market value of the Property immediately prior to the date of taking, with the balance of the proceeds paid to Borrower.

If the Property is abandoned by Borrower, or if, after notice by Lender to Borrower that the condemnor offers to make an award or settle a claim for damages, Borrower fails to respond to Lender within 30 days after the date such notice is mailed, Lender is authorized to collect and apply the proceeds, at Lender's option, either to restoration or repair of the Property or to the sums secured by this Deed of Trust.

Unless Lender and Borrower otherwise agree in writing, any such application of proceeds to principal shall not extend or postpone the due date of the monthly installments referred to in paragraphs 1 and 2 hereof or change the amount of such installments.

10. Borrower Not Released. Extension of the time for payment or modification of amortization of the sums secured by this Deed of Trust granted by Lender to any successor in interest of Borrower shall not operate to release, in any manner, the liability of the original Borrower and Borrower's successors in interest. Lender shall not be required to commence proceedings against such successor or refuse to extend time for payment or otherwise modify amortization of the sums secured by this Deed of Trust by reason of any demand made by the original Borrower and Borrower's successors in interest.

11. Forbearance by Lender Not a Waiver. Any forbearance by Lender in exercising any right or remedy hereunder, or otherwise afforded by applicable law, shall not be a waiver of or preclude the exercise of any such right or remedy. The procurement of insurance or the payment of taxes or other liens or charges by Lender shall not be a waiver of Lender's right to accelerate the maturity of the indebtedness secured by this Deed of Trust.

12. Remedies Cumulative. All remedies provided in this Deed of Trust are distinct and cumulative to any other right or remedy under this Deed of Trust or afforded by law or equity, and may be exercised concurrently, independently or successively.

13. Successors and Assigns Bound; Joint and Several Liability; Captions. The covenants and agreements herein contained shall bind, and the rights hereunder shall inure to, the respective successors and assigns of Lender and Borrower, subject to the provisions of paragraph 17 hereof. All covenants and agreements of Borrower shall be joint and several. The captions and headings of the paragraphs of this Deed of Trust are for convenience only and are not to be used to interpret or define the provisions hereof.

14. Notice. Except for any notice required under applicable law to be given in another manner, (a) any notice to Borrower provided for in this Deed of Trust shall be given by mailing such notice by certified mail addressed to Borrower at the Property Address or at such other address as Borrower may designate by notice to Lender as provided herein, and (b) any notice to Lender shall be given by certified mail, return receipt requested, to Lender's address stated herein or to such other address as Lender may designate by notice to Borrower as provided herein. Any notice provided for in this Deed of Trust shall be deemed to have been given to Borrower or Lender when given in the manner designated herein.

15. Uniform Deed of Trust; Governing Law; Severability. This form of deed of trust combines uniform covenants for national use and non-uniform covenants with limited variations by jurisdiction to constitute a uniform security instrument covering real property. This Deed of Trust shall be governed by the law of the jurisdiction in which the Property is located. In the event that any provision or clause of this Deed of Trust or the Note conflicts with applicable law, such conflict shall not affect other provisions of this Deed of Trust or the Note which can be given effect without the conflicting provision, and to this end the provisions of the Deed of Trust and the Note are declared to be severable.

16. Borrower's Copy. Borrower shall be furnished a conformed copy of the Note and of this Deed of Trust at the time of execution or after recordation hereof.

17. Transfer of the Property; Assumption. If all or any part of the Property or an interest therein is sold or transferred by Borrower without Lender's prior written consent, excluding (a) the creation of a lien or encumbrance subordinate to this Deed of Trust, (b) the creation of a purchase money security interest for household appliances, (c) a transfer by devise, descent or by operation of law upon the death of a joint tenant or (d) the grant of any leasehold interest of three years or less not containing an option to purchase, Lender may, at Lender's option, declare all the sums secured by this Deed of Trust to be immediately due and payable. Lender shall have waived such option to accelerate if, prior to the sale or transfer, Lender and the person to whom the Property is to be sold or transferred reach agreement in writing that the credit of such person is satisfactory to Lender and that the interest payable on the sums secured by this Deed of Trust shall be at such rate as Lender shall request. If Lender has waived the option to accelerate provided in this paragraph 17, and if Borrower's successor in interest has executed a written asumption agreement accepted in writing by Lender, Lender shall release Borrower from all obligations under this Deed of Trust and the Note.

If Lender exercises such option to accelerate, Lender shall mail Borrower notice of acceleration in accordance with paragraph 14 hereof. Such notice shall provide a period of not less than 30 days from the date the notice is mailed within which Borrower may pay the sums declared due. If Borrower fails to pay such sums prior to the expiration of such period, Lender may, without further notice or demand on Borrower, invoke any remedies permitted by paragraph 18 hereof.

NON—UNIFORM COVENANTS. Borrower and Lender further covenant and agree as follows:

18. Acceleration; Remedies. Except as provided in paragraph 17 hereof, upon Borrower's breach of any covenant or agreement of Borrower in this Deed of Trust, including the covenants to pay when due any sums secured by this Deed of Trust, Lender prior to acceleration shall give notice in the manner prescribed by applicable law to Borrower and to the other persons prescribed by applicable law specifying: (1) the breach; (2) the action required to cure such breach; (3) a date, not less than 30 days from the date the notice is mailed to Borrower, by which such breach must be cured; and (4) that failure to cure such breach on or before the date specified in the notice may result in acceleration of the sums secured by this Deed of Trust and sale of the property at public auction at a date not less than 120 days in the future. The notice shall further inform Borrower of (i) the right to reinstate after acceleration, (ii) the right to bring a court action to assert the non-existence of a default or any other defense of Borrower to acceleration and foreclosure and (iii) any other matter required to be included in such notice by applicable law. If the breach is not cured on or before the date specified in the notice, Lender at Lender's option may declare all of the sums secured by this Deed of Trust to be immediately due and payable without further demand and may invoke the power of sale and any other remedies permitted by applicable law. Lender shall be entitled to collect all reasonable costs and expenses incurred in pursuing the remedies provided in this paragraph 18, including, but not limited to, reasonable attorney's fees.

If Lender invokes the power of sale, Lender shall give written notice to Trustee of the occurrence of an event of default and of Lender's election to cause the Property to be sold. Trustee and Lender shall take such action regarding notice of sale and shall give such notices to Borrower and to other persons as applicable law may require. After the lapse of such time as may be required by applicable law and after publication of the notice of sale, Trustee, without demand on Borrower, shall sell the Property at public auction to the highest bidder at the time and place and under the terms designated in the notice of sale in one or more parcels and in such order as Trustee may determine. Trustee may postpone sale of the Property for a period or periods not exceeding a total of 30 days by public announcement at the time and place fixed in the notice of sale. Lender or Lender's designee may purchase the Property at any sale.

Trustee shall deliver to the purchaser Trustee's deed conveying the Proprety so sold without any covenant or warranty, expressed or implied. The recitals in the Trustee's deed shall be prima facie evidence of the truth of the statements made therein. Trustee shall apply the proceeds of the sale in the following order: (a) to all reasonable costs and expenses of the sale, including, but not limited to, reasonable Trustee's and attorney's fees and costs of title evidence; (b) to all sums secured by this Deed of Trust; and (c) the excess, if any, to the person or persons legally entitled thereto, or the clerk of the superior court of the county in which the sale took place.

19. Borrower's Right to Reinstate. Notwithstanding Lender's acceleration of the sums secured by this Deed of Trust, Borrower shall have the right to have any proceedings begun by Lender to enforce this Deed of Trust discontinued at any time prior to the earlier to occur of (i) the tenth day before sale of the Property pursuant to the power of sale contained in this Deed of Trust or (ii) entry of a judgment enforcing this Deed of Trust if: (a) Borrower pays Lender all sums which would be then due under this Deed of Trust, the Note and notes securing Future Advances, if any, had no acceleration occurred; (b) Borrower cures all breaches of any other covenants or agreements of Borrower contained in this Deed of Trust; (c) Borrower pays all reasonable expenses incurred by Lender and Trustee in enforcing the covenants and agreements of Borrower contained in this Deed of Trust and in enforcing Lender's and Trustee's remedies as provided in paragraph 18 hereof, including, but not limited to, reasonable attorney's fees; and (d) Borrower takes such action as Lender may reasonably require to assure that the lien of this Deed of Trust, Lender's interest in the Property and Borrower's obligation to pay the sums secured by this Deed of Trust shall continue unimpaired. Upon such payment and cure by Borrower, this Deed of Trust and the obligations secured hereby shall remain in full force and effect as if no acceleration had occurred.

20. Assignment of Rents; Appointment of Receiver; Lender in Possession. As additional security hereunder, Borrower hereby assigns to Lender the rents of the Property, provided that Borrower shall, prior to acceleration under paragraph 18 hereof or abandonment of the Property, have the right to collect and retain such rents as they become due and payable.

Upon acceleration under paragraph 18 hereof or abandonment of the Property, Lender, in person, by agent or by judicially appointed receiver, shall be entitled to enter upon, take possession of and manage the Property and to collect the rents of the Property, including those past due. All rents collected by Lender or the receiver shall be applied first to payment of the costs of management of the Property and collection of rents, including, but not limited to, receiver's fees, premiums on receiver's bonds and reasonable attorney's fees, and then to the sums secured by this Deed of Trust. Lender and the receiver shall be liable to account only for those rents actually received.

21. Future Advances. Upon request of Borrower, Lender, at Lender's option prior to full reconveyance of the Property by Trustee to Borrower, may make Future Advances to Borrower. Such Future Advances, with interest thereon shall be secured by this Deed of Trust when evidenced by promissory notes stating that said notes are secured hereby.

22. Reconveyance. Upon payment of all sums secured by this Deed of Trust, Lender shall request Trustee to reconvey the Property and shall surrender this Deed of Trust and all notes evidencing indebtedness secured by this Deed of Trust to Trustee. Trustee shall reconvey the Property without warranty and without charge to the person or persons legally entitled thereto. Such person or persons shall pay all costs of recordation, if any.

23. Substitute Trustee. In accordance with applciable law, Lender may from time to time appoint a successor trustee to any Trustee appointed hereunder who has ceased to act. Without conveyance of the Property, the successor trustee shall succeed to all the title, power and duties conferred upon the Trustee herein and by applicable law.

24. Use of Property. The Property is not used principally for agricultural or farming purposes.

IN WITNESS WHEREOF, BORROWER has executed this Deed of Trust.

_____   Lady N. Shoe   _Borrower_

_____   _Borrower_

STATE OF __Texas__, __Dallas_____County ss:

On this __12th__ day of __Nov.__, 19 __87__, before me the undersigned, a Notary Public in and for the State of __Texas__, duly commissioned and sworn, personally appeared __Lady N. Shoe__ _____ to me known to be the individual(s) described in and who executed the foregoing instrument, and acknowledged to me that ____she____ signed and sealed the said instrument as ___her___ free and voluntary act and deed, for the uses and purposes therein mentioned. WITNESS my hand and official seal affixed the day and year in this certificate above written.

My Commission expires:

_____

Notary Public in and for the State of _____ _residing at:_

REQUEST FOR RECONVEYANCE

To TRUSTEE:

The undersigned is the holder of the note or notes secured by this Deed of Trust. Said note or notes, together with all other indebtedness secured by this Deed of Trust, have been paid in full. You are hereby directed to cancel said note or notes and this Deed of Trust, which are delivered hereby, and to reconvey, without warranty, all the estate now held by you under this Deed of Trust to the person or persons legally entitled thereto.

Date: _____

(Space Below This Line Reserved For Lender and Recorder)

Fig. 19-3. Cont.

Prepared by the State Bar of Texas for use by lawyers only. Revised
1-1-76. Revised to include grantee's address (art 6626, RCS) 1-1-82.

DEED OF TRUST TO SECURE ASSUMPTION

(WHERE BENEFICIARY IS LIABLE ON NOTE ASSUMED)

THE STATE OF TEXAS

COUNTY OF Tarrant

KNOW ALL MEN BY THESE PRESENTS:

That   Edward J. Barnett and wife Sally S. Barnett

of   Tarrant   County, Texas, hereinafter called Grantors (whether one or more) for the purpose of securing the indebtedness hereinafter described, and in consideration of the sum of TEN DOLLARS ($10.00) to us in hand paid by the Trustee hereinafter named, the receipt of which is hereby acknowledged, and for the further consideration of the uses, purposes and trusts hereinafter set forth, have granted, sold and conveyed, and by these presents do grant, sell and convey unto Sam Kerrs , Trustee, of   Tarrant   County, Texas, and his substitutes or successors, all of the following described property situated in   Tarrant   County, Texas, to-wit:

Lot 37, Block 6/7789 Cozy Acres Addition to the City of Fort Worth,
Texas according to the Map thereof recorded in Volume 893, Page 467
Map Records of Tarrant County, Texas.

TO HAVE AND TO HOLD the above described property, together with the rights, privileges and appurtenances thereto belonging, unto the said Trustee and to his substitutes or successors forever. And Grantors named herein do hereby bind themselves, their heirs, executors, administrators and assigns to warrant and forever defend the said premises unto the said Trustee, his substitutes or successors and assigns forever, against the claim, or claims, of all persons claiming or to claim the same or any part thereof.

Fig. 19-4.

178

This conveyance, however, is made in TRUST for the following purposes:

WHEREAS, Burt W. Higgs and wife Ernestine D. Higgs

hereinafter called Beneficiary, by deed of even date herewith conveyed the herein described property to Grantors named herein, who, as part of the consideration therefor assumed and promised to pay, according to the terms thereof, all principal and interest remaining unpaid upon that one certain promissory note in the original principal sum of $ 100,000.00 , dated 9/23/79 , executed by Burt W. Higgs and wife Ernestine D. Higgs

and payable to order of Big City Mortgage Company

which said note is secured by a Deed of Trust recorded in Volume 645 , Page 743 ,

Records of Tarrant County, Texas, the obligations and covenants of the grantors named in said Deed of Trust were also assumed by Grantors named herein, and in said Deed the superior title and a vendor's lien were expressly reserved and retained by Beneficiary until said indebtedness and obligations so assumed are fully paid and satisfied, and should Grantors do and perform all of the obligations and covenants so assumed and make prompt payment of the indebtedness evidenced by said note so assumed as the same shall become due and payable, then this conveyance shall become null and void and of no further force and effect, it being agreed that a release of such indebtedness so assumed and of the liens securing the same by the legal owner and holder thereof prior to the advancement and payment thereon by Beneficiary of any sum or sums required to cure any default, shall be sufficient to release the lien created by this instrument as well as said vendor's lien so retained, without the joinder of Beneficiary. Unless, prior to the filing of a release of the indebtedness so assumed and of the liens securing the same in the office of the County Clerk of the County where said real property is situated, Beneficiary shall have filed in the office of the County Clerk of said County a sworn statement duly acknowledged and containing a legal description of the real property hereinbefore described and setting forth any and all sums that Beneficiary may have so advanced and paid, it shall be conclusively presumed that no sum or sums have been advanced and paid thereon by Beneficiary.

Grantors agree that in the event of default in the payment of any installment, principal or interest, of the note so assumed by Grantors, or in the event of default in the payment of said note when due or declared due, or of a breach of any of the obligations or covenants contained in the Deed of Trust securing said note so assumed, Beneficiary may, at his option, advance and pay such sum or sums as may be required to cure any such default, and that any and all such sums so advanced and paid by Beneficiary to cure such default shall be paid by Grantors to Beneficiary at 12345 Main Street

, in the City of Grand Prairie, Texas 66666

County, Texas, within five (5) days after the date of such payment, without notice or demand, which are expressly waived.

Grantors covenant to pay promptly to Beneficiary, without notice or demand, within the time and as provided in the foregoing paragraph, any and all sums that may, under the provisions of the foregoing paragraph, be due Beneficiary.

In the event of a breach of the foregoing covenant, it shall thereupon, or at any time thereafter, be the duty of the Trustee, or his successor or substitute as hereinafter provided, at the request of Beneficiary (which request is hereby conclusively presumed), to enforce this Trust, and after advertising the time, place and terms of the sale of the above described and conveyed property, then subject to the lien hereof, for at least twenty-one (21) days preceding the date of sale by posting written or printed notice thereof at the Courthouse door of the county where said real property is situated, which notice may be posted by the Trustee acting, or by any person acting for him, and the Beneficiary (the holder of the indebtedness secured hereby) has, at least twenty-one (21) days preceding the date of sale, served written or printed notice of the proposed sale by certified mail on each debtor obligated to pay the indebtedness secured by this Deed of Trust according to the records of Beneficiary, by the deposit of such notice, enclosed in a postpaid wrapper, properly addressed to such debtor at debtor's most recent address as shown by the records of Beneficiary, in a post office or official depository under the care and custody of the United States Postal Service, the Trustee shall sell the above described property, then subject to the lien hereof, at public auction in accordance with such notice at the Courthouse door of the county where such real property is situated (provided where said real property is situated in more than one county, the notice to be posted as herein provided shall be posted at the Courthouse door of each of such counties where said real property is situated, and said above described and conveyed property may be sold at the Courthouse door of any one of such counties, and the notices so posted shall designate the county where the property will be sold), on the first Tuesday in any month between the hours of ten o'clock A.M. and four o'clock P.M., to the highest bidder for cash, and make due conveyance to the Purchaser or Purchasers, with general warranty binding Grantors, their heirs and assigns; and out of the money arising from such sale the Trustee shall pay, first, all expenses of advertising the sale and making the conveyance, including a commission of 10% to himself and, second, to Beneficiary the full amount of all sums so advanced and paid and that are then owing to Beneficiary under the provisions hereof, rendering the balance of the sales price, if any, to the person or persons legally entitled thereto; and the recitals in the conveyance to the Purchaser or Purchasers shall be full and conclusive evidence of the truth of the matters therein stated, and all prerequisites to said sale shall be presumed to have been performed, and such sale and conveyance shall be conclusive against Grantors, their heirs and assigns; said sale and deed to be made subject to the then unpaid part of the indebtedness so assumed by Grantors and the lien or liens securing the same, and it is agreed that such sale shall not in any manner affect any indebtedness which may thereafter become due and owing to Beneficiary under the covenants and provisions of this Deed of Trust, it being agreed that this Deed of Trust and all rights of Beneficiary shall be and remain in full force and effect so long as the obligations and indebtedness so assumed by Grantors or any part thereof remains unsatisfied or unpaid; that a sale by the Trustee or Substitute Trustee hereunder shall not exhaust the right of the Trustee or Substitute Trustee in event of any subsequent default hereunder, and at the request of Beneficiary, to thereafter enforce this trust and make sale of said property as herein provided.

Beneficiary shall have the right to purchase at any sale of the property, being the highest bidder and to have the amount for which such property is sold credited on the total sums owed Beneficiary.

Beneficiary in any event is hereby authorized to appoint a substitute trustee, or a successor trustee, to act instead of the Trustee named herein without other formality than the designation in writing of a substitute or successor trustee; and the authority hereby conferred shall extend to the appointment of other successor and substitute trustees successively until the full and final payment and satisfaction of the indebtedness and obligations so assumed by Grantors, and each substitute and successor trustee shall succeed to all of the rights and powers of the original Trustee named herein.

The term "Grantors" used in this instrument shall also include any and all successors in interest of Grantors to all or any part of the herein described and conveyed property as well as any and all purchasers thereof at any sale made hereunder by the Trustee or Substitute Trustee, and the provisions of this Deed of Trust shall be covenants running with the land.

Fig. 19-4. Cont.

If this Deed of Trust is or becomes binding upon one person or upon a corporation, the plural reference to Grantors shall be held to include the singular and all of the agreements and covenants herein undertaken to be performed by and the rights conferred upon Grantors, shall be binding upon and inure to the benefit of not only Grantors respectively but also their respective heirs, executors, administrators, grantees, successors and assigns.

It is expressly stipulated that the liability of Grantors to Beneficiary, arising by virtue of the assumption by Grantors of the payment of the note herein described and of the obligations of the Deed of Trust securing said note, as well as the liability to Beneficiary of any and all persons hereafter assuming payment of said note and performance of the obligations of said Deed of Trust, shall in no wise be discharged or released by this instrument or by the exercise by Beneficiary of the rights and remedies herein provided for, it being agreed that this instrument and all rights and remedies herein accorded Beneficiary are cumulative of any and all other rights and remedies existing at law.

Grantors expressly represent that any indebtedness becoming due and payable under and by virtue of the terms and provisions of this Deed of Trust is in part payment of the purchase price of the herein described and conveyed property and that this Deed of Trust is cumulative and in addition to the Vendor's Lien expressly retained in deed of even date herewith executed by Beneficiary to Grantors, and it is expressly agreed that Beneficiary may foreclose under either or both of said liens as Beneficiary may elect, without waiving the other, said deed hereinbefore mentioned, together with its record, being here referred to and made a part of this instrument.

In the event any sale is made of the above described property, or any portion thereof, under the terms of this Deed of Trust, Grantors, their heirs and assigns, shall forthwith upon the making of such sale surrender and deliver possession of the property so sold to the Purchaser at such sale, and in the event of their failure to do so they shall thereupon from and after the making of such sale be and continue as tenants at will of such Purchaser, and in the event of their failure to surrender possession of said property upon demand, the Purchaser, his heirs or assigns, shall be entitled to institute and maintain an action for forcible detainer of said property in the Justice of the Peace Court in the Justice Precinct in which such property, or any part thereof, is situated.

EXECUTED this 12th day of November , A.D. 1987

Mailing address of trustee:

Name: Sam Kerrs
Address: 7878 Division Street
         Arlington, TX 75555

Mailing address of each beneficiary:

Name: Burt and Ernestine Higgs
Address: 12345 Main Street
         Grand Prairie, TX 66666

Name:
Address:

(Acknowledgment)

STATE OF TEXAS
COUNTY OF

    This instrument was acknowledged before me on the   day of   , 19   ,
by

My commission expires:

....

Notary Public, State of Texas
Notary's printed name:

Fig. 19-4. Cont.

20

Making the Offer

Since you will buckle fortune on my back,
To bear her burden, whether I will or no,
I must have patience to endure the load.

—Shakespeare, *Richard III.*

YOU'VE SELECTED THE RIGHT HOUSE AND ARE READY TO MAKE YOUR OFFER.
Maybe you've fallen in love with the house and are anxious to get the deal
cemented soon. Now all you need is patience to make sure the deal works best
for you. Follow Shakespeare's words, not Oren Arnold's prayer of the modern
American: "Dear God, I pray for patience. And I want it right now!"

There are several important steps that must be addressed in an agreement,
or gone over in working up the agreement, before you can begin to cement a
deal. I'll explain each one in detail:

- The verbal offer
- The written offer
- Negotiating the contract
- Earnest money
- Loan application
- Property appraisal
- Property inspection
- Closing
- Backing out

THE VERBAL OFFER

If you're dealing directly with a seller, the verbal offer can be a good way to get a feeling of the seller's motivation: his need to sell, his patience. The verbal offer is not binding, so you can make any ridiculous offer, any question inferring an offer, or propose any idea you might have for alternative seller financing that might be overly beneficial to your side of the deal.

There are different ways to make the offer, and the blunt approach will not always endear you to the seller. You must first appeal to the seller's emotions. The seller has to like you to allow you to take advantage of him. Love and patience conquers more people than animosity and anxiety. Here's what I mean. A fellow is selling a house for $130,000. A buyer drives up in his Porsche Super 1000 convertible, there's a Rolex on his wrist, and a five-carat diamond on his finger. He looks down at the seller and says, "I'll give you $110,000 and not a dime more. Take it or leave it."

The fellow might take it if he's desperate. But even if he's desperate, he might loathe the buyer's presence so much that he'd rather lose the house to foreclosure than see him get any kind of a good deal. Part of it might be jealousy, part of it anger, even hatred. You've seen it in marriage breakups. Where at one time the wife would have given her soul for her mate, she'd now rather give him a slug through the heart.

You could come along to that same seller much differently. You and your mate get out of your clean little Ford Nonpresumtious 100. You're neatly dressed, but wear no designer clothes, and no jewelry flashes before the seller's eyes. You chat with him a while, let him do as much talking as he wants. You make him feel good, and he gets to know you and like you. You want the same good deal the pretentious buyer has offered the seller. But you say, "Gosh, Mr. Smith, this is a lovely home, and my spouse and two kids would love to buy it from you, but we feel $130,000 would stretch our budget so we'd not be able to afford our little Timmy's asthma and allergy medicine. Do you think you'd consider $110,000?"

You just made a verbal offer. You have no obligation to take it even if the seller accepts. Or even if he accepts, you didn't say anything about the five points you want him to pay for your loan, or the fact that you want him to pay all of your closing costs. If he accepts, you just found out that the seller is extremely flexible in his sale price. You might also have posed the question/offer in another way. You might have said, "Gosh, Mr. Smith, this is a lovely home at a good price, but we don't think we'd qualify for a loan at a selling price of $130,000. Would you consider carrying the loan yourself at six percent interest for the first five years, then we'll be able to afford a commercial loan at a higher rate?"

182

You might have several alternatives, and pose one after the other after each rejection. You're asking each question in as nice a manner as possible, always with a smile on your face, never feeling shocked or angry after a rejection. The verbal offers are fishing expeditions. You only want to find out the seller's motivation and bottom limits. You might find that if he likes you enough, and is desperate enough for a buyer, the $130,000 house will be yours for $110,000. Because you'll have done your homework before you make your verbal offers, you'll know the house is indeed worth every bit of $130,000, and if he says he'll accept the lower offer, then you take out a contract form and begin filling it out. You want it on paper as soon as possible.

Never be afraid to make a verbal offer, and even if you're dealing with a real estate agent, ask to meet the seller and try your verbal offers with the seller as if the agent weren't there. You'll not endear yourself with the agent, but if the seller agrees on your price, get the agent to take out a contract and fill it out on the spot. The bottom line to the agent is the commission, and no matter how the sale comes about, as long as it comes about, he'll forgive your intrepid attitude.

Don't ever be afraid to make a crazy offer. Verbal offers are especially easy to make, and written offers only take a bit of very inexpensive paper to produce.

THE WRITTEN OFFER

The difference between a verbal and written offer is that a written offer, along with earnest money, signed by buyer and seller, becomes a binding contract. The seller *must* sell, but as a general rule, the buyer *does not* have to buy.

Once a seller is on contract, he can be forced to sell as long as the buyer keeps up with his end of the bargain. That's because a piece of real estate is unique. There are no two houses exactly alike. Even if the floor plan is exactly the same as another, the house is still not the same house as the other. The lot is different, the orientation, the utilities, the landscaping, and other items will be different. Very rarely can the seller back out of a contract without the buyer's consent.

If you're on contract to purchase a property, and the seller refuses to close on the deal as stipulated in the contract, you can have your signature on the contract notarized and then file the contract at the county clerk's or county recorder's office. It should put a cloud on the property's title. You won't be able to force him to sell to you without a lawsuit—a costly affair—but sometime in the future, when he does sell, he'll have to deal with you to transfer clear title to the property.

Most contracts should have one or more escape clauses for the buyer. I'll cover that later in this chapter. Even if you have no escape clause, in most places, your maximum loss if you back out of the deal is your earnest money.

The contract should contain the *entire* agreement between you and the seller. Anything the seller has promised you, such as repairs or non-real estate items that go with the deal should all be in the written agreement, or you have little chance of enforcing the inclusion of those items at closing.

An enforceable contract can be anything that's written down and signed by the buyer and seller. It does not have to be a formal document, or a preprinted form. It only has to correctly give the following:

- Contract date
- The buyer
- The seller
- Address or legal description of property
- Earnest money or down payment to firm up the contract
- Consideration—purchase price—and method of payment
- Closing date

A sheet of notebook paper written like the following would be considered an enforceable contract:

REAL ESTATE PURCHASE CONTRACT

October 1, 1990.

John and Mary Doe hereby sell 123 Main Street, Quaint City, Iowa, to Jack and Sally Brown for $75,000. $1,000 has been paid today as a down payment, and the balance is due on November 1, 1990.

_____

John Doe

_____

Mary Doe

_____

Jack Brown

_____

Sally Brown

I've seen simple contracts like this work out well (a couple of times). The buyers are familiar with the house, they know the sellers, and they simply jot down a simple contract and close on the deal when they say they will. In most cases, however, there are "ifs, ands, or buts" that must be taken care of, as you can see in the sample contracts at the end of this chapter. In other words, neither party wants to finalize the deal until all of the following questions are answered:

- Is the property condition okay?
- Is there clear title to the property?
- Does the buyer have all the money needed to close?
- What happens if someone backs out?

Consequently, contracts can be complicated because both parties want to make sure they get their part of the contract met completely. Contracts are also complicated because lawyers write most of them, and few lawyers can make anything simple. I've found the best written contracts to be those that are just a simple transcription of a verbal offer between two parties that come into a very amicable agreement. In other words, "We, John and Mary Doe, respect you Jack and Sally Brown, so we'll make sure everyone is treated fairly in this transaction for the purchase of this property. Our agreement is as follows, and we'll write it down with as many details as possible so there is no confusion and there is mutual respect from now until the consummation of this deal." The simpler the language of the written contract, the better it is. It's silly to need an interpreter—lawyer—to tell both parties the content of their agreement.

You might want to use the sample contracts at the back of this chapter as a guide. These are the contracts that were promulgated by the Texas Real Estate Commission a few years ago. They're relatively simple and easy to use, and you should be able to just fill in the blanks depending on what type of financing you're using. Unfortunately, the newer forms are more complicated, longer, and harder to use.

NEGOTIATING THE CONTRACT

I've talked about verbal and written offers, as well as written contracts. An offer is a one-sided affair. The buyer can make an offer to the seller, or vice versa. If you tell a seller, "I'll give you $175,000 for your house," you've made a verbal offer. When the seller says, "I accept," you have a verbal agreement, or contract. If you give the seller a written contract form stating your terms for the purchase of his house, you've given him a written offer. You will have signed it. He has no obligation to accept it. If you give it to him through his real estate agent, along with some earnest money, it remains an offer until it is accepted. If you make the written offer tonight, and the agent tells you he'll see the seller about it in the morning, and later tonight you change your mind, you have a right to withdraw the offer by calling the agent later that night and withdrawing the offer. The agent *must* give you your earnest money back.

Once the seller signs the written offer and it has been accepted, then both parties have made a binding contract for the sale and purchase of the property. If you back out, then you lose your earnest money. The seller could even sue you for specific performance—though he might have trouble collecting anything more than your earnest money. If the seller backs out, you can also sue for specific performance.

In negotiating the contract, you, as the buyer, must take the initiative in making the offer. Keep in mind that without you, there is no sale. So look over the contract form you'll be using, or the one the seller's agent wants to use, and make sure you understand it *completely*. Put in all of the terms that will work for you. Be fair to the seller, but be especially fair to yourself. It's *your* money that's making all this happen, and everyone must live by the golden rule: He who has the gold makes the rules.

Anything that you want included with the purchase—a refrigerator, a trash compactor, a riding lawn mower, the mule in the back forty—*must* be included in the written agreement. Make certain it's written down, even if it makes for superfluous writing. On the first shot of a written offer, ask for everything you'd like included with the sale. It doesn't matter that you're almost certain it won't be included, or that an agent tells you it's ridiculous and it won't be included. You never know until you ask.

I knew a fellow who bought an investment house on the east side of Dallas a few years ago. He paid the seller $17,000 for the equity in the house, and he assumed a fairly decent FHA loan. For a rental unit, $17,000 was a hefty equity to pay, but the seller threw in a twenty-year-old Rolls Royce along with the sale. The car was worth close to the value of the equity, but the seller didn't need the car nor the house, and the buyer wanted the house as well as the car, and he could afford the cash outlay.

Many times, investors seem to get the best deals. That's because they're the ones who ask for the most concessions and have the most patience. If you're negotiating for the purchase of a house, and you see that the seller has three or four cars parked around the house, there's no reason not to ask for the inclusion of one of them along with the real estate. You might shock the seller or his agent, but don't worry about it. There's always a chance you'll get a bonus, especially if you've offered full price for the property. Assume you're negotiating for a $60,000 property. The most you want to pay for it is $58,000. The seller has a classic little car that's worth $4,000. The seller might not care that much for the car, and he might let it go free for a full-price offer on the property. He gets his full price, and you basically get the property for $56,000.

Take your time in negotiating the offer, and do all you can not to fall in love with a property. Every time the seller counters, you should counter with a little higher offer than your first, but not quite as high as his. If neither you nor the seller want to budge, then wait a couple of weeks and give him the same offer the second time as the first. Be persistent. After a few weeks or months, the seller might realize you're his best bet. But above all, don't get angry. Everyone has a right to his own opinion of the value of a property. A house might never be worth as much to you as it is to the seller, so you must seek other properties to fill your needs.

EARNEST MONEY

To be earnest means to be sincere. When you make a written offer, you're telling the seller that you're sincere in your desire to consummate the deal. You assure him of your sincerity by offering earnest money. At closing, you'll be credited the earnest money towards the balance due on the contract price.

Most of the time, you want to make the offer using the least amount of earnest money. There's no telling when backing out of a contract and just losing the earnest money might be prudent. You might be ready to close and one of your relatives dies and leaves you a house free and clear. Do you need the one you're about to buy or should you just back out and lose your earnest money? If you can have a contract accepted with just $100 down, that's great. If the seller requests $500, that's not too bad. On a $100,000 house he might demand $1,000. On a $500,000 property, it might be $5,000. No matter what's customary in your area, go for the lowest figure possible.

On the other hand, a large, earnest money deposit can sometimes help to sway a seller to accept a low offer. If the owner has had this property on the market a while for $120,000, and has had no takers, and you come along with a $90,000 offer for a cash purchase—no financing hassles—then a large earnest money deposit might help. A $20,000 deposit with the title or escrow company will show him not only that you're serious in your offer, but that you have the cash to purchase. The only problem is that you're risking a rather nice chunk of money. If you back out, it's gone. You'll only want to do this when it will get you a very reduced price, and you don't need to get financing. You already have the money, and even if something were to happen to you, your spouse would still have the means and inclination to go through with the deal, so the earnest money would not be unduly at risk.

If you're dealing directly with the seller, the earnest money might be held by him. In a case where it's a nominal amount—$500 or less—it should be alright to allow the seller to handle it. On larger amounts, let a title or escrow company hold the earnest money. If the seller doesn't live in the property, the latter might be the best choice. A couple of years ago, a fellow in the Fort Worth area was paying for options on houses. The houses were always vacant. Once he had an option, he'd advertise the property with excellent terms and sell each property three, four, even ten times at once. Each time he'd take $500 in earnest money. Sometimes he got the buyer to put up even more. He wouldn't close on the properties. It was a great scam. He finally got caught for fraud, but not before a lot of buyers had lost their money. That wasn't the first time I'd heard of this game, so it's more prudent to let a reputable third party hold your money.

LOAN APPLICATION

If you've already made the loan application before you write up the written agreement, you're ahead of the game. If not, state in the contract how long you have to apply for a loan, and what will happen if you're rejected for the loan. There are lenders who insist on having a completed contract on hand before you make formal application. Most will take your loan application before you're on contract, and many will give you a definite commitment on a loan amount before you purchase. That's almost like having the cash on hand for the purchase. The only step needed after the signing of a contract to purchase is to have the house appraised. If the house appraises, the only thing left is the closing.

PROPERTY APPRAISAL

One of the steps of obtaining a loan on a certain property is getting an appraisal for a value at least the amount of the sales price. Whether it's a first lien, or a second lien loan, the lender wants to know there's enough value to warrant the size loan he's providing. You also need to know the property is worth what you're paying for it.

If the sales price is $100,000, and a professional appraisal comes in at $90,000, there must be a provision in the contract to either lower the amount of the sales price, or cancel the contract. Some contracts call for a second appraisal in case the property doesn't appraise at first.

On a conventional appraisal, you'll know exactly what the property appraises for. On FHA appraisals, you often only get a value that agrees with the contract price. If you're paying $80,000, the appraiser will work up his figures as if he were working a conventional appraisal and perhaps come up with a $90,000 value. Although, on his final Certificate of Reasonable Value, he might only state that the house is worth $80,000. That's all FHA wants to know, and that's all the appraiser might tell you.

If you're taking over somebody's loan and paying cash for the seller's equity, or even if he's financing the equity, you might want to obtain an appraisal to make sure the property is worth what you're paying for it. Do this only once you're on contract and are committed to the property's purchase. For two or three hundred dollars (less in some areas), you can get a professional opinion of value. Even if there are no outside lenders to deal with, it's a good idea to have a clause in the contract that either lowers the selling price if the appraisal comes in low, or to allow you to withdraw from the contract.

The contract should state who's to pay for the appraisal. It's best to let the seller pay for it. Naturally, it's best if he pays for all costs of the sale—best for you anyway. Also, if you fail to qualify for a loan on the property, an appraisal to the seller's house is hardly going to do you any good later on, but the seller should be able to use it with the next buyer.

PROPERTY INSPECTION ——

Other than your own preliminary property inspection, you needn't pay for any professional house inspection until you have a firm contract. As with the appraisal, it's best if the seller pays for the inspection. If the deal with you doesn't go through, he can use it with the next buyer.

There should be provisions in the contract that require the seller to make needed repairs on the structure, or its systems, that are found deficient. On most standard contract forms there are provisions for inserting a maximum amount the seller will pay. If the needed repairs exceed that amount, the buyer has the right to pay the additional amounts himself, or accept the property with only the limited repairs, or the seller has the right to pay additional amounts to complete the repairs. The contract should also state that if the needed repairs exceed the stipulated maximum, and neither the buyer nor the seller agree to pay, that the buyer has a right to cancel the contract.

CLOSING

You should specify in the contract where you want the closing to take place, who should provide a title policy if one is to be obtained, the date of the closing, what happens if the closing doesn't take place at the required time, and that you expect to receive a copy of the closing documents for review at least 24 hours before the time of closing.

The closing is the last important part of the purchase. If there's no closing, there is no purchase. Some real estate agents have a favorite closer, or a favorite title company. There are good closers and there are some very mediocre ones. You might want to put a provision in the contract that allows you to change closing or title companies at your discretion. If you see poor service from the escrow or title company before the closing, you can switch to another.

BACKING OUT

For years, I've been an advocate of making sure there's a back door before I go in the front door. There are all kinds of escape clauses, but the most widely used one is the one that cancels the contract if the buyer doesn't obtain financing. No financing means no money to buy, which means no sale. If you're in a contract that you want out of but have run out of ways to escape, then simply short-circuit the financing to get out of it. For example, assume you qualify for the $1,000 payment required for your loan. You desperately want to cancel the contract because of any number of legitimate reasons, but if you simply pull out, you'll lose your earnest money. Just call the lender and ask if it matters that you have a loan from your parents for $15,000 and that you make $300 per month payments on it. The loan officer will ask you why you'd not mentioned it before. You just tell her that you didn't think it was important, but your lawyer advised you that to not claim it could be construed as fraud. You insist that the loan application be modified. Naturally, you'll now not qualify because of payment ratios. You'll be denied the loan and the contract will cancel.

If you don't like that ploy, then simply go out and actually borrow as much as you can from a bank, then insist that the loan application be modified to reflect that new loan. After you're denied the home loan and you receive your earnest money back, then pay off the new loan in full and you're ready to try for another home loan whenever you want.

Sneaky? Yes, it certainly is. It's also not very fair to the seller. I've seen people back out of purchases many, many times, however, including a few rare times right at the closing table. When I've worked with sellers, I've always stressed that they did not have a sale until they had the sale proceeds in their hands, and to not commit to any other home purchase until the closing on their current property was consummated. Whether it's fair or not, as a buyer, you never know when you'll need to back out of a deal.

Every part of the contract should give you an escape clause. If the property condition is found to be substandard, you can back out. If there is no clear title to the property, you can back out. If you're not approved for a loan, you can back out. How about this: if you're transferred by your company, you can back out. If you or your spouse are laid off at work, you can back out.

UNDERSTANDING CONTRACT FORMS

In the remainder of this chapter, I have analyzed, line-by-line, the most common contract forms. Read each contract description over thoroughly until you understand what each element means.

VA Contract Form

Figure 20-1 shows a completed contract to purchase using a VA-guaranteed loan and a blank contract you can use, if you're a veteran. The following is a line-by-line explanation of the contract:

VA GUARANTEED LOAN — RESIDENTIAL EARNEST MONEY CONTRACT (RESALE)

1. PARTIES: _DARRELL D. DYKES AND WIFE LINDA L. DYKES_ (Seller) agrees
to sell and convey to _SID T. SIMONS AND BROTHER JULES SIMONS_ (Buyer)
and Buyer agrees to buy from Seller the following property situated in _DALLAS_ County, Texas,
known as _8300 CENTER ST. GARLAND, TX 88888_ (Address).

2. PROPERTY: Lot _6R_, Block _12_, _HAY FIELD_
_#3_ Addition, City of _GARLAND_, or as described on attached exhibit,
together with the following fixtures, if any: curtain rods, drapery rods, venetian blinds, window shades, screens and shutters, awnings, wall-to-wall carpeting, mirrors fixed in place, attic fans, permanently installed heating and air conditioning units and equipment, lighting and plumbing fixtures, TV antennas, mail boxes, water softeners, shrubbery and all other property owned by Seller and attached to the above described real property. All property sold by this contract is called "Property".

3. CONTRACT SALES PRICE:
   A. Cash down payment payable at closing .... $ _-0-_
   B. Note described in 4 below (the Note) in the amount of .... $ _50,000.00_
   C. Sales Price payable to Seller on Loan funding after closing (Sum of A and B) ...... $ _50,000.00_

4. FINANCING CONDITIONS: This contract is subject to approval for Buyer of a VA loan (the Loan) of not less than the amount of the Note, amortizable monthly for not less than _30_ years, with interest at maximum rate allowable at time of Loan funding. Buyer shall apply for the Loan within _10_ days from the effective date of this contract and shall make every reasonable effort to obtain approval. If the Loan has not been approved by the Closing Date, this contract shall terminate and the Earnest Money shall be refunded to Buyer without delay. VA NOTICE TO BUYER: "It is expressly agreed that, notwithstanding any other provisions of this contract, the Buyer shall not incur any penalty by forfeiture of earnest money or otherwise or be obligated to complete the purchase of the Property described herein, if the contract purchase price or cost exceeds the reasonable value of the Property established by the Veterans Administration. The Buyer shall, however, have the privilege and option of proceeding with the consummation of this contract without regard to the amount of the reasonable value established by the Veterans Administration." Buyer agrees that should Buyer elect to complete the purchase at an amount in excess of the reasonable value established by VA, Buyer shall pay such excess amount in cash from a source which Buyer agrees to disclose to the VA and which Buyer represents will not be from borrowed funds except as approved by VA. If VA reasonable value is less than the Sales Price (3C above), Seller may reduce the Sales Price to an amount equal to the VA reasonable value and both parties agree to close the sale at such lower Sales Price with appropriate adjustments to 3A and 3B above.

5. EARNEST MONEY: $ _500_ is herewith tendered and is to be deposited as Earnest Money with _ABC TITLE COMPANY_, as Escrow Agent, upon execution of the contract by both parties. Additional Earnest Money, if any, shall be deposited with the Escrow Agent on or before _____, 19 ____, in the amount of $_____.

6. TITLE: Seller at Seller's expense shall furnish either:
   [X] A. Owner's Policy of Title Insurance (the Title Policy) issued by _ABC TITLE CO._
   in the amount of the Sales Price and dated at or after closing: OR
   [ ] B. Complete Abstract of Title (the Abstract) certified by _____ to current date.
   NOTICE TO BUYER: AS REQUIRED BY LAW, Broker advises that YOU should have the Abstract covering the Property examined by an attorney of YOUR selection, or YOU should be furnished with or obtain a Title Policy.

7. PROPERTY CONDITION (Check "A" or "B"):
   [ ] A. Buyer accepts the Property in its present condition, subject only to VA required repairs and _____

   [X] B. Buyer requires inspections and repairs required by the Property Condition Addendum (the Addendum) and those required by VA. Upon Seller's receipt of the Loan approval and inspection reports Seller shall commence and complete prior to closing all required repairs at Seller's expense.
   All inspections, reports and repairs required of Seller by this contract and the Addendum shall not exceed $_____. If Seller fails to complete such requirements, Buyer may do so and Seller shall be liable up to the amount specified and the same paid from the proceeds of the sale. If such expenditures exceed the stated amount and Seller refuses to pay such excess, Buyer may pay the additional cost or accept the Property with the limited repairs and this sale shall be closed as scheduled, or Buyer may terminate this contract and the Earnest Money shall be refunded to Buyer. Broker and sales associates have no responsibility or liability for repair or replacement of any of the Property.

8. BROKER'S FEE: _N/A_ Listing Broker (____%) and _____
   _____ Co-Broker (____%), as Real Estate Broker (the Broker), has negotiated this sale and Seller agrees to pay Broker in _____ County, Texas, on consummation of this sale or on Seller's default (unless otherwise provided herein) a total cash fee of _____ of the total Sales Price, which Escrow Agent may pay from the sale proceeds.

9. CLOSING: The closing of the sale (the Closing Date) shall be on or before _JULY 30_, 19 _88_ or within 7 days after objections to title have been cured, whichever date is later; however, if necessary to complete Loan requirements, the Closing Date shall be extended daily up to 15 days.

10. POSSESSION: The possession of the Property shall be delivered to Buyer on _2 DAYS AFTER CLOSING_ in its present or required improved condition, ordinary wear and tear excepted. Any possession by Buyer prior to or by Seller after Closing Date shall establish a landlord-tenant at sufferance relationship between the parties.

11. SPECIAL PROVISIONS:

ALL WINDOW TREATMENTS TO REMAIN WITH THE PROPERTY.

(Insert terms and conditions of a factual nature applicable to this sale, e.g., prior purchase or sale of other property, lessee's surrender of possession, and the like.)

№ 65

Fig. 20-1.

12. SALES EXPENSES TO BE PAID IN CASH AT OR PRIOR TO CLOSING:
   A. Loan appraisal fees shall be paid by ___SELLER___.
   B. Seller's Expenses:
      (1) Seller's Loan discount points not exceeding __2% OF LOAN AMOUNT__ and in the Addendum.
      (2) VA required repairs and any other inspections, reports and repairs required of Seller herein, and in the Addendum.
      (3) Releases of existing loans, including prepayment penalties and recordation; escrow fee; tax statements; preparation of Deed, Note and Deed of Trust; expenses VA prohibits Buyer to pay, (e.g., copies of restrictions, photos, excess cost of survey of Property); other expenses stipulated to be paid by Seller under other provisions of this contract.
   C. Buyer's Expenses: Expenses incident to Loan (e.g., credit reports; recording fees; Mortgagee's Title Policy; Loan origination fee; that portion of survey cost Buyer can pay by VA regulation; Loan related inspection fees; premiums for 1 year's hazard insurance and any flood insurance; required reserve deposits for insurance premiums, ad valorem taxes and special assessments; interest from date of disbursement to 1 month prior to date of first monthly payment on the Note); premiums on non-required insurance; expenses stipulated to be paid by Buyer under other provisions of this contract.
   D. If any sales expenses exceed the maximum amount herein stipulated to be paid by either party, either party may terminate this contract unless the other party agrees to pay such excess. In no event shall Buyer pay charges and fees other than those expressly permitted by VA Regulations.
13. PRORATIONS: Insurance (at Buyer's option), taxes and any rents and maintenance fees shall be prorated to the Closing Date.
14. TITLE APPROVAL: If Abstract is furnished, Seller shall deliver same to Buyer within 20 days from the effective date hereof. Buyer shall have 20 days from date of receipt of Abstract to deliver a copy of the title opinion to Seller, stating any objections to title, and only objections so stated shall be considered. If Title Policy is furnished, the Title Policy shall guarantee Buyer's title to be good and indefeasible subject only to (i) restrictive covenants affecting the Property (ii) any discrepancies, conflicts or shortages in area or boundary lines or any encroachments, or any overlapping of improvements (iii) all taxes for the current and subsequent years (iv) any existing building and zoning ordinances (v) rights of parties in possession (vi) any liens created as security for the sale consideration and (vii) any reservations or exceptions contained in the Deed. In either instance, if title objections are disclosed, Seller shall have 30 days to cure the same. Exceptions permitted in the Deed and zoning ordinances shall not be valid objections to title. Seller shall furnish at Seller's expense tax statements showing no delinquent taxes and a General Warranty Deed conveying title subject only to liens securing debt created as part of the consideration, taxes for the current year, usual restrictive covenants and utility easements common to the platted subdivision of which the Property is a part and any other reservations or exceptions acceptable to Buyer. The Note shall be secured by Vendor's and Deed of Trust liens. In case of dispute as to the form of Deed, such shall be upon a form prepared by the State Bar of Texas.
15. CASUALTY LOSS: If any part of Property is damaged or destroyed by fire or other casualty loss, Seller shall restore the same to its previous condition as soon as reasonably possible, but in any event by Closing Date; and if Seller is unable to do so without fault, this contract shall terminate and Earnest Money shall be refunded with no Broker's fee due.
16. DEFAULT: If Buyer fails to comply herewith, Seller may either enforce specific performance or terminate this contract and receive the Earnest Money as liquidated damages, one-half of which (but not exceeding the herein recited Broker's fee) shall be paid by Seller to Broker in full payment for Broker's services. If Seller is unable without fault to deliver Abstract or Title Policy or to make any non-casualty repairs required herein within the time herein specified, Buyer may either terminate this contract and receive the Earnest Money as the sole remedy, and no Broker's fee shall be earned, or extend the time up to 30 days. If Seller fails to comply herewith for any other reason, Buyer may (i) terminate this contract and receive the Earnest Money, thereby releasing Seller from this contract (ii) enforce specific performance hereof or (iii) seek such other relief as may be provided by law. If completion of sale is prevented by Buyer's default, and Seller elects to enforce specific performance, the Broker's fee is payable only if and when Seller collects damages for such default by suit, compromise, settlement or otherwise, and after first deducting the expenses of collection, and then only in an amount equal to one-half of that portion collected, but not exceeding the amount of Broker's fee.
17. ATTORNEY'S FEES: Any signatory to this contract who is the prevailing party in any legal proceeding against any other signatory brought under or with relation to this contract or transaction shall be additionally entitled to recover court costs and reasonable attorney fees from the non-prevailing party.
   ESCROW: Earnest Money is deposited with Escrow Agent with the understanding that Escrow Agent (i) does not assume or have any liability for performance or nonperformance of any party (ii) has the right to require the receipt, release and authorization in writing of all parties before paying the deposit to any party and (iii) is not liable for interest or other charge on the funds held. If any party unreasonably fails to agree in writing to an appropriate release of Earnest Money, then such party shall be liable to the other parties to the extent provided in paragraph 17. At closing, Earnest Money shall be applied to any cash down payment required, next to Buyer's closing costs and any excess refunded to Buyer. Before Buyer shall be entitled to refund of Earnest Money, any actual and VA allowable expenses incurred or paid on Buyer's behalf shall be deducted therefrom and paid to the creditors entitled thereto.
19. REPRESENTATIONS: Seller represents that there will be no Title I liens, unrecorded liens or Uniform Commercial Code liens against any of the Property on Closing Date. If any representation above is untrue this contract may be terminated by Buyer and the Earnest Money shall be refunded without delay. Representations shall survive closing.
20. AGREEMENT OF PARTIES: This contract contains the entire agreement of the parties and cannot be changed except by their written consent.
21. CONSULT YOUR ATTORNEY: This is intended to be a legally binding contract. **READ IT CAREFULLY.** If you do not understand the effect of any part, consult your attorney BEFORE signing. The Broker cannot give you legal advice — only factual and business details concerning land and improvements. Attorneys to represent parties may be designated below, and, so employment may be accepted, Broker shall promptly deliver a copy of this contract to such attorneys.

Seller's Atty: ___N/A___   Buyer's Atty: ___N/A___

EXECUTED in multiple originals effective the _30th_ day of ___MAY___, 19 _88_ (BROKER FILL IN THE DATE LAST PARTY SIGNS).

Listing Broker	License No.	Seller _Darrell D. Dykes_
By _____		Seller _Linda L. Dykes_
		Seller's Address _8300 CENTER, GARLAND_ _222-2222_ Tel.
Co-Broker	License No.	Buyer _Sid T. Simons_
By _____		Buyer _Jules Simons_
Receipt of $ _500_ Earnest Money is acknowledged in the form		Buyer's Address _287 S.W. 5TH, DALLAS_ _666-2354_ Tel.
of _CHECK_.		
ABC TITLE CO. _5/30/88_		
Escrow Agent Date		
By _____		

Fig. 20-1. Cont.

VA GUARANTEED LOAN — RESIDENTIAL EARNEST MONEY CONTRACT (RESALE)

1. PARTIES: _____ (Seller) agrees
to sell and convey to _____ (Buyer
and Buyer agrees to buy from Seller the following property situated in _____ County,
known as _____ (Address).

2. PROPERTY: Lot _____, Block _____, _____
_____ Addition, City of _____, or as described on attached exhibit,
together with the following fixtures, if any: curtain rods, drapery rods, venetian blinds, window shades, screens and shutters, awnings, wall-to-wall carpeting, mirrors fixed in place, attic fans, permanently installed heating and air conditioning units and equipment, lighting and plumbing fixtures, TV antennas, mail boxes, water softeners, shrubbery and all other property owned by Seller and attached to the above described real property. All property sold by this contract is called "Property".

3. CONTRACT SALES PRICE:
   A. Cash down payment payable at closing . . . . $_____

   B. Note described in 4 below (the Note) in the amount of . . . . $_____

   C. Sales Price payable to Seller on Loan funding after closing (Sum of A and B) . . . . $_____

4. FINANCING CONDITIONS: This contract is subject to approval for Buyer of a VA loan (the Loan) of not less than the amount of the Note, amortizable monthly for not less than _____ years, with interest at maximum rate allowable at time of Loan funding. Buyer shall apply for the Loan within _____ days from the effective date of this contract and shall make every reasonable effort to obtain approval. If the Loan has not been approved by the Closing Date, this contract shall terminate and the Earnest Money shall be refunded to Buyer without delay.
VA NOTICE TO BUYER: "It is expressly agreed that, notwithstanding any other provisions of this contract, the Buyer shall not incur any penalty by forfeiture of earnest money or otherwise or be obligated to complete the purchase of the Property described herein, if the contract purchase price or cost exceeds the reasonable value of the Property established by the Veterans Administration. The Buyer shall, however, have the privilege and option of proceeding with the consummation of this contract without regard to the amount of the reasonable value established by the Veterans Administration." Buyer agrees that should Buyer elect to complete the purchase at an amount in excess of the reasonable value established by VA, Buyer shall pay such excess amount in cash from a source which Buyer agrees to disclose to the VA and which Buyer represents will not be from borrowed funds except as approved by VA. If VA reasonable value of the Property is less than the Sales Price (3C above), Seller may reduce the Sales Price to an amount equal to the VA reasonable value and both parties agree to close the sale at such lower Sales Price with appropriate adjustments to 3A and 3B above.

5. EARNEST MONEY: $_____ is herewith tendered and is to be deposited as Earnest Money with _____
_____, as Escrow Agent, upon execution of the contract by both parties. Additional Earnest Money, if any, shall be deposited with the Escrow Agent on or before _____, 19____, in the amount of $_____.

6. TITLE: Seller at Seller's expense shall furnish either:
   ☐ A. Owner's Policy of Title Insurance (the Title Policy) issued by _____
   in the amount of the Sales Price and dated at or after closing: OR
   ☐ B. Complete Abstract of Title (the Abstract) certified by _____ to current date.
NOTICE TO BUYER: AS REQUIRED BY LAW. Broker advises that YOU should have the Abstract covering the Property examined by an attorney of YOUR selection, or YOU should be furnished with or obtain a Title Policy.

7. PROPERTY CONDITION (Check "A" or "B"):
   ☐ A. Buyer accepts the Property in its present condition, subject only to VA required repairs and _____
   _____.
   ☐ B. Buyer requires inspections and repairs required by the Property Condition Addendum (the Addendum) and those required by VA. Upon Seller's receipt of the Loan approval and inspection reports Seller shall commence and complete prior to closing all required repairs at Seller's expense.
All inspections, reports and repairs required of Seller by this contract and the Addendum shall not exceed $_____. If Seller fails to complete such requirements, Buyer may do so and Seller shall be liable up to the amount specified and the same paid from the proceeds of the sale. If such expenditures exceed the stated amount and Seller refuses to pay such excess, Buyer may pay the additional cost or accept the Property with the limited repairs and this sale shall be closed as scheduled, or Buyer may terminate this contract and the Earnest Money shall be refunded to Buyer. Broker and sales associates have no responsibility or liability for repair or replacement of any of the Property.

8. BROKER'S FEE: _____ Listing Broker (____%) and _____
_____ Co-Broker (____%), as Real Estate Broker (the Broker), has negotiated this sale and Seller agrees to pay Broker in _____ County, on consummation of this sale or on Seller's default (unless otherwise provided herein) a total cash fee of _____ of the total Sales Price, which Escrow Agent may pay from the sale proceeds.

9. CLOSING: The closing of the sale (the Closing Date) shall be on or before _____, 19____, or within 7 days after objections to title have been cured, whichever date is later; however, if necessary to complete Loan requirements, the Closing Date shall be extended daily up to 15 days.

10. POSSESSION: The possession of the Property shall be delivered to Buyer on _____ in its present or required improved condition, ordinary wear and tear excepted. Any possession by Buyer prior to or by Seller after Closing Date shall establish a landlord-tenant at sufferance relationship between the parties.

11. SPECIAL PROVISIONS:

(Insert terms and conditions of a factual nature applicable to this sale, e.g., prior purchase or sale of other property, lessee's surrender of possession, and the like.)

Fig. 20-1. Cont.

12. SALES EXPENSES TO BE PAID IN CASH AT OR PRIOR TO CLOSING:

    A.   Loan appraisal fees shall be paid by _____

    B.   Seller's Expenses:

        (1) Seller's Loan discount points not exceeding _____

        (2) VA required repairs and any other inspections, reports and repairs required of Seller herein, and in the Addendum.

        (3) Releases of existing loans, including prepayment penalties and recordation: escrow fee; tax statements; preparation of Deed, Note and Deed of Trust; expenses VA prohibits Buyer to pay; (e.g., copies of restrictions, photos, excess cost of survey of Property); other expenses stipulated to be paid by Seller under other provisions of this contract.

    C.   Buyer's Expenses: Expenses incident to Loan (e.g., credit reports; recording fees; Mortgagee's Title Policy; Loan origination fee; that portion of survey cost Buyer can pay by VA regulation; Loan related inspection fees; premiums for 1 year's hazard insurance and any flood insurance; required reserve deposits for insurance premiums, ad valorem taxes and special assessments; interest from date of disbursement to 1 month prior to date of first monthly payment on the Note); premiums on non-required insurance; expenses stipulated to be paid by Buyer under other provisions of this contract.

    D.   If any sales expenses exceed the maximum amount herein stipulated to be paid by either party, either party may terminate this contract unless the other party agrees to pay such excess. In no event shall Buyer pay charges and fees other than those expressly permitted by VA Regulations.

13. PRORATIONS: Insurance (at Buyer's option), taxes and any rents and maintenance fees shall be prorated to the Closing Date.

14. TITLE APPROVAL: If Abstract is furnished, Seller shall deliver same to Buyer within 20 days from the effective date hereof. Buyer shall have 20 days from date of receipt of Abstract to deliver a copy of the title opinion to Seller, stating any objections to title, and only objections so stated shall be considered. If Title Policy is furnished, the Title Policy shall guarantee Buyer's title to be good and indefeasible subject only to (i) restrictive covenants affecting the Property (ii) any discrepancies, conflicts or shortages in area or boundary lines or any encroachments, or any overlapping of improvements (iii) all taxes for the current and subsequent years (iv) any existing building and zoning ordinances (v) rights of parties in possession (vi) any liens created as security for the sale consideration and (vii) any reservations or exceptions contained in the Deed. In either instance, if title objections are disclosed, Seller shall have 30 days to cure the same. Exceptions permitted in the Deed and zoning ordinances shall not be valid objections to title. Seller shall furnish at Seller's expense tax statements showing no delinquent taxes and a General Warranty Deed conveying title subject only to liens securing debt created as part of the consideration, taxes for the current year, usual restrictive covenants and utility easements common to the platted subdivision of which the Property is a part and any other reservations or exceptions acceptable to Buyer. The Note shall be secured by Vendor's and Deed of Trust liens. In case of dispute as to the form of Deed, such shall be upon a form prepared by the State Bar of

15. CASUALTY LOSS: If any part of Property is damaged or destroyed by fire or other casualty loss, Seller shall restore the same to its previous condition as soon as reasonably possible, but in any event by Closing Date; and if Seller is unable to do so without fault, this contract shall terminate and Earnest Money shall be refunded with no Broker's fee due.

16. DEFAULT: If Buyer fails to comply herewith, Seller may either enforce specific performance or terminate this contract and receive the Earnest Money as liquidated damages, one-half of which (but not exceeding the herein recited Broker's fee) shall be paid by Seller to Broker in full payment for Broker's services. If Seller is unable without fault to deliver Abstract or Title Policy or to make any non-casualty repairs required herein within the time herein specified, Buyer may either terminate this contract and receive the Earnest Money as the sole remedy, and no Broker's fee shall be earned, or extend the time up to 30 days. If Seller fails to comply herewith for any other reason, Buyer may (i) terminate this contract and receive the Earnest Money, thereby releasing Seller from this contract (ii) enforce specific performance hereof or (iii) seek such other relief as may be provided by law. If completion of sale is prevented by Buyer's default, and Seller elects to enforce specific performance, the Broker's fee is payable only if and when Seller collects damages for such default by suit, compromise, settlement or otherwise, and after first deducting the expenses of collection, and then only in an amount equal to one-half of that portion collected, but not exceeding the amount of Broker's fee.

17. ATTORNEY'S FEES: Any signatory to this contract who is the prevailing party in any legal proceeding against any other signatory brought under or with relation to this contract or transaction shall be additionally entitled to recover court costs and reasonable attorney fees from the non-prevailing party.

    ESCROW: Earnest Money is deposited with Escrow Agent with the understanding that Escrow Agent (i) does not assume or have any liability for performance or nonperformance of any party (ii) has the right to require the receipt, release and authorization in writing of all parties before paying the deposit to any party and (iii) is not liable for interest or other charge on the funds held. If any party unreasonably fails to agree in writing to an appropriate release of Earnest Money, then such party shall be liable to the other parties to the extent provided in paragraph 17. At closing, Earnest Money shall be applied to any cash down payment required, next to Buyer's closing costs and any excess refunded to Buyer. Before Buyer shall be entitled to refund of Earnest Money, any actual and VA allowable expenses incurred or paid on Buyer's behalf shall be deducted therefrom and paid to the creditors entitled thereto.

19. REPRESENTATIONS: Seller represents that there will be no Title I liens, unrecorded liens or Uniform Commercial Code liens against any of the Property on Closing Date. If any representation above is untrue this contract may be terminated by Buyer and the Earnest Money shall be refunded without delay. Representations shall survive closing.

20. AGREEMENT OF PARTIES: This contract contains the entire agreement of the parties and cannot be changed except by their written consent.

21. CONSULT YOUR ATTORNEY: This is intended to be a legally binding contract. READ IT CAREFULLY. If you do not understand the effect of any part, consult your attorney BEFORE signing. The Broker cannot give you legal advice — only factual and business details concerning land and improvements. Attorneys to represent parties may be designated below, and, so employment may be accepted, Broker shall promptly deliver a copy of this contract to such attorneys.

Seller's Atty: _____   Buyer's Atty: _____

EXECUTED in multiple originals effective the _____ day of _____, 19 _____. **(BROKER FILL IN THE DATE LAST PARTY SIGNS).**

Listing Broker License No.	Seller _____
By _____	Seller _____
Co-Broker License No.	Seller's Address _____ Tel.
By _____	Buyer _____
Receipt of $ _____ Earnest Money is acknowledged in the form	Buyer _____
of _____ .	Buyer's Address _____ Tel.
Escrow Agent Date	
By _____	

Fig. 20-1. Cont.

Paragraph #1. Write the sellers' legal names on the first line, and your legal names as buyers on the next line. Remember to note the marital status of all parties. For example:

- If one of the parties is a married couple, you would write "John M. Doe and wife Mary M. Doe."
- For a single person, you can simply write "John M. Doe," or you can write "John M. Doe, a single person."
- For a divorced person, write "John M. Doe, a divorced person since May 23, 1985."
- For a widower, write "John M. Doe, a widower since May 23, 1985."
- For a corporation, you would write JMD Industries, Inc., a Texas Corporation."
- For a partnership, you would write "Doe Properties, a Texas General Partnership," or "Doe Properties, a Texas Limited Partnership."
- For a pension and profit-sharing plan, you would write "JMD Industries, Inc., Pension & Profit-Sharing Trust."
- For two individuals not related or married, you would write "John M. Doe and John R. Smith, in indiscriminate interest."

The next blank asks for the name of the county in which the real estate is located. Fill this in, then place the two-letter abbreviation for the state after the word "County."

The last blank requests the address of the property.

Paragraph #2. This paragraph asks for the legal description of the property. This information is available in the seller's copies of his original closing papers. Make *certain* you have the correct description. Write the lot number, the block number, then the name of the addition in the first three blanks. On the fourth blank insert the city in which the property is located.

Paragraph #3.

A. In this space, most of the time you'll want to put "0," because most VA loans are processed with no money down. In some cases, there will be a down payment (if the loan is to be for more than $144,000).

B. Insert the amount of the note here. If you've put a "0" in A above, then you'll put the purchase price here, otherwise deduct the down payment from the purchase price.

C. Put the sales price here.

Paragraph #4. The first blank will have the number of years the loan will run. Most loans are made for 30 years, so you'll write "30."

On the second blank, insert the number of days from the contract date the buyer will take to go for financing. Generally, 5 to 10 days is enough.

Paragraph #5. Give the least amount of earnest money possible. One percent of the sales price should be the maximum, preferably no more than $500. Put the amount in the first blank. On the second blank, indicate who will hold the earnest money. Depending on the custom in your state, it could be a title or escrow company, an attorney, or even a real estate broker. Write the seller's name if he'll hold the earnest money, but avoid that as much as possible.

If there will be additional earnest money at a future date before the closing, then indicate the date and the amount of the additional funds on the remaining blanks. Except in unusual situations, there should not be any additional earnest money.

Paragraph #6. Check box A if the seller will furnish a title insurance policy, and indicate the name of the company that will issue the policy. Check box B if the seller will provide an abstract of title, and indicate the abstractor or abstract company that will provide it.

Paragraph #7. Check box A if you're purchasing the property "as is" except for any repairs that might be required by a lender, or other conditions you'll indicate in the blank in the first paragraph.

Check box B if you will be allowed to inspect the property before closing. If you check this box—which you should—then you will include a Property Condition Addendum form (Fig. 20-2).

Paragraph #8. If one or more brokers are to receive a commission, this paragraph will be used. In most situations, you won't be using this contract form if a real estate agent or broker is involved. Brokers will use their own forms.

Paragraph #9. Fill in the closing date. Make sure you give yourself enough time to find financing. Check with several mortgage companies to see how long to allow. If you run out of time and have not been approved, this contract will become null and void, so you or the seller could back out of the deal.

Paragraph #10. Indicate when you'll take possession of the property. If you put in an exact date predicated on the closing date and don't make that date, then there will be confusion. Rather, indicate whether possession will be "on date of closing," "three days after closing," or other such date that is agreeable between you and the seller. Naturally, the sooner after closing the better.

Paragraph #11. Include here any special provisions that are important to your agreement with the seller. For example, include any personal property that's included with the property, such as "refrigerator and all window treatments to remain with property." Any personal property that looks like it is

FHA INSURED LOAN — RESIDENTIAL EARNEST MONEY CONTRACT (RESALE)

1. PARTIES: __JOE J. DOE AND WIFE MARY B. DOE__ (Seller) agrees to sell and convey to __EDDIE E. EDWARDS, AND WIFE JO EDWARDS__ (Buyer) and Buyer agrees to buy from Seller the following property situated in __TARRANT__ County, Texas, known as __1807 MESQUITE LN., ARLINGTON, TX 33333__ (Address).

2. PROPERTY: Lot __106__, Block __77__, __McBRIDE OAKS__ Addition, City of __ARLINGTON__, or as described on attached exhibit, together with the following fixtures, if any: curtain rods, drapery rods, venetian blinds, window shades, screens and shutters, awnings, wall-to-wall carpeting, mirrors fixed in place, attic fans, permanently installed heating and air conditioning units and equipment, lighting and plumbing fixtures, TV antennas, mail boxes, water softeners, shrubbery and all other property owned by Seller and attached to the above described real property. All property sold by this contract is called "Property".

3. CONTRACT SALES PRICE:
   A. Cash down payment payable at closing .... $ __3,500.00__
   B. Amount of Note (the Note) described in 4-A below .... $ __76,500.00__
   C. Sales Price payable to Seller on Loan funding after closing (Sum of A plus B) .... $ __80,000.00__

4. FINANCING CONDITIONS:
   A. This contract is subject to approval for Buyer of a Section __203 B__ FHA Insured Loan (the Loan) of not less than the amount of the Note, amortizable monthly for not less than __30__ years, with interest at maximum rate allowable at time of Loan funding. Buyer shall apply for the Loan within __10__ days from the effective date of this contract and shall make every reasonable effort to obtain approval of the Loan. If the Loan has not been approved by the Closing Date, this contract shall terminate and Earnest Money shall be refunded to Buyer without delay.
   B. As required by HUD-FHA regulation, if FHA valuation is unknown, "It is expressly agreed that, notwithstanding any other provisions of this contract, the Purchaser (Buyer) shall not be obligated to complete the purchase of the Property described herein or to incur any penalty by forfeiture of Earnest Money deposits or otherwise unless the Seller has delivered to the Purchaser (Buyer) a written statement issued by the Federal Housing Commissioner setting forth the appraised value of the Property (excluding closing costs) of not less than $ __80,000__, which statement the Seller hereby agrees to deliver to the Purchaser (Buyer) promptly after such appraised value statement is made available to the Seller. The Purchaser (Buyer) shall, however, have the privilege and option of proceeding with the consummation of this contract without regard to the amount of the appraised valuation made by the Federal Housing Commissioner. The appraised valuation is arrived at to determine the maximum mortgage the Department of Housing and Urban Development will insure. HUD does not warrant the value or the condition of the property. The purchaser should satisfy himself/herself that the price and the condition of the property are acceptable."

5. EARNEST MONEY: $ __500__ is herewith tendered and is to be deposited as Earnest Money with __LIBERTY TITLE CO.__, as Escrow Agent, upon execution of the contract by both parties. Additional Earnest Money, if any, shall be deposited with the Escrow Agent on or before __N/A__, 19___, in the amount of $_____.

6. TITLE: Seller at Seller's expense shall furnish either:
   ☒ A. Owner's Policy of Title Insurance (the Title Policy) issued by __LIBERTY TITLE CO.__ in the amount of the Sales Price and dated at or after closing: OR
   ☐ B. Complete Abstract of Title (the Abstract) certified by _____ to current date.
   NOTICE TO BUYER: AS REQUIRED BY LAW, Broker advises that YOU should have the Abstract covering the Property examined by an attorney of YOUR selection, or YOU should be furnished with or obtain a Title Policy.

7. PROPERTY CONDITION (Check "A" or "B"):
   ☒ A. Buyer accepts the Property in its present condition, subject only to FHA required repairs and _____

   ☐ B. Buyer requires inspections and repairs required by the Property Condition Addendum (the Addendum) and those required by FHA. Upon Seller's receipt of the Loan approval and inspection reports Seller shall commence and complete prior to closing all required repairs at Seller's expense.
   All inspections, reports and repairs required of Seller by this contract and the Addendum shall not exceed $ __500__. If Seller fails to complete such requirements, Buyer may do so and Seller shall be liable up to the amount specified and the same paid from the proceeds of the sale. If such expenditures exceed the stated amount and Seller refuses to pay such excess, Buyer may pay the additional cost or accept the Property with the limited repairs and this sale shall be closed as scheduled, or Buyer may terminate this contract and the Earnest Money shall be refunded to Buyer. Broker and sales associates have no responsibility or liability for repair or replacement of any of the Property.

8. BROKER'S FEE: __N/A__ Listing Broker (____%) and _____ Co-Broker (____%), as Real Estate Broker (the Broker), has negotiated this sale and Seller agrees to pay Broker in _____ County, Texas, on consummation of this sale or on Seller's default (unless otherwise provided herein) a total cash fee of _____ of the total Sales Price, which Escrow Agent may pay from the sale proceeds.

9. CLOSING: The closing of the sale (the Closing Date) shall be on or before __3/30__, 19 __88__, or within 7 days after objections to title have been cured, whichever date is later; however, if necessary to complete Loan requirements, the Closing Date shall be extended daily up to 15 days.

10. POSSESSION: The possession of the Property shall be delivered to Buyer on __DATE OF CLOSING__ in its present or required improved condition, ordinary wear and tear excepted. Any possession by Buyer prior to or by Seller after Closing Date shall establish a landlord-tenant at sufferance relationship between the parties.

11. SPECIAL PROVISIONS:

    ANTIQUE FAN IN LIVING ROOM WILL NOT REMAIN WITH PROPERTY. SELLER TO INSTALL NEW FAN OF EQUAL SIZE AND SIMILAR DESIGN.

    № 65

(Insert terms and conditions of a factual nature applicable to this sale, e.g., prior purchase or sale of other property, lessee's surrender of possession, and the like.)

Fig. 20-2.

2. SALES EXPENSES TO BE PAID IN CASH AT OR PRIOR TO CLOSING:
    A.   Loan appraisal fee (FHA application fee) shall be paid by __BUYER__
    B.   Seller's Expenses:
        (1) Seller's Loan discount points not exceeding __$2,300.00__ .
        (2) FHA required repairs and any other inspections, reports and repairs required of Seller herein, and in the Addendum.
        (3) Expenses incident to Loan (e.g., preparation of Loan documents, survey, recording fees, copies of restrictions and easements, amortization schedule, Mortgagee's Title Policy, Loan origination fee, credit reports, photographs).
        (4) Releases of existing loans, including prepayment penalties and recordation; tax statements; preparation of Deed; escrow fee; and other expenses stipulated to be paid by Seller under other provisions of this contract.
    C.   Buyer's Expenses: All prepaid items required by applicable HUD-FHA or other regulations (e.g., required premiums for flood and hazard insurance; required reserve deposits for FHA and other insurance, ad valorem taxes and special assessments); interest on the Note from date of disbursement to one month prior to date of first monthly payment; expenses stipulated to be paid by Buyer under other provisions of this contract.
    D   If any sales expenses exceed the maximum amount herein stipulated to be paid by either party, either party may terminate this Contract unless other party agrees to pay such excess. In no event shall Buyer pay charges and fees other than those expressly permitted by FHA regulation.

13. PRORATIONS: Insurance (at Buyer's option), taxes, and any rents and maintenance fees shall be prorated to the Closing Date.

14. TITLE APPROVAL: If Abstract is furnished, Seller shall deliver same to Buyer within 20 days from the effective date hereof. Buyer shall have 20 days from date of receipt of Abstract to deliver a copy of the title opinion to Seller, stating any objections to title, and only objections so stated shall be considered. If Title Policy is furnished, the Title Policy shall guarantee Buyer's title to be good and indefeasible subject only to (i) restrictive covenants affecting the Property (ii) any discrepancies, conflicts or shortages in area or boundary lines or any encroachments, or any overlapping of improvements (iii) all taxes for the current and subsequent years (iv) any existing building and zoning ordinances (v) rights of parties in possession (vi) any liens created as security for the sale consideration and (vii) any reservations or exceptions contained in the Deed. In either instance, if title objections are disclosed, Seller shall have 30 days to cure the same. Exceptions permitted in the Deed and zoning ordinances shall not be valid objections to title. Seller shall furnish at Seller's expense tax statements showing no delinquent taxes and a General Warranty Deed conveying title subject only to liens securing debt created as part of the consideration, taxes for the current year, usual restrictive covenants and utility easements common to the platted subdivision of which the Property is a part and any other reservations or exceptions acceptable to Buyer. The Note shall be secured by Vendor's and Deed of Trust liens. In case of dispute as to the form of Deed, such shall be upon a form prepared by the State Bar of Texas.

15. CASUALTY LOSS: If any part of Property is damaged or destroyed by fire or other casualty loss, Seller shall restore the same to its previous condition as soon as reasonably possible, but in any event by Closing Date; and if Seller is unable to do so without fault, this contract shall terminate and Earnest Money shall be refunded with no Broker's fee due.

16. DEFAULT: If Buyer fails to comply herewith, Seller may either enforce specific performance or terminate this contract and receive the Earnest Money as liquidated damages, one-half of which (but not exceeding the herein recited Broker's fee) shall be paid by Seller to Broker in full payment for Broker's services. If Seller is unable without fault to deliver Abstract or Title Policy or to make any non-casualty repairs required herein within the time herein specified, Buyer may either terminate this contract and receive the Earnest Money as the sole remedy, and no Broker's fee shall be earned, or extend the time up to 30 days. If Seller fails to comply herewith for any other reason, Buyer may (i) terminate this contract and receive the Earnest Money, thereby releasing Seller from this contract (ii) enforce specific performance hereof or (iii) seek such other relief as may be provided by law. If completion of sale is prevented by Buyer's default, and Seller elects to enforce specific performance, the Broker's fee is payable only if and when Seller collects damages for such default by suit, compromise, settlement or otherwise, and after first deducting the expenses of collection, and then only in an amount equal to one-half of that portion collected, but not exceeding the amount of Broker's fee.

17. ATTORNEY'S FEES: Any signatory to this contract who is the prevailing party in any legal proceeding against any other signatory brought under or with relation to this contract or transaction shall be additionally entitled to recover court costs and reasonable attorney fees from the non-prevailing party.

18. ESCROW: Earnest Money is deposited with Escrow Agent with the understanding that Escrow Agent (i) does not assume or have any liability for performance or nonperformance of any party (ii) has the right to require the receipt, release and authorization in writing of all parties before paying the deposit to any party and (iii) is not liable for interest or other charge on the funds held. If any party unreasonably fails to agree in writing to an appropriate release of Earnest Money, then such party shall be liable to the other parties to the extent provided in paragraph 17. At closing, Earnest Money shall be applied to any cash down payment required, next to Buyer's closing costs and any excess refunded to Buyer. Before Buyer shall be entitled to refund of Earnest Money, any actual and FHA allowable expenses incurred or paid on Buyer's behalf shall be deducted therefrom and paid to the creditors entitled thereto.

19. REPRESENTATIONS: Seller represents that there will be no Title I liens, unrecorded liens or Uniform Commercial Code liens against any of the Property on Closing Date. If any representation above is untrue this contract may be terminated by Buyer and the Earnest Money shall be refunded without delay. Representations shall survive closing.

20. AGREEMENT OF PARTIES: This contract contains the entire agreement of the parties and cannot be changed except by their written consent.

21. CONSULT YOUR ATTORNEY: This is intended to be a legally binding contract. READ IT CAREFULLY. If you do not understand the effect of any part, consult your attorney BEFORE signing. The Broker cannot give you legal advice — only factual and business details concerning land and improvements. Attorneys to represent parties may be designated below, and, so employment may be accepted, Broker shall promptly deliver a copy of this contract to such attorneys.

Seller's Atty: ___N/A___   Buyer's Atty: ___N/A___

EXECUTED in multiple originals effective the __15th__ day of __JAN__, 19 __88__   **(BROKER FILL IN THE DATE LAST PARTY SIGNS).**

Listing Broker _____	License No. _____	_Joe J. Doe_ Seller
By _____		_Mary B. Doe_ Seller
Co-Broker _____	License No. _____	2600 MESQUITE LN., ARLINGTON Seller's Address 555-2345 Tel.
By _____		_Eddie E. Edwards_ Buyer
Receipt of $ _500_ Earnest Money is acknowledged in the form		_Edwards_ Buyer
of __CHECK__ .		
LIBERTY TITLE CO. 1/15/88		2607 B MAIN ST., FT. WORTH
Escrow Agent Date		Buyer's Address 123-4567 Tel.
By _Harry Vernon_		

Fig. 20-2. Cont.

FHA INSURED LOAN — RESIDENTIAL EARNEST MONEY CONTRACT (RESALE)

1. PARTIES: _____ (Seller) agrees
to sell and convey to _____ (Buyer)
and Buyer agrees to buy from Seller the following property situated in _____ County,
known as _____ (Address).

2. PROPERTY: Lot _____, Block _____, _____,
_____ Addition, City of _____, or as described on attached exhibit, together
with the following fixtures, if any: curtain rods, drapery rods, venetian blinds, window shades, screens and shutters, awnings, wall-to-wall
carpeting, mirrors fixed in place, attic fans, permanently installed heating and air conditioning units and equipment, lighting and plumbing fixtures, TV antennas, mail boxes, water softeners, shrubbery and all other property owned by Seller and attached to the above described real property. All property sold by this contract is called "Property".

3. CONTRACT SALES PRICE:
   A. Cash down payment payable at closing .... $ _____
   B. Amount of Note (the Note) described in 4-A below............................... $ _____
   C. Sales Price payable to Seller on Loan funding after closing (Sum of A plus B)........................ $ _____

4. FINANCING CONDITIONS:
   A. This contract is subject to approval for Buyer of a Section _____ FHA Insured Loan (the Loan) of not less
       than the amount of the Note, amortizable monthly for not less than _____ years, with interest at maximum rate allowable at time of
       Loan funding. Buyer shall apply for the Loan within _____ days from the effective date of this contract and shall make every
       reasonable effort to obtain approval of the Loan. If the Loan has not been approved by the Closing Date, this contract shall terminate and
       Earnest Money shall be refunded to Buyer without delay.
   B. As required by HUD-FHA regulation, if FHA valuation is unknown, "It is expressly agreed that, notwithstanding any other provisions of
       this contract, the Purchaser (Buyer) shall not be obligated to complete the purchase of the Property described herein or to incur any penalty
       by forfeiture of Earnest Money deposits or otherwise unless the Seller has delivered to the Purchaser (Buyer) a written statement issued by
       the Federal Housing Commissioner setting forth the appraised value of the Property (excluding closing costs) of not less than
       $ _____ , which statement the Seller hereby agrees to deliver to the Purchaser (Buyer) promptly after such appraised value statement
       is made available to the Seller. The Purchaser (Buyer) shall, however, have the privilege and option of proceeding with the consummation
       of this contract without regard to the amount of the appraised valuation made by the Federal Housing Commissioner. The appraised valu-
       ation is arrived at to determine the maximum mortgage the Department of Housing and Urban Development will insure. HUD does not
       warrant the value or the condition of the property. The purchaser should satisfy himself/herself that the price and the condition of the pro-
       perty are acceptable."

5. EARNEST MONEY: $_____ is herewith tendered and is to be deposited as Earnest Money with _____
   _____, as Escrow Agent, upon execution of the contract by both parties. Additional Earnest
   Money, if any, shall be deposited with the Escrow Agent on or before _____, 19 _____, in the amount of $_____.

6. TITLE: Seller at Seller's expense shall furnish either:
   ☐ A. Owner's Policy of Title Insurance (the Title Policy) issued by _____
          in the amount of the Sales Price and dated at or after closing: OR
   ☐ B. Complete Abstract of Title (the Abstract) certified by _____ to current date.
   NOTICE TO BUYER: AS REQUIRED BY LAW, Broker advises that YOU should have the Abstract covering the Property examined by an
   attorney of YOUR selection, or YOU should be furnished with or obtain a Title Policy.

7. PROPERTY CONDITION (Check "A" or "B"):
   ☐ A. Buyer accepts the Property in its present condition, subject only to FHA required repairs and _____
       _____
   ☐ B. Buyer requires inspections and repairs required by the Property Condition Addendum (the Addendum) and those required by FHA.
   Upon Seller's receipt of the Loan approval and inspection reports Seller shall commence and complete prior to closing all required repairs at
   Seller's expense.
   All inspections, reports and repairs required of Seller by this contract and the Addendum shall not exceed $_____. If Seller fails to com-
   plete such requirements, Buyer may do so and Seller shall be liable up to the amount specified and the same paid from the proceeds of the sale.
   If such expenditures exceed the stated amount and Seller refuses to pay such excess, Buyer may pay the additional cost or accept the Property
   with the limited repairs and this sale shall be closed as scheduled, or Buyer may terminate this contract and the Earnest Money shall be refunded
   to Buyer. Broker and sales associates have no responsibility or liability for repair or replacement of any of the Property.

8. BROKER'S FEE: _____ Listing Broker (_____%) and
   _____ Co-Broker (_____%), as Real Estate Broker (the Broker), has negotiated this sale and Seller
   agrees to pay Broker in _____ County, on consummation of this sale or on Seller's default (unless
   otherwise provided herein) a total cash fee of _____ of the total Sales Price, which Escrow Agent may pay from the sale proceeds.

9. CLOSING: The closing of the sale (the Closing Date) shall be on or before _____, 19 _____, or within 7 days after objections to title have been cured, whichever date is later; however, if necessary to complete Loan requirements, the Closing Date shall be extended
   daily up to 15 days.

10. POSSESSION: The possession of the Property shall be delivered to Buyer on _____ in its present or required
    improved condition, ordinary wear and tear excepted. Any possession by Buyer prior to or by Seller after Closing Date shall establish a landlord-
    tenant at sufferance relationship between the parties.

11. SPECIAL PROVISIONS:

    (Insert terms and conditions of a factual nature applicable to this sale, e.g., prior purchase or sale of other property, lessee's surrender of posses-
    sion, and the like.)

Fig. 20-2. Cont.

12. **SALES EXPENSES TO BE PAID IN CASH AT OR PRIOR TO CLOSING:**
   A.   Loan appraisal fee (FHA application fee) shall be paid by _____.
   B.   Seller's Expenses:
      (1) Seller's Loan discount points not exceeding _____
      (2) FHA required repairs and any other inspections, reports and repairs required of Seller herein, and in the Addendum.
      (3) Expenses incident to Loan (e.g., preparation of Loan documents, survey, recording fees, copies of restrictions and easements, amortization schedule, Mortgagee's Title Policy, Loan origination fee, credit reports, photographs).
      (4) Releases of existing loans, including prepayment penalties and recordation; tax statements; preparation of Deed; escrow fee; and other expenses stipulated to be paid by Seller under other provisions of this contract.
   C.   Buyer's Expenses: All prepaid items required by applicable HUD-FHA or other regulations (e.g., required premiums for flood and hazard insurance; required reserve deposits for FHA and other insurance, ad valorem taxes and special assessments); interest on the Note from date of disbursement to one month prior to date of first monthly payment; expenses stipulated to be paid by Buyer under other provisions of this contract.
   D.   If any sales expenses exceed the maximum amount herein stipulated to be paid by either party, either party may terminate this Contract unless other party agrees to pay such excess. In no event shall Buyer pay charges and fees other than those expressly permitted by FHA regulation.

13. **PRORATIONS:** Insurance (at Buyer's option), taxes, and any rents and maintenance fees shall be prorated to the Closing Date.

14. **TITLE APPROVAL:** If Abstract is furnished, Seller shall deliver same to Buyer within 20 days from the effective date hereof. Buyer shall have 20 days from date of receipt of Abstract to deliver a copy of the title opinion to Seller, stating any objections to title, and only objections so stated shall be considered. If Title Policy is furnished, the Title Policy shall guarantee Buyer's title to be good and indefeasible subject only to (i) restrictive covenants affecting the Property (ii) any discrepancies, conflicts or shortages in area or boundary lines or any encroachments, or any overlapping of improvements (iii) all taxes for the current and subsequent years (iv) any existing building and zoning ordinances (v) rights of parties in possession (vi) any liens created as security for the sale consideration and (vii) any reservations or exceptions contained in the Deed. In either instance, if title objections are disclosed, Seller shall have 30 days to cure the same. Exceptions permitted in the Deed and zoning ordinances shall not be valid objections to title. Seller shall furnish at Seller's expense tax statements showing no delinquent taxes and a General Warranty Deed conveying title subject only to liens securing debt created as part of the consideration, taxes for the current year, usual restrictive covenants and utility easements common to the platted subdivision of which the Property is a part and any other reservations or exceptions acceptable to Buyer. The Note shall be secured by Vendor's and Deed of Trust liens. In case of dispute as to the form of Deed, such shall be upon a form prepared by the State Bar of

15. **CASUALTY LOSS:** If any part of Property is damaged or destroyed by fire or other casualty loss, Seller shall restore the same to its previous condition as soon as reasonably possible, but in any event by Closing Date; and if Seller is unable to do so without fault, this contract shall terminate and Earnest Money shall be refunded with no Broker's fee due.

16. **DEFAULT:** If Buyer fails to comply herewith, Seller may either enforce specific performance or terminate this contract and receive the Earnest Money as liquidated damages, one-half of which (but not exceeding the herein recited Broker's fee) shall be paid by Seller to Broker in full payment for Broker's services. If Seller is unable without fault to deliver Abstract or Title Policy or to make any non-casualty repairs required herein within the time herein specified, Buyer may either terminate this contract and receive the Earnest Money as the sole remedy, and no Broker's fee shall be earned, or extend the time up to 30 days. If Seller fails to comply herewith for any other reason, Buyer may (i) terminate this contract and receive the Earnest Money, thereby releasing Seller from this contract (ii) enforce specific performance hereof or (iii) seek such other relief as may be provided by law. If completion of sale is prevented by Buyer's default, and Seller elects to enforce specific performance, the Broker's fee is payable only if and when Seller collects damages for such default by suit, compromise, settlement or otherwise, and after first deducting the expenses of collection, and then only in an amount equal to one-half of that portion collected, but not exceeding the amount of Broker's fee.

17. **ATTORNEY'S FEES:** Any signatory to this contract who is the prevailing party in any legal proceeding against any other signatory brought under or with relation to this contract or transaction shall be additionally entitled to recover court costs and reasonable attorney fees from the non-prevailing party.

18. **ESCROW:** Earnest Money is deposited with Escrow Agent with the understanding that Escrow Agent (i) does not assume or have any liability for performance or nonperformance of any party (ii) has the right to require the receipt, release and authorization in writing of all parties before paying the deposit to any party and (iii) is not liable for interest or other charge on the funds held. If any party unreasonably fails to agree in writing to an appropriate release of Earnest Money, then such party shall be liable to the other parties to the extent provided in paragraph 17. At closing, Earnest Money shall be applied to any cash down payment required, next to Buyer's closing costs and any excess refunded to Buyer. Before Buyer shall be entitled to refund of Earnest Money, any actual and FHA allowable expenses incurred or paid on Buyer's behalf shall be deducted therefrom and paid to the creditors entitled thereto.

19. **REPRESENTATIONS:** Seller represents that there will be no Title I liens, unrecorded liens or Uniform Commercial Code liens against any of the Property on Closing Date. If any representation above is untrue this contract may be terminated by Buyer and the Earnest Money shall be refunded without delay. Representations shall survive closing.

20. **AGREEMENT OF PARTIES:** This contract contains the entire agreement of the parties and cannot be changed except by their written consent.

21. **CONSULT YOUR ATTORNEY:** This is intended to be a legally binding contract. READ IT CAREFULLY. If you do not understand the effect of any part, consult your attorney BEFORE signing. The Broker cannot give you legal advice — only factual and business details concerning land and improvements. Attorneys to represent parties may be designated below, and, so employment may be accepted, Broker shall promptly deliver a copy of this contract to such attorneys.

Seller's Atty: _____   Buyer's Atty: _____

EXECUTED in multiple originals effective the _____ day of _____, 19 _____.   **(BROKER FILL IN THE DATE LAST PARTY SIGNS).**

Listing Broker _____	License No. _____	Seller _____
By _____		Seller _____
Co-Broker _____	License No. _____	Seller's Address _____ Tel. ____
By _____		Buyer _____
Receipt of $_____ Earnest Money is acknowledged in the form		Buyer _____
of _____.		Buyer's Address _____ Tel. ____
Escrow Agent _____	Date _____	
By _____		

Fig. 20-2. Cont.

attached to the property, but which the seller will take with him, should be included here.

You can also show other terms of purchase or financing that don't fit anywhere else, such as "First five payments on owner financing to be made in the amount of $250, to cover principal only. Interest to begin on the sixth month."

Paragraph #12.

A. The loan appraisal fees are often paid by the seller, because he'll want to keep the appraisal if you don't get your financing. Insert "buyer" or "seller" in this space.

B.(1) On this line, you want to insert the discount points. Check with the lenders and see what is a reasonable number of points you must pay. Three or four should generally be sufficient.

Paragraph #21. There are two spaces at the end of this paragraph for the name of the buyer's or seller's attorneys. Write in their names if attorneys will represent either party. Often on simple transactions, attorneys will not be used and you'll mark out these lines.

On the blanks that ask for the date, fill in the effective date of the contract, which is when all parties have affixed their signatures.

FHA Contract Form

Use the blank contract to purchase using an FHA-insured loan shown in Fig. 20-2 when you're using an FHA contract. The following is a line-by-line explanation of the contract:

Paragraph #1. Write the sellers' legal names on the first line, and your legal names as buyers on the next line. Remember to note the marital status of all parties. For example:

- If one of the parties is a married couple, you would write "John M. Doe and wife Mary M. Doe."
- For a single person, you can simply write "John M. Doe," or you can write "John M. Doe, a single person."
- For a divorced person, write "John M. Doe, a divorced person since May 23, 1985."
- For a widower, write "John M. Doe, a widower since May 23, 1985."
- For a corporation, you would write JMD Industries, Inc., a Texas Corporation."
- For a partnership, you would write "Doe Properties, a Texas General Partnership," or "Doe Properties, a Texas Limited Partnership."

- For a pension and profit-sharing plan, you would write "JMD Industries, Inc., Pension & Profit-Sharing Trust."
- For two individuals not related or married, you would write "John M. Doe and John R. Smith, in indiscriminate interest."

The next blank asks for the name of the county in which the real estate is located. Fill this in, then place the two letter abbreviation for the state after the word "County."

The last blank requests the address of the property.

Paragraph #2. This paragraph asks for the legal description of the property. This information is available in the seller's copies of his original closing papers. Make *certain* you have the correct description. Write the lot number, the block number, then the name of the addition in the first three blanks. Insert the city in which the property is located on the fourth blank.

Paragraph #3. On an FHA loan, if the sales price is $50,000 or higher, the required down payment is 3 percent of the first $25,000, and 5 percent of everything above that. If the sales price is under $50,000, then the down payment is only 3 percent of the total purchase price. Let's look at some examples:

- Sales price of $47,000. The down payment is $1,410 (3 percent of the selling price). The loans are made in $50 increments, so you would round up to $1,450. In A, you would enter $1,450. In B, you would enter $45,550, and in C, you would enter the sales price, $47,000.
- Sales price of $82,000. The down payment is 3 percent of the first $25,000 ($750) and 5 percent of the $57,000 balance ($2,850). The total down payment is $3,600. There is an easy way to figure this without much confusion: On any house that's under $50,000, simply figure 3 percent. On any house over $50,000, figure 5 percent of the sales price and deduct $500. So on the $82,000 example above, you would figure $82,000 × 5 percent = $4,100. Then deduct $500 from that and you would come up with $3,600.

Paragraph #4.

A. In the first blank, you'll usually put in "203b." Most FHA programs are the 203b type. If you're working a 245 program, then you'd use that number. The second blank will more than likely be "30," because most loans are written for 30 years. On the third blank, put in anywhere between 5 and 10. You'll want to apply for a loan as soon as possible.

B. Fill in the purchase price here.

Paragraph #5. Give the least amount of earnest money possible. One percent of the sales price should be the maximum, preferably no more than $500. Put the amount in the first blank. On the second blank indicate who will hold the earnest money. Depending on the custom in your state, it could be a title or escrow company, an attorney, or even a real estate broker. Write the seller's name if he'll hold the earnest money, but avoid that as much as possible.

If there will be additional earnest money at a future date before the closing, then indicate the date and the amount of the additional funds on the remaining blanks. Except in unusual situations, there should not be any additional earnest money.

Paragraph #6. Check box A if the seller will furnish a title insurance policy, and indicate the name of the company that will issue the policy. Check box B if the seller will provide an abstract of title, and indicate the abstractor or abstract company that will provide it.

Paragraph #7. Check box A if you're purchasing the property ''as is'' except for any repairs that might be required by a lender, or other conditions you'll indicate in the blank in the first paragraph.

Check box B if you'll be allowed to inspect the property before closing. If you check this box, which you should, then you will include a Property Condition Addendum form (Figure 20-6).

Paragraph #8. If one or more brokers are to receive a commission, use this paragraph. In most situations, you won't be using this contract form if a real estate agent or broker is involved. Brokers will use their own forms.

Paragraph #9. Fill in the closing date. Make sure you give yourself enough time to find financing. Check with several mortgage companies to see how long to allow. If you run out of time and have not been approved, this contract will become null and void, so you or the seller could back out of the deal.

Paragraph #10. Indicate when you'll take possession of the property. If you put in an exact date predicated on the closing date and don't make that date, then there will be confusion. Rather, indicate whether possession will be ''on date of closing,'' ''three days after closing,'' or other such date that is agreeable between you and the seller. Naturally, the sooner after closing the better.

Paragraph #11. Include here any special provisions that are important to your agreement with the seller. For example, include any personal property that's included with the property, such as ''refrigerator and all window treatments to remain with property.'' Any personal property that looks like it is attached to the property, but which the seller will take with him, should be included here.

You can also show other terms of purchase or financing that don't fit anywhere else, such as "First five payments on owner financing to be made in the amount of $250, to cover principal only. Interest to begin on the sixth month."

Paragraph #12.

A. The loan appraisal fees are often paid by the seller, because he'll want to keep the appraisal if you don't get your financing. Insert "buyer" or "seller" in this space.

B.(1) On this line you want to insert the discount points. Check with the lenders and see what is a reasonable number of points you must pay. Three or four should generally be sufficient.

Paragraph #21. There are two spaces at the end of this paragraph for the name of the buyer's or seller's attorneys. Write in their names if attorneys will represent either party. Often on simple transactions, attorneys will not be used and you'll mark out these lines.

On the blanks that ask for the date, fill in the effective date of the contract, which is when all parties have affixed their signatures.

Conventional Loan Contract Form

Use the blank contract shown in Fig. 20-3 to purchase using conventional financing. The following is a line-by-line explanation of the contract. Figure 20-3 also shows a sample of a completed contract.

Paragraph #1. Write the sellers' legal names on the first line, and your legal names as buyers on the next line. Remember to note the marital status of all parties. For example:

- If one of the parties is a married couple, you would write "John M. Doe and wife Mary M. Doe."
- For a single person, you can simply write "John M. Doe," or you can write "John M. Doe, a single person."
- For a divorced person, write "John M. Doe, a divorced person since May 23, 1985."
- For a widower, write "John M. Doe, a widower since May 23, 1985."
- For a corporation, you would write JMD Industries, Inc., a Texas Corporation."
- For a partnership, you would write "Doe Properties, a Texas General Partnership," or "Doe Properties, a Texas Limited Partnership."
- For a pension and profit-sharing plan, you would write "JMD Industries, Inc., Pension & Profit-Sharing Trust."

CONVENTIONAL LOAN — RESIDENTIAL EARNEST MONEY CONTRACT (RESALE)

1. PARTIES: _JACK B. NIMBLE AND WIFE, SANDY W. NIMBLE_ (Seller) agrees
   to sell and convey to _LADY N. SHOE, A SINGLE WOMAN_ (Buyer)
   and Buyer agrees to buy from Seller the following property situated in _TARRANT_ County, Texas,
   known as _1717 WILSON LANE, FOREST HILL, TX 66666_ (Address).

2. PROPERTY: Lot _75_, Block _N_, _SUNNY_
   HILLS Addition, City of _FOREST HILL_, or as described on attached exhibit,
   together with the following fixtures, if any: curtain rods, drapery rods, venetian blinds, window shades, screens and shutters, awnings, wall-to-
   wall carpeting, mirrors fixed in place, attic fans, permanently installed heating and air conditioning units and equipment, lighting and plumbing
   fixtures, TV antennas, mail boxes, water softeners, shrubbery and all other property owned by Seller and attached to the above described real
   property. All property sold by this contract is called ''Property''.

3. CONTRACT SALES PRICE:
   A. Cash down payment payable at closing . . . . $_50,000.00_
   B. Note described in 4 below (the Note) in the amount of . . . . $_200,000.00_
   C. Any balance of Sales Price to be evidenced by a second lien note (the Second Note)payable to [check (1) or
      (2) below]:
      ☐ (1) Seller, bearing interest at the rate of _____ % per annum, in
         ☐ lump sum on or before _____
         ☐ principal and interest installments of $_____, or more per _____,
         with first installment payable on _____
      ☐ (2) Third Party in principal and interest installments not in excess of $_____ per month
      in the principal amount of . . . . $_____
   D. Sales Price payable to Seller on Loan funding after closing (Sum of A, B & C) . . . . $_250,000.00_

4. FINANCING CONDITIONS: This contract is subject to approval for Buyer of a ☒ Conventional or ☐ Conventional private mortgage
   insured third party loan (the Loan) of not less than the amount of the Note, amortizable monthly for not less than _20_ years,
   with interest not to exceed _10_ percent per annum, and approval of any third party Second Note. Buyer shall apply for all financing within _5_ days from the effective date of this contract and shall make every reasonable effort to obtain approval. If all
   financing cannot be approved within _60_ days from effective date of this contract, this contract shall terminate and Earnest
   Money shall be refunded to Buyer without delay.

5. EARNEST MONEY: $_2,500_ is herewith tendered and is to be deposited as Earnest Money with _FRIENDLY_
   TITLE COMPANY, as Escrow Agent, upon execution of the contract by both parties. Additional Earnest
   Money, if any, shall be deposited with the Escrow Agent on or before _N/A_, 19___, in the amount of $_____.

6. TITLE: Seller at Seller's expense shall furnish either:
   ☒ A. Owner's Policy of Title Insurance (the Title Policy) issued by _FRIENDLY TITLE CO._
      in the amount of the Sales Price and dated at or after closing: OR
   ☐ B. Complete Abstract of Title (the Abstract) certified by _____ to current date.
   NOTICE TO BUYER: AS REQUIRED BY LAW, Broker advises that YOU should have the Abstract covering the Property examined by an
   attorney of YOUR selection, or YOU should be furnished with or obtain a Title Policy.

7. PROPERTY CONDITION (Check ''A'' or ''B''):
   ☒ A. Buyer accepts the Property in its present condition, subject only to lender required repairs and _INSTALLATION_
      OF NEW #1 CEDAR SHINGLE ROOF
   ☐ B. Buyer requires inspections and repairs required by the Property Condition Addendum (the Addendum) and any lender.
   Upon Seller's receipt of all loan approvals and inspection reports Seller shall commence and complete prior to closing all required repairs at
   Seller's expense.
   All inspections, reports and repairs required of Seller by this contract and the Addendum shall not exceed $_1,000_. If Seller fails to com-
   plete such requirements, Buyer may do so and Seller shall be liable up to the amount specified and the same paid from the proceeds of the sale.
   If such expenditures exceed the stated amount and Seller refuses to pay such excess, Buyer may pay the additional cost or accept the Property
   with the limited repairs and this sale shall be closed as scheduled, or Buyer may terminate this contract and the Earnest Money shall be refunded to Buyer. Broker and sales associates have no responsibility or liability for repair or replacement of any of the Property.

8. BROKER'S FEE: _N/A_ Listing Broker (____%) and _____
   _____ Co-Broker (____%), as Real Estate Broker (the Broker), has negotiated this sale and Seller
   agrees to pay Broker in _____ County, Texas, on consummation of this sale or on Seller's default (unless
   otherwise provided herein) a total cash fee of _____ of the total Sales Price, which Escrow Agent may pay from the sale proceeds.

9. CLOSING: The closing of the sale (the Closing Date) shall be on or before _3/15_, 19_88_, or within 7 days after objections to title have been cured, whichever date is later; however, if necessary to complete Loan requirements, the Closing Date shall be extended
   daily up to 15 days.

10. POSSESSION: The possession of the Property shall be delivered to Buyer on _3 DAYS AFTER CLOSING_ in its present or required
    improved condition, ordinary wear and tear excepted. Any possession by Buyer prior to or by Seller after Closing Date shall establish a landlord-
    tenant at sufferance relationship between the parties.

11. SPECIAL PROVISIONS:

    ALL WINDOW TREATMENTS TO REMAIN
    WITH THE PROPERTY

(Insert terms and conditions of a factual nature applicable to this sale, e.g., personal property included in sale [curtains, draperies, valances, etc.],
prior purchase or sale of other property, lessee's surrender of possession, and the like.) №   65

Fig. 20-3.

12. **SALES EXPENSES TO BE PAID IN CASH AT OR PRIOR TO CLOSING:**
   A. Loan appraisal fees shall be paid by ___SELLER___
   B. Seller's Expenses:
      (1) Seller's loan discount points not exceeding ___2% OF LOAN AMOUNT___.
      (2) Lender required repairs and any other inspections, reports and repairs required of Seller herein and in the Addendum.
      (3) Prepayment penalties on any existing loans, plus cost of releasing such loans and recording releases; tax statements; 1/2 of any escrow fee; preparation of Deed; other expenses stipulated to be paid by Seller under other provisions of this contract.
   C. Buyer's Expenses:
      (1) Fees for loans (e.g., any private mortgage insurance premiums; loan and mortgage application, origination and commitment fees; Buyer's loan discount points) not exceeding $ ___4,000.00___.
      (2) Expenses incident to loan(s) (e.g., preparation of any Note, Deed of Trust and other loan documents, survey, recording fees, copies of restrictions and easements, Mortgagee's Title Policies, credit reports, photos); 1/2 of any escrow fee; any required premiums for flood and hazard insurance; any required reserve deposits for insurance premiums, ad valorem taxes and special assessments; interest on all monthly installment payment notes from date of disbursements to 1 month prior to dates of first monthly payments; expenses stipulated to be paid by Buyer under other provisions of this contract.
   D. If any sales expenses exceed the maximum amount herein stipulated to be paid by either party, either party may terminate this contract unless the other party agrees to pay such excess.

13. **PRORATIONS:** Insurance (at Buyer's option), taxes and any rents and maintenance fees shall be prorated to the Closing Date.

14. **TITLE APPROVAL:** If Abstract is furnished, Seller shall deliver same to Buyer within 20 days from the effective date hereof. Buyer shall have 20 days from date of receipt of Abstract to deliver a copy of the title opinion to Seller, stating any objections to title, and only objections so stated shall be considered. If Title Policy is furnished, the Title Policy shall guarantee Buyer's title to be good and indefeasible subject only to (i) restrictive covenants affecting the Property (ii) any discrepancies, conflicts or shortages in area or boundary lines or any encroachments, or any overlapping of improvements (iii) all taxes for the current and subsequent years (iv) any existing building and zoning ordinances (v) rights of parties in possession (vi) any liens created as security for the sale consideration and (vii) any reservations or exceptions contained in the Deed. In either instance, if title objections are disclosed, Seller shall have 30 days to cure the same. Exceptions permitted in the Deed and zoning ordinances shall not be valid objections to title. Seller shall furnish at Seller's expense tax statements showing no delinquent taxes and a General Warranty Deed conveying title subject only to liens securing debt created as part of the consideration, taxes for the current year, usual restrictive covenants and utility easements common to the platted subdivision of which the Property is a part and any other reservations or exceptions acceptable to Buyer. Each note herein provided shall be secured by Vendor's and Deed of Trust liens. In case of dispute as to the form of Deed, Note(s) or Deed(s) of Trust, such shall be upon a form prepared by the State Bar of Texas.

15. **CASUALTY LOSS:** If any part of Property is damaged or destroyed by fire or other casualty loss, Seller shall restore the same to its previous condition as soon as reasonably possible, but in any event by Closing Date; and if Seller is unable to do so without fault, this contract shall terminate and Earnest Money shall be refunded with no Broker's fee due.

16. **DEFAULT:** If Buyer fails to comply herewith, Seller may either enforce specific performance or terminate this contract and receive the Earnest Money as liquidated damages, one-half of which (but not exceeding the herein recited Broker's fee) shall be paid by Seller to Broker in full payment for Broker's services. If Seller is unable without fault to deliver Abstract or Title Policy or to make any non-casualty repairs required herein within the time herein specified, Buyer may either terminate this contract and receive the Earnest Money as the sole remedy, and no Broker's fee shall be earned, or extend the time up to 30 days. If Seller fails to comply herewith for any other reason, Buyer may (i) terminate this contract and receive the Earnest Money, thereby releasing Seller from this contract (ii) enforce specific performance hereof or (iii) seek such other relief as may be provided by law. If completion of sale is prevented by Buyer's default, and Seller elects to enforce specific performance, the Broker's fee is payable only if and when Seller collects damages for such default by suit, compromise, settlement or otherwise, and after first deducting the expenses of collection, and then only in an amount equal to one-half of that portion collected, but not exceeding the amount of Broker's fee.

17. **ATTORNEY'S FEES:** Any signatory to this contract who is the prevailing party in any legal proceeding against any other signatory brought under or with relation to this contract or transaction shall be additionally entitled to recover court costs and reasonable attorney fees from the non-prevailing party.

18. **ESCROW:** Earnest Money is deposited with Escrow Agent with the understanding that Escrow Agent (i) does not assume or have any liability for performance or nonperformance of any party (ii) has the right to require the receipt, release and authorization in writing of all parties before paying the deposit to any party and (iii) is not liable for interest or other charge on the funds held. If any party unreasonably fails to agree in writing to an appropriate release of Earnest Money, then such party shall be liable to the other parties to the extent provided in paragraph 17. At closing, Earnest Money shall be applied to any cash down payment required, next to Buyer's closing costs and any excess refunded to Buyer. Before Buyer shall be entitled to refund of Earnest Money, any actual expenses incurred or paid on Buyer's behalf shall be deducted therefrom and paid to the creditors entitled thereto.

19. **REPRESENTATIONS:** Seller represents that unless securing payment of the Note there will be no Title I liens, unrecorded liens or Uniform Commercial Code liens against any of the Property on Closing Date. If any representation above is untrue this contract may be terminated by Buyer and the Earnest Money shall be refunded without delay. Representations shall survive closing.

20. **AGREEMENT OF PARTIES:** This contract contains the entire agreement of the parties and cannot be changed except by their written consent.

21. **CONSULT YOUR ATTORNEY:** This is intended to be a legally binding contract. READ IT CAREFULLY. If you do not understand the effect of any part, consult your attorney BEFORE signing. The Broker cannot give you legal advice — only factual and business details concerning land and improvements. Attorneys to represent parties may be designated below, and, so employment may be accepted, Broker shall promptly deliver a copy of this contract to such attorneys.

Seller's Atty: ___N/A___   Buyer's Atty: ___N/A___

EXECUTED in multiple originals effective the ___10TH___ day of ___JAN___, 19 ___88___. **(BROKER FILL IN THE DATE LAST PARTY SIGNS).**

Listing Broker _____ License No. _____	*Jack B. Nimble*
By _____	Seller
	Sandy W. Nimble
	Seller
	___1717 WILSON LN., FOREST HILL___
Co-Broker _____ License No. _____	Seller's Address ___66-7777___ Tel.
By _____	*Lady N. Shoe*
	Buyer
Receipt of $ ___2,500___ Earnest Money is acknowledged in the form	
	Buyer
of ___CASH___.	___666 HIGH HILL, FT. WORTH___
	Buyer's Address ___222-7676___ Tel.
___FRIENDLY TITLE CO. 1/11/88___	
Escrow Agent _____ Date	
By _____	

Fig. 20-3. Cont.

CONVENTIONAL LOAN — RESIDENTIAL EARNEST MONEY CONTRACT (RESALE)

1. PARTIES: _____ (Seller) agrees
to sell and convey to _____ (Buyer)
and Buyer agrees to buy from Seller the following property situated in _____ County,
known as _____ (Address).

2. PROPERTY: Lot _____, Block _____, _____,
_____ Addition, City of _____, or as described on attached exhibit,
together with the following fixtures, if any: curtain rods, drapery rods, venetian blinds, window shades, screens and shutters, awnings, wall-to-wall carpeting, mirrors fixed in place, attic fans, permanently installed heating and air conditioning units and equipment, lighting and plumbing fixtures, TV antennas, mail boxes, water softeners, shrubbery and all other property owned by Seller and attached to the above described real property. All property sold by this contract is called ''Property''.

3. CONTRACT SALES PRICE:
   A. Cash down payment payable at closing. . . . . $_____

   B. Note described in 4 below (the Note) in the amount of . . . . $_____
   C. Any balance of Sales Price to be evidenced by a second lien note (the Second Note)payable to [check (1) or (2) below]:
      ☐ (1) Seller, bearing interest at the rate of _____ % per annum, in
         ☐ lump sum on or before _____.
         ☐ principal and interest installments of $_____, or more per _____,
            with first installment payable on _____
      ☐ (2) Third Party in principal and interest installments not in excess of $_____ per month
      in the principal amount of. . . . . $_____

   D. Sales Price payable to Seller on Loan funding after closing (Sum of A, B & C) . . . . $_____

4. FINANCING CONDITIONS: This contract is subject to approval for Buyer of a ☐ Conventional or ☐ Conventional private mortgage insured third party loan (the Loan) of not less than the amount of the Note, amortizable monthly for not less than _____ years, with interest not to exceed _____ percent per annum, and approval of any third party Second Note. Buyer shall apply for all financing within _____ days from the effective date of this contract and shall make every reasonable effort to obtain approval. If all financing cannot be approved within _____ days from effective date of this contract, this contract shall terminate and Earnest Money shall be refunded to Buyer without delay.

5. EARNEST MONEY: $_____ is herewith tendered and is to be deposited as Earnest Money with _____
_____, as Escrow Agent, upon execution of the contract by both parties. Additional Earnest Money, if any, shall be deposited with the Escrow Agent on or before _____, 19____, in the amount of $_____.

6. TITLE: Seller at Seller's expense shall furnish either:
   ☐ A. Owner's Policy of Title Insurance (the Title Policy) issued by _____
      in the amount of the Sales Price and dated at or after closing: OR
   ☐ B. Complete Abstract of Title (the Abstract) certified by _____ to current date.
   NOTICE TO BUYER: AS REQUIRED BY LAW, Broker advises that YOU should have the Abstract covering the Property examined by an attorney of YOUR selection, or YOU should be furnished with or obtain a Title Policy.

7. PROPERTY CONDITION (Check "A" or "B"):
   ☐ A. Buyer accepts the Property in its present condition, subject only to lender required repairs and _____
   _____
   ☐ B. Buyer requires inspections and repairs required by the Property Condition Addendum (the Addendum) and any lender.
   Upon Seller's receipt of all loan approvals and inspection reports Seller shall commence and complete prior to closing all required repairs at Seller's expense.
   All inspections, reports and repairs required of Seller by this contract and the Addendum shall not exceed $_____. If Seller fails to complete such requirements, Buyer may do so and Seller shall be liable up to the amount specified and the same paid from the proceeds of the sale. If such expenditures exceed the stated amount and Seller refuses to pay such excess, Buyer may pay the additional cost or accept the Property with the limited repairs and this sale shall be closed as scheduled, or Buyer may terminate this contract and the Earnest Money shall be refunded to Buyer. Broker and sales associates have no responsibility or liability for repair or replacement of any of the Property.

8. BROKER'S FEE: _____ Listing Broker (____%) and _____
_____ Co-Broker (____%), as Real Estate Broker (the Broker), has negotiated this sale and Seller
agrees to pay Broker in _____ County, on consummation of this sale or on Seller's default (unless otherwise provided herein) a total cash fee of _____ of the total Sales Price, which Escrow Agent may pay from the sale proceeds.

9. CLOSING: The closing of the sale (the Closing Date) shall be on or before _____, 19____, or within 7 days after objections to title have been cured, whichever date is later; however, if necessary to complete Loan requirements, the Closing Date shall be extended daily up to 15 days.

10. POSSESSION: The possession of the Property shall be delivered to Buyer on _____ in its present or required improved condition, ordinary wear and tear excepted. Any possession by Buyer prior to or by Seller after Closing Date shall establish a landlord-tenant at sufferance relationship between the parties.

11. SPECIAL PROVISIONS:

(Insert terms and conditions of a factual nature applicable to this sale, e.g., personal property included in sale [curtains, draperies, valances, etc.], prior purchase or sale of other property, lessee's surrender of possession, and the like.)

Fig. 20-3. Cont.

12. SALES EXPENSES TO BE PAID IN CASH AT OR PRIOR TO CLOSING:
   A. Loan appraisal fees shall be paid by _____
   B. Seller's Expenses:
      (1) Seller's loan discount points not exceeding _____.
      (2) Lender required repairs and any other inspections, reports and repairs required of Seller herein and in the Addendum.
      (3) Prepayment penalties on any existing loans, plus cost of releasing such loans and recording releases; tax statements; 1/2 of any escrow fee; preparation of Deed; other expenses stipulated to be paid by Seller under other provisions of this contract.
   C. Buyer's Expenses:
      (1) Fees for loans (e.g., any private mortgage insurance premiums; loan and mortgage application, origination and commitment fees; Buyer's loan discount points) not exceeding $_____
      (2) Expenses incident to loan(s) (e.g., preparation of any Note, Deed of Trust and other loan documents, survey, recording fees, copies of restrictions and easements, Mortgagee's Title Policies, credit reports, photos); 1/2 of any escrow fee; any required premiums for flood and hazard insurance; any required reserve deposits for insurance premiums, ad valorem taxes and special assessments; interest on all monthly installment payment notes from date of disbursements to 1 month prior to dates of first monthly payments; expenses stipulated to be paid by Buyer under other provisions of this contract.
   D. If any sales expenses exceed the maximum amount herein stipulated to be paid by either party, either party may terminate this contract unless the other party agrees to pay such excess.
13. PRORATIONS: Insurance (at Buyer's option), taxes and any rents and maintenance fees shall be prorated to the Closing Date.
14. TITLE APPROVAL: If Abstract is furnished, Seller shall deliver same to Buyer within 20 days from the effective date hereof. Buyer shall have 20 days from date of receipt of Abstract to deliver a copy of the title opinion to Seller, stating any objections to title, and only objections so stated shall be considered. If Title Policy is furnished, the Title Policy shall guarantee Buyer's title to be good and indefeasible subject only to (i) restrictive covenants affecting the Property (ii) any discrepancies, conflicts or shortages in area or boundary lines or any encroachments, or any overlapping of improvements (iii) all taxes for the current and subsequent years (iv) any existing building and zoning ordinances (v) rights of parties in possession (vi) any liens created as security for the sale consideration and (vii) any reservations or exceptions contained in the Deed. In either instance, if title objections are disclosed, Seller shall have 30 days to cure the same. Exceptions permitted in the Deed and zoning ordinances shall not be valid objections to title. Seller shall furnish at Seller's expense tax statements showing no delinquent taxes and a General Warranty Deed conveying title subject only to liens securing debt created as part of the consideration, taxes for the current year, usual restrictive covenants and utility easements common to the platted subdivision of which the Property is a part and any other reservations or exceptions acceptable to Buyer. Each note herein provided shall be secured by Vendor's and Deed of Trust liens. In case of dispute as to the form of Deed, Note(s) or Deed(s) of Trust, such shall be upon a form prepared by the State Bar of

15. CASUALTY LOSS: If any part of Property is damaged or destroyed by fire or other casualty loss, Seller shall restore the same to its previous condition as soon as reasonably possible, but in any event by Closing Date; and if Seller is unable to do so without fault, this contract shall terminate and Earnest Money shall be refunded with no Broker's fee due.
16. DEFAULT: If Buyer fails to comply herewith, Seller may either enforce specific performance or terminate this contract and receive the Earnest Money as liquidated damages, one-half of which (but not exceeding the herein recited Broker's fee) shall be paid by Seller to Broker in full payment for Broker's services. If Seller is unable without fault to deliver Abstract or Title Policy or to make any non-casualty repairs required herein within the time herein specified, Buyer may either terminate this contract and receive the Earnest Money as the sole remedy, and no Broker's fee shall be earned, or extend the time up to 30 days. If Seller fails to comply herewith for any other reason, Buyer may (i) terminate this contract and receive the Earnest Money, thereby releasing Seller from this contract (ii) enforce specific performance hereof or (iii) seek such other relief as may be provided by law. If completion of sale is prevented by Buyer's default, and Seller elects to enforce specific performance, the Broker's fee is payable only if and when Seller collects damages for such default by suit, compromise, settlement or otherwise, and after first deducting the expenses of collection, and then only in an amount equal to one-half of that portion collected, but not exceeding the amount of Broker's fee.
17. ATTORNEY'S FEES: Any signatory to this contract who is the prevailing party in any legal proceeding against any other signatory brought under or with relation to this contract or transaction shall be additionally entitled to recover court costs and reasonable attorney fees from the non-prevailing party.
18. ESCROW: Earnest Money is deposited with Escrow Agent with the understanding that Escrow Agent (i) does not assume or have any liability for performance or nonperformance of any party (ii) has the right to require the receipt, release and authorization in writing of all parties before paying the deposit to any party and (iii) is not liable for interest or other charge on the funds held. If any party unreasonably fails to agree in writing to an appropriate release of Earnest Money, then such party shall be liable to the other parties to the extent provided in paragraph 17. At closing, Earnest Money shall be applied to any cash down payment required, next to Buyer's closing costs and any excess refunded to Buyer. Before Buyer shall be entitled to refund of Earnest Money, any actual expenses incurred or paid on Buyer's behalf shall be deducted therefrom and paid to the creditors entitled thereto.
19. REPRESENTATIONS: Seller represents that unless securing payment of the Note there will be no Title I liens, unrecorded liens or Uniform Commercial Code liens against any of the Property on Closing Date. If any representation above is untrue this contract may be terminated by Buyer and the Earnest Money shall be refunded without delay. Representations shall survive closing.
20. AGREEMENT OF PARTIES: This contract contains the entire agreement of the parties and cannot be changed except by their written consent.
21. CONSULT YOUR ATTORNEY: This is intended to be a legally binding contract. READ IT CAREFULLY. If you do not understand the effect of any part, consult your attorney BEFORE signing. The Broker cannot give you legal advice — only factual and business details concerning land and improvements. Attorneys to represent parties may be designated below, and, so employment may be accepted, Broker shall promptly deliver a copy of this contract to such attorneys.

Seller's Atty: _____   Buyer's Atty: _____

EXECUTED in multiple originals effective the _____ day of _____, 19 ____.   (BROKER FILL IN THE DATE LAST PARTY SIGNS).

_____
Listing Broker   License No.

By _____

_____
Co-Broker   License No.

By _____

Receipt of $ _____ Earnest Money is acknowledged in the form

of _____.

_____
Escrow Agent   Date

By _____

_____
Seller

_____
Seller

_____
Seller's Address   Tel.

_____
Buyer

_____
Buyer

_____
Buyer's Address   Tel.

Fig. 20-3. Cont.

- For two individuals not related or married, you would write "John M. Doe and John R. Smith, in indiscriminate interest."

The next blank asks for the name of the county in which the real estate is located. Fill this in, then place the two letter abbreviation for the state after the word "County."

The last blank requests the address of the property.

Paragraph #2. This paragraph asks for the legal description of the property. This information is available in the seller's copies of his original closing papers. Make *certain* you have the correct description. Write the lot number, the block number, then the name of the addition in the first three blanks. Insert the city in which the property is located on the fourth blank.

Paragraph #3.

A. Insert the cash down payment you will pay. It should be at least 5 percent of the purchase price if the financing is a conventional commercial loan. The less the better if the owner is providing the financing.

B. Write the amount of the first lien you will obtain from the mortgage company.

C. Check the first box (1) if the seller will be carrying a second lien. Then on the first blank show the interest rate. Check the next box if the second lien will be paid in a lump sum, and indicate the date the lump sum is due. Normally, though, you'll check the box indicating payments will be made in installments. Include the amount of each installment (on the first blank). On the second blank, you'll more than likely write "monthly," and show when the first installment will be made on the last blank.

Check the "Third Party" box (2) if there will be a second lien provided by a commercial lien lender, and in the first blank indicate the maximum monthly payment you are willing to pay for the second lien. On the second blank, show the amount of the second lien.

D. Indicate the total of all the liens and the down payment for the final sales price here.

Paragraph #4. Check the first box if the first lien will be for 80 percent or less of the sales price. Check the second box if the first lien will be for 81 percent or more of the sales price, in which case there will be private mortgage insurance (PMI). Indicate the number of years of the first lien on the first blank, and on the second blank, show the maximum interest rate you are willing to pay. If it looks like rates are climbing fast, lock in your points with the lender, or show a rate $1/4$ percent to $1/2$ percent above the existing rate at the time you sign the contract.

On the third blank, insert anywhere from "5" to "10." That should be enough time for you to apply for a loan.

On the last blank, put in a realistic figure for financing approval. Generally, 60 days should be enough. Just remember that, if approval doesn't come within that time, the seller could back out of the deal and sell to someone else.

Paragraph #5. Give the least amount of earnest money possible. One percent of the sales price should be the maximum, preferably no more than $500. Put the amount in the first blank. Indicate who will hold the earnest money on the second blank. Depending on the custom in your state, it could be a title or escrow company, an attorney, or even a real estate broker. Write the seller's name if he'll hold the earnest money but avoid that as much as possible.

If there will be additional earnest money at a future date before the closing, then indicate the date and the amount of the additional funds on the remaining blanks. Except in unusual situations, there should not be any additional earnest money.

Paragraph #6. Check box A if the seller will furnish a title insurance policy, and indicate the name of the company that will issue the policy. Check box B if the seller will provide an abstract of title, and indicate the abstractor or abstract company that will provide it.

Paragraph #7. Check box A if you're purchasing the property "as is" except for any repairs that might be required by a lender, or other conditions you'll indicate in the blank in the first paragraph.

Check box B if you will be allowed to inspect the property before closing. If you check this box, which you should, then you will include a Property Condition Addendum form (Fig. 20-6).

Paragraph #8. If one or more brokers are to receive a commission, use this paragraph. In most situations, you won't be using this contract form if a real estate agent or broker is involved. Brokers will use their own forms.

Paragraph #9. Fill in the closing date. Make sure you give yourself enough time to find financing. Check with several mortgage companies to see how long to allow. If you run out of time and have not been approved, this contract will become null and void, so you or the seller could back out of the deal.

Paragraph #10. Indicate when you'll take possession of the property. If you put in an exact date predicated on the closing date and don't make that date, then there will be confusion. Rather, indicate whether possession will be "on date of closing," "three days after closing," or other such date that is agreeable between you and the seller. Naturally, the sooner after closing the better.

Paragraph #11. Include here any special provisions that are important to your agreement with the seller. For example, include any personal property that's included with the property, such as "refrigerator and all window treatments to remain with property." Any personal property that looks like it is attached to the property, but which the seller will take with him, should be included here.

You can also show other terms of purchase or financing that don't fit anywhere else, such as "First five payments on owner financing to be made in the amount of $250, to cover principal only. Interest to begin on the sixth month."

Paragraph #12.

A. The loan appraisal fees are often paid by the seller, because he'll want to keep the appraisal if you don't get your financing. Insert "buyer" or "seller" in this space.

B.(1) Insert the discount points on this line. Check with the lenders and see what is a reasonable number of points you must pay. Three or four should generally be sufficient.

Paragraph #21. There are two spaces at the end of this paragraph for the name of the buyer's or seller's attorneys. Write in their names if attorneys will represent either party. Often on simple transactions, attorneys will not be used and you'll mark out these lines.

On the blanks that ask for the date, fill in the effective date of the contract, which is when all parties have affixed their signatures.

Cash or Owner-Financed Contract Form

Use the blank contract shown in Fig. 20-4 when you have a cash buyer, or when you are getting owner financing with no third-party financing. Figure 20-4 also shows a sample completed contract. The following is a line-by-line explanation of this type of contract.

Paragraph #1. Write the sellers' legal names on the first line, and your legal names as buyers on the next line. Remember to note the marital status of all parties. For example:

- If one of the parties is a married couple, you would write "John M. Doe and wife Mary M. Doe."
- For a single person, you can simply write "John M. Doe," or you can write "John M. Doe, a single person."
- For a divorced person, write "John M. Doe, a divorced person since May 23, 1985."

- For a widower, write "John M. Doe, a widower since May 23, 1985."
- For a corporation, you would write JMD Industries, Inc., a Texas Corporation."
- For a partnership, you would write "Doe Properties, a Texas General Partnership," or "Doe Properties, a Texas Limited Partnership."
- For a pension and profit-sharing plan, you would write "JMD Industries, Inc., Pension & Profit-Sharing Trust."
- For two individuals not related or married, you would write "John M. Doe and John R. Smith, in indiscriminate interest."

The next blank asks for the name of the county in which the real estate is located. Fill this in, then place the two letter abbreviation for the state after the word "County."

The last blank requests the address of the property.

Paragraph #2. This paragraph asks for the legal description of the property. This information is available in the seller's copies of his original closing papers. Make *certain* you have the correct description. Write the lot number, the block number, then the name of the addition in the first three blanks. On the fourth blank insert the city in which the property is located.

Paragraph #3.
A. Write the amount of the down payment here.
B. Write the amount of the note the seller will be carrying here.
C. This is the sum of A and B, and the final sales price.

Paragraph #4.
A. Check this box if the deal is all cash.
B. Check this box if the seller will be doing owner financing. On the first blank, insert the interest rate. Check box (1) if the payments will be made in installments. If they're monthly, indicate this in the first blank, showing the amount of each payment on the second blank. On the last blank, you can indicate a date, or write something like 30 days after closing, or whenever you want the first payment to start after the closing date. Then check box "a" if the payments will continue for the entire term of the loan—20 to 30 years, or whatever you've negotiated with the seller. You would check box "b" if you want to make regular payments for several months or years, then have a balloon due on a certain date, which you would show on the blanks.

Check box (2) if there will only be one lump sum due at a future date, which you will specify in the blank.

C. The seller might want you to check this box. Leave it at his discretion.

ALL CASH OR OWNER FINANCED — RESIDENTIAL EARNEST MONEY CONTRACT (RESALE)

1. PARTIES: _JACK B. NIMBLE AND WIFE, SANDY W. NIMBLE_ (Seller) agrees to sell and convey to _LADY N. SHOE, A SINGLE WOMAN_ (Buyer) and Buyer agrees to buy from Seller the following property situated in _DALLAS_ County, Texas, known as _123 CANDLESTICK LANE, DALLAS, TX 77777_ (Address).

2. PROPERTY: Lot _2_, Block _7/1653_, _FOREST PARK_ Addition, City of _DALLAS_, or as described on attached exhibit, together with the following fixtures, if any: curtain rods, drapery rods, venetian blinds, window shades, screens and shutters, awnings, wall-to-wall carpeting, mirrors fixed in place, attic fans, permanently installed heating and air conditioning units and equipment, lighting and plumbing fixtures, TV antennas, mail boxes, water softeners, shrubbery and all other property owned by Seller and attached to the above described real property. All property sold by this contract is called "Property".

3. CONTRACT SALES PRICE:
   A. Cash payment payable at closing .... $ _10,000.00_
   B. Note described in 4 B below (the Note) .... $ _90,000.00_
   C. Sales Price payable to Seller (Sum of A and B) .... $ _100,000.00_

4. FINANCING CONDITIONS:
   ☐ A. This is an all cash sale; no financing is involved.
   ☒ B. The Note in the principal sum shown in 3 B above, dated as of the Closing Date, to be executed and delivered by Buyer and payable to the order of Seller, bearing interest at the rate of _9½_ percent per annum from date thereof until maturity, matured unpaid principal and interest to bear interest at the rate of 10% per annum, principal and interest to be due and payable
   ☒ (1) In _MONTHLY_ installments of $ _756.77_ or more each, beginning on or before _2/1/88_ after date of the Note, and (Check "a" or "b")
   　☒ a. continuing regularly and at the same intervals thereafter until fully paid.
   　☐ b. continuing regularly and at the same intervals thereafter until _____, 19 _____, when the entire balance of principal and accrued interest shall be due and payable.
   ☐ (2) In a lump sum on or before _____ after date of the Note,
   ☒ C. This contract is subject to Buyer furnishing Seller evidence that Buyer has a history of good credit.

5. EARNEST MONEY: $ _1,000_ is herewith tendered and is to be deposited as Earnest Money with _ABC TITLE COMPANY_, as Escrow Agent, upon execution of the contract by both parties. Additional Earnest Money, if any, shall be deposited with the Escrow Agent on or before _N/A_, 19 _____, in the amount of $ _____.

6. TITLE: Seller at Seller's expense shall furnish either:
   ☒ A. Owner's Policy of Title Insurance (the Title Policy) issued by _ABC TITLE COMPANY_ in the amount of the Sales Price and dated at or after closing: OR
   ☐ B. Complete Abstract of Title (the Abstract) certified by _____ to current date.
   NOTICE TO BUYER: AS REQUIRED BY LAW, Broker advises that YOU should have the Abstract covering the Property examined by an attorney of YOUR selection, or YOU should be furnished with or obtain a Title Policy.

7. PROPERTY CONDITION (Check "A" or "B"):
   ☐ A. Buyer accepts the Property in its present condition, subject only to _____

   ☒ B. Buyer requires inspections and repairs required by the Property Condition Addendum (the Addendum).
   Seller shall commence and complete prior to closing all required repairs at Seller's expense.
   All inspections, reports and repairs required of Seller by this contract and the Addendum shall not exceed $_____. If Seller fails to complete such requirements, Buyer may do so and Seller shall be liable up to the amount specified and the same paid from the proceeds of the sale. If such expenditures exceed the stated amount and Seller refuses to pay such excess, Buyer may pay the additional cost or accept the Property with the limited repairs and this sale closed as scheduled, or Buyer may terminate this contract and the Earnest Money shall be refunded to Buyer. Broker and sales associates have no responsibility or liability for repair or replacement of any of the Property.

8. BROKER'S FEE: _N/A_ Listing Broker (_____%) and _____ Co-Broker (_____%), as Real Estate Broker (the Broker), has negotiated this sale and Seller agrees to pay Broker in _____ County, Texas, on consummation of this sale or on Seller's default (unless otherwise provided herein) a total cash fee of _____ of the total Sales Price, which Escrow Agent may pay from the sale proceeds.

9. CLOSING: The closing of the sale (the Closing Date) shall be on or before _12/30_, 19 _87_, or within 7 days after objections to title have been cured, whichever date is later.

10. POSSESSION: The possession of the Property shall be delivered to Buyer on _DATE OF CLOSING_ in its present or required improved condition, ordinary wear and tear excepted. Any possession by Buyer prior to or by Seller after Closing Date shall establish a landlord-tenant at sufferance relationship between the parties.

11. SPECIAL PROVISIONS:

    CHEST FREEZER IN GARAGE AND POOL TABLE IN GAME ROOM WILL REMAIN WITH THE PROPERTY.

    (Insert terms and conditions of a factual nature applicable to this sale, e.g., personal property included in sale [curtains, draperies, valances, etc.], prior purchase or sale of other property, lessee's surrender of possession, and the like.)

    № 65

Fig. 20-4.

12. SALES EXPENSES TO BE PAID IN CASH AT OR PRIOR TO CLOSING:
   A. Seller's Expenses:
   (1) Any inspections, reports and repairs required of Seller herein, and in the Addendum.
   (2) All cost of releasing existing loans and recording the releases; tax statements; 1/2 of any escrow fee; preparation of Deed; copies of restrictions and easements; other expenses stipulated to be paid by Seller under other provisions of this contract.
   B. Buyer's Expenses: All expenses incident to any loan (e.g., preparation of Note, Deed of Trust and other loan documents, recording fees, Mortgagee's Title Policy, credit reports); 1/2 of any escrow fee; one year premium for hazard insurance unless insurance is prorated; and expenses stipulated to be paid by Buyer under other provisions of this contract.
   C. If any sales expenses exceed the maximum amount herein stipulated to be paid by either party, either party may terminate this contract unless the other party agrees to pay such excess.

13. PRORATIONS: Insurance (at Buyer's option), taxes and any rents and maintenance fees, shall be prorated to the Closing Date.

14. TITLE APPROVAL: If Abstract is furnished, Seller shall deliver same to Buyer within 20 days from the effective date hereof. Buyer shall have 20 days from date of receipt of Abstract to deliver a copy of the title opinion to Seller, stating any objections to title, and only objections so stated shall be considered. If Title Policy is furnished, the Title Policy shall guarantee Buyer's title to be good and indefeasible subject only to (i) restrictive covenants affecting the Property (ii) any discrepancies, conflicts or shortages in area or boundary lines or any encroachments, or any overlapping of improvements (iii) all taxes for the current and subsequent years (iv) any existing building and zoning ordinances (v) rights of parties in possession (vi) any liens created as security for the sale consideration and (vii) any reservations or exceptions contained in the Deed. In either instance, if title objections are disclosed, Seller shall have 30 days to cure the same. Exceptions permitted in the Deed and zoning ordinances shall not be valid objections to title. Seller shall furnish at Seller's expense tax statements showing no delinquent taxes and a General Warranty Deed conveying title subject only to liens securing debt created as part of the consideration, taxes for the current year, usual restrictive covenants and utility easements common to the platted subdivision of which the Property is a part and any other reservations or exceptions acceptable to Buyer. The Note shall be secured by Vendor's and Deed of Trust liens. In case of dispute as to the form of Deed, Deed of Trust or Note, such shall be upon a form prepared by the State Bar of Texas.

15. CASUALTY LOSS: If any part of Property is damaged or destroyed by fire or other casualty loss, Seller shall restore the same to its previous condition as soon as reasonably possible, but in any event by Closing Date; and if Seller is unable to do so without fault, this contract shall terminate and Earnest Money shall be refunded with no Broker's fee due.

16. DEFAULT: If Buyer fails to comply herewith, Seller may either enforce specific performance or terminate this contract and receive the Earnest Money as liquidated damages, one-half of which (but not exceeding the herein recited Broker's fee) shall be paid by Seller to Broker in full payment for Broker's services. If Seller is unable without fault to deliver Abstract or Title Policy or to make any non-casualty repairs required herein within the time herein specified, Buyer may either terminate this contract and receive the Earnest Money as the sole remedy, and no Broker's fee shall be earned, or extend the time up to 30 days. If Seller fails to comply herewith for any other reason, Buyer may (i) terminate this contract and receive the Earnest Money, thereby releasing Seller from this contract (ii) enforce specific performance hereof or (iii) seek such other relief as may be provided by law. If completion of sale is prevented by Buyer's default, and Seller elects to enforce specific performance, the Broker's fee is payable only if and when Seller collects damages for such default by suit, compromise, settlement or otherwise, and after first deducting the expenses of collection, and then only in an amount equal to one-half of that portion collected, but not exceeding the amount of Broker's fee.

17. ATTORNEY'S FEES: Any signatory to this contract who is the prevailing party in any legal proceeding against any other signatory brought under or with relation to this contract or transaction shall be additionally entitled to recover court costs and reasonable attorney fees from the non-prevailing party.

18. ESCROW: Earnest Money is deposited with Escrow Agent with the understanding that Escrow Agent (i) does not assume or have any liability for performance or nonperformance of any party (ii) has the right to require the receipt, release and authorization in writing of all parties before paying the deposit to any party and (iii) is not liable for interest or other charge on the funds held. If any party unreasonably fails to agree in writing to an appropriate release of Earnest Money, then such party shall be liable to the other parties to the extent provided in paragraph 17. At closing, Earnest Money shall be applied to any cash down payment required, next to Buyer's closing costs and any excess refunded to Buyer. Before Buyer shall be entitled to refund of Earnest Money, any actual expenses incurred or paid on Buyer's behalf shall be deducted therefrom and paid to the creditors entitled thereto.

19. REPRESENTATIONS: Seller represents that there will be no Title I liens, unrecorded liens or Uniform Commercial Code liens against any of the Property on Closing Date. If any representation above is untrue this contract may be terminated by Buyer and the Earnest Money shall be refunded without delay. Representations shall survive closing.

20. AGREEMENT OF PARTIES: This contract contains the entire agreement of the parties and cannot be changed except by their written consent.

21. CONSULT YOUR ATTORNEY: This is intended to be a legally binding contract. READ IT CAREFULLY. If you do not understand the effect of any part, consult your attorney BEFORE signing. The Broker cannot give you legal advice — only factual and business details concerning land and improvements. Attorneys to represent parties may be designated below, and, so employment may be accepted, Broker shall promptly deliver a copy of this contract to such attorneys.

Seller's Atty: __EDWARD BARRISTER__   Buyer's Atty: __JOHNNY JOHNS__

EXECUTED in multiple originals effective the __23rd__ day of __NOV.__ , 19 __87__. **(BROKER FILL IN THE DATE LAST PARTY SIGNS).**

_____ Listing Broker	License No.	_Jack B Nimble_ Seller
By _____		_Sandy W. Nimble_ Seller
		25 CEDAR LN., DALLAS 123-4444 Seller's Address Tel.
_____ Co-Broker	License No.	_Jacky N. Shae_ Buyer
By _____		_____ Buyer
Receipt of $ _1,000_ Earnest Money is acknowledged in the form		_1000 PINECREST, KELLER 333-555_ Buyer's Address Tel.
of __CHECK__ .		
__ABC TITLE CO.__ __11/23/87__ Escrow Agent Date		
By _____		

Fig. 20-4. Cont.

ALL CASH OR OWNER FINANCED — RESIDENTIAL EARNEST MONEY CONTRACT (RESALE)

1. PARTIES: _____ (Seller) agrees
    to sell and convey to _____ (Buyer)
    and Buyer agrees to buy from Seller the following property situated in _____ County,
    known as _____ (Address).

2. PROPERTY: Lot _____, Block _____, _____
    _____ Addition, City of _____, or as described on attached exhibit, together
    with the following fixtures, if any: curtain rods, drapery rods, venetian blinds, window shades, screens and shutters, awnings, wall-to-wall
    carpeting, mirrors fixed in place, attic fans, permanently installed heating and air conditioning units and equipment, lighting and plumbing fix-
    tures, TV antennas, mail boxes, water softeners, shrubbery and all other property owned by Seller and attached to the above described real pro-
    perty. All property sold by this contract is called "Property".

3. CONTRACT SALES PRICE:
    A. Cash payment payable at closing . . . . $_____

    B. Note described in 4 B below (the Note) . . . . $_____

    C. Sales Price payable to Seller (Sum of A and B) . . . . $_____

4. FINANCING CONDITIONS:
    ☐ A. This is an all cash sale; no financing is involved.
    ☐ B. The Note in the principal sum shown in 3 B above, dated as of the Closing Date, to be executed and delivered by Buyer and payable to
    the order of Seller, bearing interest at the rate of _____ percent per annum from date thereof until maturity, matured unpaid
    principal and interest to bear interest at the rate of 10% per annum, principal and interest to be due and payable
    ☐ (1) In _____ installments of $_____ or more each, beginning on or before _____
    after date of the Note, and (Check "a" or "b")
    ☐ a. continuing regularly and at the same intervals thereafter until fully paid.
    ☐ b. continuing regularly and at the same intervals thereafter until _____, 19 _____, when the entire balance
    of principal and accrued interest shall be due and payable.
    ☐ (2) In a lump sum on or before _____ after date of the Note,
    ☐ C. This contract is subject to Buyer furnishing Seller evidence that Buyer has a history of good credit.

5. EARNEST MONEY: $_____ is herewith tendered and is to be deposited as Earnest Money with _____
    _____, as Escrow Agent, upon execution of the contract by both parties. Additional Earnest
    Money, if any, shall be deposited with the Escrow Agent on or before _____, 19 _____, in the amount of $_____.

6. TITLE: Seller at Seller's expense shall furnish either:
    ☐ A. Owner's Policy of Title Insurance (the Title Policy) issued by _____
    in the amount of the Sales Price and dated at or after closing: OR
    ☐ B. Complete Abstract of Title (the Abstract) certified by _____ to current date.
    NOTICE TO BUYER: AS REQUIRED BY LAW, Broker advises that YOU should have the Abstract covering the Property examined by an
    attorney of YOUR selection, or YOU should be furnished with or obtain a Title Policy.

7. PROPERTY CONDITION (Check "A" or "B"):
    ☐ A. Buyer accepts the Property in its present condition, subject only to _____
    _____.

    ☐ B. Buyer requires inspections and repairs required by the Property Condition Addendum (the Addendum).
    Seller shall commence and complete prior to closing all required repairs at Seller's expense.
    All inspections, reports and repairs required of Seller by this contract and the Addendum shall not exceed $_____. If Seller fails to complete
    such requirements, Buyer may do so and Seller shall be liable up to the amount specified and the same paid from the proceeds of the sale.
    If such expenditures exceed the stated amount and Seller refuses to pay such excess, Buyer may pay the additional cost or accept the Property
    with the limited repairs and this sale shall be closed as scheduled, or Buyer may terminate this contract and the Earnest Money shall be refunded
    to Buyer. Broker and sales associates have no responsibility or liability for repair or replacement of any of the Property.

8. BROKER'S FEE: _____ Listing Broker (_____%) and _____
    _____ Co-Broker (_____%), as Real Estate Broker (the Broker), has negotiated this sale and Seller
    agrees to pay Broker in _____ County, on consummation of this sale or on Seller's default (unless
    otherwise provided herein) a total cash fee of _____ of the total Sales Price, which Escrow Agent may pay from the sale proceeds.

9. CLOSING: The closing of the sale (the Closing Date) shall be on or before _____, 19 _____, or within 7 days after objections
    to title have been cured, whichever date is later.

10. POSSESSION: The possession of the Property shall be delivered to Buyer on _____ in its present or required
    improved condition, ordinary wear and tear excepted. Any possession by Buyer prior to or by Seller after Closing Date shall establish a landlord-
    tenant at sufferance relationship between the parties.

11. SPECIAL PROVISIONS:

    (Insert terms and conditions of a factual nature applicable to this sale, e.g., personal property included in sale [curtains, draperies, valances, etc.],
    prior purchase or sale of other property, lessee's surrender of possession, and the like.)

Fig. 20-4. Cont.

12. SALES EXPENSES TO BE PAID IN CASH AT OR PRIOR TO CLOSING:
   A. Seller's Expenses:
      (1) Any inspections, reports and repairs required of Seller herein, and in the Addendum.
      (2) All cost of releasing existing loans and recording the releases; tax statements; 1/2 of any escrow fee; preparation of Deed; copies of restrictions and easements; other expenses stipulated to be paid by Seller under other provisions of this contract.
   B. Buyer's Expenses: All expenses incident to any loan (e.g., preparation of Note, Deed of Trust and other loan documents, recording fees, Mortgagee's Title Policy, credit reports); 1/2 of any escrow fee; one year premium for hazard insurance unless insurance is prorated; and expenses stipulated to be paid by Buyer under other provisions of this contract.
   C. If any sales expenses exceed the maximum amount herein stipulated to be paid by either party, either party may terminate this contract unless the other party agrees to pay such excess.

13. PRORATIONS: Insurance (at Buyer's option), taxes and any rents and maintenance fees, shall be prorated to the Closing Date

14. TITLE APPROVAL: If Abstract is furnished, Seller shall deliver same to Buyer within 20 days from the effective date hereof. Buyer shall have 20 days from date of receipt of Abstract to deliver a copy of the title opinion to Seller, stating any objections to title, and only objections so stated shall be considered. If Title Policy is furnished, the Title Policy shall guarantee Buyer's title to be good and indefeasible subject only to (i) restrictive covenants affecting the Property (ii) any discrepancies, conflicts or shortages in area or boundary lines or any encroachments, or any overlapping of improvements (iii) all taxes for the current and subsequent years (iv) any existing building and zoning ordinances (v) rights of parties in possesion (vi) any liens created as security for the sale consideration and (vii) any reservations or exceptions contained in the Deed. In either instance, if title objections are disclosed, Seller shall have 30 days to cure the same. Exceptions permitted in the Deed and zoning ordinances shall not be valid objections to title. Seller shall furnish at Seller's expense tax statements showing no delinquent taxes and a General Warranty Deed conveying title subject only to liens securing debt created as part of the consideration, taxes for the current year, usual restrictive covenants and utility easements common to the platted subdivision of which the Property is a part and any other reservations or exceptions acceptable to Buyer. The Note shall be secured by Vendor's and Deed of Trust liens. In case of dispute as to the form of Deed, Deed of Trust or Note, such shall be upon a form prepared by the State Bar of

15. CASUALTY LOSS: If any part of Property is damaged or destroyed by fire or other casualty loss, Seller shall restore the same to its previous condition as soon as reasonably possible, but in any event by Closing Date; and if Seller is unable to do so without fault, this contract shall terminate and Earnest Money shall be refunded with no Broker's fee due.

16. DEFAULT: If Buyer fails to comply herewith, Seller may either enforce specific performance or terminate this contract and receive the Earnest Money as liquidated damages, one-half of which (but not exceeding the herein recited Broker's fee) shall be paid by Seller to Broker in full payment for Broker's services. If Seller is unable without fault to deliver Abstract or Title Policy or to make any non-casualty repairs required herein within the time herein specified, Buyer may either terminate this contract and receive the Earnest Money as the sole remedy, and no Broker's fee shall be earned, or extend the time up to 30 days. If Seller fails to comply herewith for any other reason, Buyer may (i) terminate this contract and receive the Earnest Money, thereby releasing Seller from this contract (ii) enforce specific performance hereof or (iii) seek such other relief as may be provided by law. If completion of sale is prevented by Buyer's default, and Seller elects to enforce specific performance, the Broker's fee is payable only if and when Seller collects damages for such default by suit, compromise, settlement or otherwise, and after first deducting the expenses of collection, and then only in an amount equal to one-half of that portion collected, but not exceeding the amount of Broker's fee.

17. ATTORNEY'S FEES: Any signatory to this contract who is the prevailing party in any legal proceeding against any other signatory brought under or with relation to this contract or transaction shall be additionally entitled to recover court costs and reasonable attorney fees from the non-prevailing party.

18. ESCROW: Earnest Money is deposited with Escrow Agent with the understanding that Escrow Agent (i) does not assume or have any liability for performance or nonperformance of any party (ii) has the right to require the receipt, release and authorization in writing of all parties before paying the deposit to any party and (iii) is not liable for interest or other charge on the funds held. If any party unreasonably fails to agree in writing to an appropriate release of Earnest Money, then such party shall be liable to the other parties to the extent provided in paragraph 17. At closing, Earnest Money shall be applied to any cash down payment required, next to Buyer's closing costs and any excess refunded to Buyer. Before Buyer shall be entitled to refund of Earnest Money, any actual expenses incurred or paid on Buyer's behalf shall be deducted therefrom and paid to the creditors entitled thereto.

19. REPRESENTATIONS: Seller represents that there will be no Title I liens, unrecorded liens or Uniform Commercial Code liens against any of the Property on Closing Date. If any representation above is untrue this contract may be terminated by Buyer and the Earnest Money shall be refunded without delay. Representations shall survive closing.

20. AGREEMENT OF PARTIES: This contract contains the entire agreement of the parties and cannot be changed except by their written consent

21. CONSULT YOUR ATTORNEY: This is intended to be a legally binding contract. READ IT CAREFULLY. If you do not understand the effect of any part, consult your attorney BEFORE signing. The Broker cannot give you legal advice — only factual and business details concerning land and improvements. Attorneys to represent parties may be designated below, and, so employment may be accepted, Broker shall promptly deliver a copy of this contract to such attorneys.

Seller's Atty: _____ Buyer's Atty: _____

EXECUTED in multiple originals effective the _____ day of _____, 19 _____. **(BROKER FILL IN THE DATE LAST PARTY SIGNS).**

Listing Broker	License No.	Seller
By _____		Seller
Co-Broker	License No.	Seller's Address Tel.
By _____		Buyer
Receipt of $_____ Earnest Money is acknowledged in the form		Buyer
of _____		Buyer's Address Tel.
Escrow Agent	Date	
By _____		

Fig. 20-4. Cont.

Paragraph #5. Give the least amount of earnest money possible. One percent of the sales price should be the maximum, preferably no more than $500. Put the amount in the first blank. On the second blank, indicate who will hold the earnest money. Depending on the custom in your state, it could be a title or escrow company, an attorney, or even a real estate broker. Write the seller's name if he'll hold the earnest money, but avoid this as much as possible.

If there will be additional earnest money at a future date before the closing, then indicate the date and the amount of the additional funds on the remaining blanks. Except in unusual situations, there should not be any additional earnest money.

Paragraph #6. Check box A if the seller will furnish a title insurance policy, and indicate the name of the company that will issue the policy. Check box B if the seller will provide an abstract of title, and indicate the abstractor or abstract company that will provide it.

Paragraph #7. Check box A if you're purchasing the property ''as is'' except for any repairs that might be required by a lender, or other conditions you'll indicate in the blank in the first paragraph.

Check box B if you will be allowed to inspect the property before closing. If you check this box, which you should, then you will include a Property Condition Addendum form (Fig. 20-6).

Paragraph #8. If one or more brokers are to receive a commission, use this paragraph. In most situations, you won't be using this contract form if a real estate agent or broker is involved. Brokers will use their own forms.

Paragraph #9. Fill in the closing date.

Paragraph #10. Indicate when you'll take possession of the property. If you put in an exact date predicated on the closing date and don't make that date, then there will be confusion. Rather indicate whether possession will be ''on date of closing,'' ''three days after closing,'' or other such date that is agreeable between you and the seller. Naturally, the sooner after closing, the better.

Paragraph #11. Include here any special provisions that are important to your agreement with the seller. For example, include any personal property that's included with the property, such as ''refrigerator and all window treatments to remain with property.'' Any personal property that looks like it is attached to the property, but which the seller will take with him, should be included here.

You can also show other terms of purchase or financing that don't fit anywhere else, such as ''First five payments on owner financing to be made in the amount of $250, to cover principal only. Interest to begin on the sixth month.''

Paragraph #21. There are two spaces at the end of this paragraph for the name of the buyer's or seller's attorneys. Write in their names if attorneys will represent either party. Often on simple transactions, attorneys will not be used and you'll mark out these lines.

On the blanks that ask for the date, fill in the effective date of the contract, which is when all parties have affixed their signatures.

Assumption-of-Loan Contract Form

Use the blank contract shown in Fig. 20-5 when assuming an existing loan. Figure 20-5 also includes a completed sample contract. The following is a line-by-line explanation of the contract.

Paragraph #1. Write the sellers' legal names on the first line, and your legal names as buyers on the next line. Remember to note the marital status of all parties. For example:

- If one of the parties is a married couple, you would write "John M. Doe and wife Mary M. Doe."
- For a single person, you can simply write "John M. Doe," or you can write "John M. Doe, a single person."
- For a divorced person, write "John M. Doe, a divorced person since May 23, 1985."
- For a widower, write "John M. Doe, a widower since May 23, 1985."
- For a corporation, you would write JMD Industries, Inc., a Texas Corporation."
- For a partnership, you would write "Doe Properties, a Texas General Partnership," or "Doe Properties, a Texas Limited Partnership."
- For a pension and profit-sharing plan, you would write "JMD Industries, Inc., Pension & Profit-Sharing Trust."
- For two individuals not related or married, you would write "John M. Doe and John R. Smith, in indiscriminate interest."

The next blank asks for the name of the county in which the real estate is located. Fill this in, then place the two letter abbreviation for the state after the word "County."

The last blank requests the address of the property.

Paragraph #2. This paragraph asks for the legal description of the property. This information is available in the seller's copies of his original closing papers. Make *certain* you have the correct description. Write the lot number, the

ASSUMPTION OF LOAN — RESIDENTIAL EARNEST MONEY CONTRACT

1. PARTIES: _BOBBY McGEE AND WIFE LEA E. McGEE_ (Seller) agrees to sell and convey to _SMITH ENTERPRISES, INC., A TEXAS CORP._ (Buyer) and Buyer agrees to buy from Seller the following property situated in _DALLAS_ County, Texas, known as _8543 AVENUE C, DUNCANVILLE, TX 55555_ (Address).

2. PROPERTY: Lot _111_, Block _2A_, _CEDAR TREES_ Addition, City of _DUNCANVILLE_, or as described on attached exhibit, together with the following fixtures, if any: curtain rods, drapery rods, venetian blinds, window shades, screens and shutters, awnings, wall-to-wall carpeting, mirrors fixed in place, attic fans, permanently installed heating and air conditioning units and equipment, lighting and plumbing fixtures, TV antennas, mail boxes, water softeners, shrubbery and all other property owned by Seller and attached to the above described real property. All property sold by this contract is called "Property".

3. CONTRACT SALES PRICE:
   A. The ☒ Exact ☐ Approximate   Cash down payment payable at closing .... $ _5,000.00_
   B. Buyer's assumption of the unpaid balance of a promissory note (the Note) payable in present monthly installments of $ _237.55_, including principal and interest and any reserve deposits, with Buyer's first installment payable to _MAURY MORTGAGE CO._ on _JUNE 1_, 19 _88_, the assumed principal balance of which at closing (allowing for an agreed $250 variance) will be .... $ _22,600.00_
   C. Any balance of Sales Price to be evidenced by a second lien note payable to [check (1) or (2) below]:
      ☒ (1) Seller, bearing interest at the rate of _9_ % per annum, in
         ☐ lump sum on or before _____
         ☒ principal and interest installments of $ _126.68_, or more per _MONTH_, with first installment payable on _JUNE 1, 1988_
      ☐ (2) Third Party in principal and interest installments not in excess of $ _____ per month and in the ☐ Exact ☐ Approximate (check "Approximate" only if A above and D below are "Exact") amount of .... $ _10,000.00_
   D. The ☒ Exact ☐ Approximate total Sales Price of (Sum of A, B and C above) .... $ _37,600.00_

4. FINANCING CONDITIONS: If a Noteholder on assumption (i) requires Buyer to pay an assumption fee in excess of $ _50.00_ and Seller declines to pay such excess (ii) raises the existing interest rate above _8_ % or (iii) requires approval of Buyer or can accelerate the Note and Buyer does not receive from the Noteholder written approval and acceleration waiver prior to the Closing Date, Buyer may terminate this contract and the Earnest Money shall be refunded. Buyer shall apply for the approval and waiver under (iii) above within 7 days from the effective date hereof and shall make every reasonable effort to obtain the same.

5. EARNEST MONEY: $ _500_ is herewith tendered and is to be deposited as Earnest Money with _FRIENDLY TITLE CO._, as Escrow Agent, upon execution of the contract by both parties. Additional Earnest Money, if any, shall be deposited with the Escrow Agent on or before _APRIL 15_, 19 _88_, in the amount of $ _500_.

6. TITLE: Seller at Seller's expense shall furnish either:
   ☒ A. Owner's Policy of Title Insurance (the Title Policy) issued by _FRIENDLY TITLE CO._ in the amount of the Sales Price and dated at or after closing: OR
   ☐ B. Complete Abstract of Title (the Abstract) certified by _____ to current date.
   NOTICE TO BUYER: AS REQUIRED BY LAW, Broker advises that YOU should have the Abstract covering the Property examined by an attorney of YOUR selection, or YOU should be furnished with or obtain a Title Policy.

7. PROPERTY CONDITION (Check "A" or "B"):
   ☐ A. Buyer accepts the Property in its present condition, subject only to _____

   ☒ B. Buyer requires inspections and repairs required by the Property Condition Addendum (the Addendum).
   Upon Seller's receipt of all loan approvals and inspection reports Seller shall commence and complete prior to closing all required repairs at Seller's expense.
   All inspections, reports and repairs required of Seller by this contract and the Addendum shall not exceed $ _____. If Seller fails to complete such requirements, Buyer may do so and Seller shall be liable up to the amount specified and the same paid from the proceeds of the sale. If such expenditures exceed the stated amount and Seller refuses to pay such excess, Buyer may pay the additional cost or accept the Property with the limited repairs and this sale shall be closed as scheduled, or Buyer may terminate this contract and the Earnest Money shall be refunded to Buyer. Broker and sales associates have no responsibility or liability for repair or replacement of any of the Property.

8. BROKER'S FEE: _N/A_ _____ Listing Broker (____%) and _____ Co-Broker (____%), as Real Estate Broker (the Broker), has negotiated this sale and Seller agrees to pay Broker in _____ County, Texas, on consummation of this sale or on Seller's default (unless otherwise provided herein) a total cash fee of _____ of the total Sales Price, which Escrow Agent may pay from the sale proceeds.

9. CLOSING: The closing of the sale (the Closing Date) shall be on or before _APRIL 30_, 19 _88_, or within 7 days after objections to title have been cured, whichever date is later.

10. POSSESSION: The possession of the Property shall be delivered to Buyer on _DATE OF CLOSING_ in its present or required improved condition, ordinary wear and tear excepted. Any possession by Buyer prior to or by Seller after Closing Date shall establish a landlord-tenant at sufferance relationship between the parties.

11. SPECIAL PROVISIONS:

    PAYMENT IN #3C ABOVE WILL VARY DEPENDING ON FINAL AMOUNT OF SECOND LIEN NOTE.

    (Insert terms and conditions of a factual nature applicable to this sale, e.g., personal property included in sale [curtains, draperies, valances, etc.], prior purchase or sale of other property, lessee's surrender of possession, and the like.)

    № 315

Fig. 20-5.

12. **PRORATION:** Taxes, insurance, rents, interest and maintenance fees, if any, ☐ SHALL ☐ SHALL NOT be prorated to the Closing Date. If these are not prorated, all funds held in reserve for payment of taxes, maintenance fees and insurance and the insurance policy shall be transferred to the Buyer by Seller without cost to Buyer.

13. **SALES EXPENSES TO BE PAID IN CASH AT OR PRIOR TO CLOSING:** Preparing Deed, preparing and recording Deed of Trust to Secure Assumption, all inspections, reports and repairs required of Seller herein and in the Addendum and 1/2 of escrow fee shall be Seller's expense. All other costs and expenses incurred in connection with this contract which are not recited herein to be the obligation of Seller, shall be the obligation of Buyer. Unless otherwise paid, before Buyer shall be entitled to refund of Earnest Money, any such costs and expenses shall be deducted therefrom and paid to the creditors entitled thereto. If any sales expenses exceed the maximum amount herein stipulated to be paid by either party, either party may terminate this contract unless the other party agrees to pay such excess.

14. **TITLE APPROVAL:** If Abstract is furnished, Seller shall deliver same to Buyer within 20 days from the effective date hereof. Buyer shall have 20 days from date of receipt of Abstract to deliver a copy of the title opinion to Seller, stating any objections to title, and only objections so stated shall be considered. If Title Policy is furnished, the Title Policy shall guarantee Buyer's title to be good and indefeasible subject only to (i) restrictive covenants affecting the Property (ii) any discrepancies, conflicts or shortages in area or boundary lines or any encroachments, or any overlapping of improvements (iii) all taxes for the current and subsequent years (iv) any existing building and zoning ordinances (v) rights of parties in possession (vi) any liens assumed or created as security for the sale consideration and (vii) any reservations or exceptions contai~ ed in the Deed. In either instance, if title objections are disclosed, Seller shall have 30 days to cure the same. Exceptions permitted in the Deed and zoning ordinances shall not be valid objections to title. Seller shall furnish at Seller's expense tax statements showing no delinquent taxes and a General Warranty Deed conveying title subject only to liens securing debt created or assumed as part of the consideration, taxes for the current year, usual restrictive covenants and utility easements common to the platted subdivision of which the Property is a part and any other reservations or exceptions acceptable to Buyer. Each note herein provided shall be secured by Vendor's and Deed of Trust liens. A Vendor's lien shall be retained and a Deed of Trust to Secure Assumption required, which shall be automatically released on execution and delivery of a release by noteholder. In the case of dispute as to the form of Deed, Note(s) or Deed(s) of Trust, such shall be upon a form prepared by the State Bar of Texas.

15. **CASUALTY LOSS:** If any part of Property is damaged or destroyed by fire or other casualty loss, Seller shall restore the same to its previous condition as soon as reasonably possible, but in any event by Closing Date; and if Seller is unable to do so without fault, this contract shall terminate and Earnest Money shall be refunded with no Broker's fee due.

16. **DEFAULT:** If Buyer fails to comply herewith, Seller may either enforce specific performance or terminate this contract and receive the Earnest Money as liquidated damages, one-half of which (but not exceeding the herein recited Broker's fee) shall be paid by Seller to Broker in full payment for Broker's services. If Seller is unable without fault to deliver Abstract or Title Policy or to make any non-casualty repairs required herein within the time herein specified, Buyer may either terminate this contract and receive the Earnest Money as the sole remedy, and no Broker's fee shall be earned, or extend the time up to 30 days. If Seller fails to comply herewith for any other reason, Buyer may (i) terminate this contract and receive the Earnest Money, thereby releasing Seller from this contract (ii) enforce specific performance hereof or (iii) seek such other relief as may be provided by law. If completion of sale is prevented by Buyer's default, and Seller elects to enforce specific performance, the Broker's fee is payable only if and when Seller collects damages for such default by suit, compromise, settlement or otherwise, and after first deducting the expenses of collection, and then only in an amount equal to one-half of that portion collected, but not exceeding the amount of Broker's fee.

17. **ATTORNEY'S FEES:** Any signatory to this contract who is the prevailing party in any legal proceeding against any other signatory brought under or with relation to this contract or transaction shall be additionally entitled to recover court costs and reasonable attorney fees from the non-prevailing party.

18. **ESCROW:** Earnest Money is deposited with Escrow Agent with the understanding that Escrow Agent (i) does not assume or have any liability for performance or nonperformance of any party (ii) has the right to require the receipt, release and authorization in writing of all parties before paying the deposit to any party and (iii) is not liable for interest or other charge on the funds held. If any party unreasonably fails to agree in writing to an appropriate release of Earnest Money, then such party shall be liable to the other parties to the extent provided in paragraph 17. At closing, Earnest Money shall be applied to any cash down payment required, next to Buyer's closing costs and any excess refunded to Buyer. Before Buyer shall be entitled to refund of Earnest Money, any actual expenses incurred or paid on Buyer's behalf shall be deducted therefrom and paid to the creditors entitled thereto.

19. **REPRESENTATIONS:** Seller represents that unless securing payment of the Note there will be no Title I liens, unrecorded liens or Uniform Commerical Code liens against any of the Property on Closing Date, that loan(s) will be without default, and reserve deposits will not be deficient. If any representation above is untrue this contract may be terminated by Buyer and the Earnest Money shall be refunded without delay. Representations shall survive closing.

20. **THIRD PARTY FINANCING:** If financing by Third Party under 3C(2) above is required herein, Buyer shall have 15 days from effective date hereof to obtain the same, and failure to secure the same after reasonable effort shall render this contract null and void, and the Earnest Money refunded without delay.

21. **AGREEMENT OF PARTIES:** This contract contains the entire agreement of the parties and cannot be changed except by their written consent.

22. **CONSULT YOUR ATTORNEY:** This is intended to be a legally binding contract. **READ IT CAREFULLY.** If you do not understand the effect of any part, consult your attorney BEFORE signing. The Broker cannot give you legal advice — only factual and business details concerning land and improvements. Attorneys to represent parties may be designated below, and, so employment may be accepted, Broker shall promptly deliver a copy of this contract to such attorneys.

Seller's Atty: _____N/A_____   Buyer's Atty: _____N/A_____

EXECUTED in multiple originals effective the 1ST day of _APRIL_, 19 88 **(BROKER FILL IN THE DATE LAST PARTY SIGNS).**

Listing Broker _____	License No. _____	_Molly M Lee_ (signature)
		Seller
By _____		_Lea E. M Lee_ (signature)
		Seller
Co-Broker _____	License No. _____	12345 AUDELIA, DALLAS 77777
		Seller's Address 222-3333 Tel.
By _____		_Ted Armstrong Pres._ (signature)
		Buyer
Receipt of $ 500 Earnest Money is acknowledged in the form		
of CHECK _____		Buyer _____
		6704 ABRAMS, SUITE 210
FRIENDLY TITLE CO. 4/1/88		Buyer's Address
Escrow Agent Date		DALLAS 77777 666-7777 Tel.
By _____		

Fig. 20-5. Cont.

ASSUMPTION OF LOAN — RESIDENTIAL EARNEST MONEY CONTRACT

1. PARTIES: _____ (Seller) agrees
   to sell and convey to _____ (Buyer)
   and Buyer agrees to buy from Seller the following property situated in _____ County,
   known as _____ (Address).

2. PROPERTY: Lot _____, Block _____, _____
   _____ Addition, City of _____, or as described on attached exhibit,
   together with the following fixtures, if any: curtain rods, drapery rods, venetian blinds, window shades, screens and shutters, awnings, wall-to-wall carpeting, mirrors fixed in place, attic fans, permanently installed heating and air conditioning units and equipment, lighting and plumbing fixtures, TV antennas, mail boxes, water softeners, shrubbery and all other property owned by Seller and attached to the above described real property. All property sold by this contract is called "Property".

3. CONTRACT SALES PRICE:
   A. The ☐ Exact ☐ Approximate   Cash down payment payable at closing .... $ _____
   B. Buyer's assumption of the unpaid balance of a promissory note (the Note) payable in present monthly instal-
      lments of $ _____, including principal and interest and any reserve deposits, with Buyer's first
      installment payable to _____
      on _____, 19_____ , the assumed principal balance of which at closing
      (allowing for an agreed $250 variance) will be .... $ _____
   C. Any balance of Sales Price to be evidenced by a second lien note payable to [check (1) or (2) below]:
      ☐ (1) Seller, bearing interest at the rate of _____% per annum, in
         ☐ lump sum on or before _____.
         ☐ principal and interest installments of $ _____, or more per _____,
         with first installment payable on _____
      ☐ (2) Third Party in principal and interest installments not in excess of $ _____ per month
      and in the ☐ Exact ☐ Approximate (check "Approximate" only if A above and D below are "Exact")
      amount of .... $ _____

   D. The ☐ Exact ☐ Approximate total Sales Price of (Sum of A, B and C above) .... $ _____

4. FINANCING CONDITIONS: If a Noteholder on assumption (i) requires Buyer to pay an assumption fee in excess of $ _____
   and Seller declines to pay such excess (ii) raises the existing interest rate above _____% or (iii) requires approval of Buyer or can accelerate the Note and Buyer does not receive from the Noteholder written approval and acceleration waiver prior to the Closing Date, Buyer
   may terminate this contract and the Earnest Money shall be refunded. Buyer shall apply for the approval and waiver under (iii) above within 7
   days from the effective date hereof and shall make every reasonable effort to obtain the same.

5. EARNEST MONEY: $_____ is herewith tendered and is to be deposited as Earnest Money with _____
   _____, as Escrow Agent, upon execution of the contract by both parties. Additional Earnest
   Money, if any, shall be deposited with the Escrow Agent on or before _____, 19_____ , in the amount of $_____.

6. TITLE: Seller at Seller's expense shall furnish either:
   ☐ A. Owner's Policy of Title Insurance (the Title Policy) issued by _____
      in the amount of the Sales Price and dated at or after closing: OR
   ☐ B. Complete Abstract of Title (the Abstract) certified by _____ to current date.
   NOTICE TO BUYER: AS REQUIRED BY LAW, Broker advises that YOU should have the Abstract covering the Property examined by an
   attorney of YOUR selection, or YOU should be furnished with or obtain a Title Policy.

7. PROPERTY CONDITION (Check "A" or "B"):
   ☐ A. Buyer accepts the Property in its present condition, subject only to _____
      _____.
   ☐ B. Buyer requires inspections and repairs required by the Property Condition Addendum (the Addendum).
   Upon Seller's receipt of all loan approvals and inspection reports Seller shall commence and complete prior to closing all required repairs at
   Seller's expense.
   All inspections, reports and repairs required of Seller by this contract and the Addendum shall not exceed $_____. If Seller fails to com-
   plete such requirements, Buyer may do so and Seller shall be liable up to the amount specified and the same paid from the proceeds of the sale.
   If such expenditures exceed the stated amount and Seller refuses to pay such excess, Buyer may pay the additional cost or accept the Property
   with the limited repairs and this sale shall be closed as scheduled, or Buyer may terminate this contract and the Earnest Money shall be refunded
   to Buyer. Broker and sales associates have no responsibility or liability for repair or replacement of any of the Property.

8. BROKER'S FEE: _____ Listing Broker (_____%) and _____
   _____ Co-Broker (_____%), as Real Estate Broker (the Broker), has negotiated this sale and Seller
   agrees to pay Broker in _____ County,   on consummation of this sale or on Seller's default (unless
   otherwise provided herein) a total cash fee of _____ of the total Sales Price, which Escrow Agent may pay from the sale proceeds.

9. CLOSING: The closing of the sale (the Closing Date) shall be on or before _____, 19_____ , or within 7 days after objections to title have been cured, whichever date is later.

10. POSSESSION: The possession of the Property shall be delivered to Buyer on _____ in its present or required
    improved condition, ordinary wear and tear excepted. Any possession by Buyer prior to or by Seller after Closing Date shall establish a landlord-
    tenant at sufferance relationship between the parties.

11. SPECIAL PROVISIONS:

    (Insert terms and conditions of a factual nature applicable to this sale, e.g., personal property included in sale [curtains, draperies, valances, etc.],
    prior purchase or sale of other property, lessee's surrender of possession, and the like.)

Fig. 20-5. Cont.

12. **PRORATION:** Taxes, insurance, rents, interest and maintenance fees, if any, ☐ SHALL ☐ SHALL NOT be prorated to the Closing Date. If these are not prorated, all funds held in reserve for payment of taxes, maintenance fees and insurance and the insurance policy shall be transferred to the Buyer by Seller without cost to Buyer.

13. **SALES EXPENSES TO BE PAID IN CASH AT OR PRIOR TO CLOSING:** Preparing Deed, preparing and recording Deed of Trust to Secure Assumption, all inspections, reports and repairs required of Seller herein and in the Addendum and 1/2 of escrow fee shall be Seller's expense. All other costs and expenses incurred in connection with this contract which are not recited herein to be the obligation of Seller, shall be the obligation of Buyer. Unless otherwise paid, before Buyer shall be entitled to refund of Earnest Money, any such costs and expenses shall be deducted therefrom and paid to the creditors entitled thereto. If any sales expenses exceed the maximum amount herein stipulated to be paid by either party, either party may terminate this contract unless the other party agrees to pay such excess.

14. **TITLE APPROVAL:** If Abstract is furnished, Seller shall deliver same to Buyer within 20 days from the effective date hereof. Buyer shall have 20 days from date of receipt of Abstract to deliver a copy of the title opinion to Seller, stating any objections to title, and only objections so stated shall be considered. If Title Policy is furnished, the Title Policy shall guarantee Buyer's title to be good and indefeasible subject only to (i) restrictive covenants affecting the Property (ii) any discrepancies, conflicts or shortages in area or boundary lines or any encroachments, or any overlapping of improvements (iii) all taxes for the current and subsequent years (iv) any existing building and zoning ordinances (v) rights of parties in possession (vi) any liens assumed or created as security for the sale consideration and (vii) any reservations or exceptions contai ed in the Deed. In either instance, if title objections are disclosed, Seller shall have 30 days to cure the same. Exceptions permitted in the Deed and zoning ordinances shall not be valid objections to title. Seller shall furnish at Seller's expense tax statements showing no delinquent taxes and a General Warranty Deed conveying title subject only to liens securing debt created or assumed as part of the consideration, taxes for the current year, usual restrictive covenants and utility easements common to the platted subdivision of which the Property is a part and any other reservations or exceptions acceptable to Buyer. Each note herein provided shall be secured by Vendor's and Deed of Trust liens. A Vendor's lien shall be retained and a Deed of Trust to Secure Assumption required, which shall be automatically released on execution and delivery of a release by noteholder. In the case of dispute as to the form of Deed, Note(s) or Deed(s) of Trust, such shall be upon a form prepared by the State Bar of

15. **CASUALTY LOSS:** If any part of Property is damaged or destroyed by fire or other casualty loss, Seller shall restore the same to its previous condition as soon as reasonably possible, but in any event by Closing Date; and if Seller is unable to do so without fault, this contract shall terminate and Earnest Money shall be refunded with no Broker's fee due.

16. **DEFAULT:** If Buyer fails to comply herewith, Seller may either enforce specific performance or terminate this contract and receive the Earnest Money as liquidated damages, one-half of which (but not exceeding the herein recited Broker's fee) shall be paid by Seller to Broker in full payment for Broker's services. If Seller is unable without fault to deliver Abstract or Title Policy or to make any non-casualty repairs required herein within the time herein specified, Buyer may either terminate this contract and receive the Earnest Money as the sole remedy, and no Broker's fee shall be earned, or extend the time up to 30 days. If Seller fails to comply herewith for any other reason, Buyer may (i) terminate this contract and receive the Earnest Money, thereby releasing Seller from this contract (ii) enforce specific performance hereof or (iii) seek such other relief as may be provided by law. If completion of sale is prevented by Buyer's default, and Seller elects to enforce specific performance, the Broker's fee is payable only if and when Seller collects damages for such default by suit, compromise, settlement or otherwise, and after first deducting the expenses of collection, and then only in an amount equal to one-half of that portion collected, but not exceeding the amount of Broker's fee.

17. **ATTORNEY'S FEES:** Any signatory to this contract who is the prevailing party in any legal proceeding against any other signatory brought under or with relation to this contract or transaction shall be additionally entitled to recover court costs and reasonable attorney fees from the non-prevailing party.

18. **ESCROW:** Earnest Money is deposited with Escrow Agent with the understanding that Escrow Agent (i) does not assume or have any liability for performance or nonperformance of any party (ii) has the right to require the receipt, release and authorization in writing of all parties before paying the deposit to any party and (iii) is not liable for interest or other charge on the funds held. If any party unreasonably fails to agree in writing to an appropriate release of Earnest Money, then such party shall be liable to the other parties to the extent provided in paragraph 17. At closing, Earnest Money shall be applied to any cash down payment required, next to Buyer's closing costs and any excess refunded to Buyer. Before Buyer shall be entitled to refund of Earnest Money, any actual expenses incurred or paid on Buyer's behalf shall be deducted therefrom and paid to the creditors entitled thereto.

19. **REPRESENTATIONS:** Seller represents that unless securing payment of the Note there will be no Title I liens, unrecorded liens or Uniform Commerical Code liens against any of the Property on Closing Date, that loan(s) will be without default, and reserve deposits will not be deficient. If any representation above is untrue this contract may be terminated by Buyer and the Earnest Money shall be refunded without delay. Representations shall survive closing.

20. **THIRD PARTY FINANCING:** If financing by Third Party under 3C(2) above is required herein, Buyer shall have 15 days from effective date hereof to obtain the same, and failure to secure the same after reasonable effort shall render this contract null and void, and the Earnest Money refunded without delay.

21. **AGREEMENT OF PARTIES:** This contract contains the entire agreement of the parties and cannot be changed except by their written consent.

22. **CONSULT YOUR ATTORNEY:** This is intended to be a legally binding contract. READ IT CAREFULLY. If you do not understand the effect of any part, consult your attorney BEFORE signing. The Broker cannot give you legal advice — only factual and business details concerning land and improvements. Attorneys to represent parties may be designated below, and, so employment may be accepted, Broker shall promptly deliver a copy of this contract to such attorneys.

Seller's Atty: _____ Buyer's Atty: _____

EXECUTED in multiple originals effective the _____ day of _____, 19 _____. **(BROKER FILL IN THE DATE LAST PARTY SIGNS).**

Listing Broker	License No.	Seller

By _____

Seller _____

Co-Broker	License No.	Seller's Address	Tel.

By _____

Buyer _____

Receipt of $ _____ Earnest Money is acknowledged in the form

of _____.

Buyer _____

Buyer's Address _____ Tel.

Escrow Agent	Date

By _____

Fig. 20-5. Cont.

block number, then the name of the addition in the first three blanks. Insert the city in which the property is located on the fourth blank.

Paragraph #3.

A. If you check the first box "Exact," then you will have to check the "Approximate" box in D below and vice-versa. The reason for this is that you won't know the exact balance *to the day of closing* on the existing loan that you are assuming from the seller. Therefore, if you want the amount of the down payment to be exact, the final sales price will have to be approximate, and if you want the sales price to be exact, the amount of the down payment will have to vary (up to $250 as is stated at the end of B). Check the appropriate box, and insert the amount of down payment you will pay out of your own funds.

B. On the first blank, include the seller's total payment for principal, interest, taxes, and insurance. On the second blank, include the name of the mortgage company. On the next two blanks is the date you will make your first payment. Remember that all payments are made in arrears. If you close at the end of August, the payment due September first is the payment for the month of August. To make sure all's fair, the payment due September first should be the seller's responsibility.

If the seller is doing any owner financing—such as a second or third lien—the seller can gain up to $250 by indicating on the last blank a figure that's $250 less than what he knows his mortgage balance is, and checking the "Exact" box in A and D. At closing, the true sales price will be increased by $250, to be shown as an increase in the owner financing.

C. Check box (1) if the seller will be carrying a second lien, then on the first blank show the interest rate. Check the lump-sum box if the second lien will be paid in a lump sum, and indicate the date the lump sum is due. Normally, you'll check the next box when payments are made in installments. On the first blank include the amount of each installment, on the second blank, you'll more than likely want to write "monthly," and on the last blank show when the first installment will be made.

Check the second box if there will be a second lien provided by a commercial lender, and in the first blank indicate the maximum monthly payment you are willing to pay for the second lien. See the instructions for Paragraph #3A to determine if you will check the "Exact" box or the "Approximate" box.

Paragraph #4. On the first blank, you need to check $50. The cost to transfer a loan is generally $50 if it is a nonqualifying, fully-assumable loan. If it is a conventional assumable loan, then you'll need to check with the lender to see what he'll require for you to assume it. On the second blank, insert the existing interest rate if the loan is a nonqualifying, fully assumable loan. If it is a conventional loan, check with the lender to make sure the rate won't change. If it will change, then write in the new rate.

Paragraph #5. Give the least amount of earnest money possible. One percent of the sales price should be the maximum, preferably no more than $500. Put the amount in the first blank. On the second blank indicate who will hold the earnest money. Depending on the custom in your state, it could be a title or escrow company, an attorney, or even a real estate broker. Write the seller's name if he'll hold the earnest money, but avoid this as much as possible.

If there will be additional earnest money at a future date before the closing, then indicate the date and the amount of the additional funds on the remaining blanks. Except in unusual situations, there should not be any additional earnest money.

Paragraph #6. Check box A if the seller will furnish a title insurance policy, and indicate the name of the company that will issue the policy. Check box B if the seller will provide an abstract of title, and indicate the abstractor or abstract company that will provide it.

Paragraph #7. Check box A if you're purchasing the property "as is" except for any repairs that may be required by a lender, or other conditions you'll indicate in the blank in the first paragraph.

Check box B if you will be allowed to inspect the property before closing. If you check this box, which you should, then you will include a Property Condition Addendum form (Fig. 20-6).

Paragraph #8. If one or more brokers are to receive a commission, you can use this paragraph. In most situations, you won't be using this contract form if a real estate agent or broker is involved. Brokers will use their own forms.

Paragraph #9. Fill in the closing date. Make sure you give yourself enough time to find financing if a second lien is needed. Check with several mortgage companies to see how long to allow. If you run out of time and have not been approved, this contract will become null and void, so you or the seller could back out of the deal.

Paragraph #10. Indicate when you'll take possession of the property. If you put in an exact date predicated on the closing date and don't make that date, then there will be confusion. Rather, indicate whether possession will be "on date of closing," "three days after closing," or other such date that is agreeable between you and the seller. Naturally, the sooner after closing the better.

Paragraph #11. Include here any special provisions that are important to your agreement with the seller. For example, include any personal property

PROPERTY CONDITION ADDENDUM

**ADDENDUM TO EARNEST MONEY CONTRACT BETWEEN THE UNDERSIGNED PARTIES
CONCERNING THE PROPERTY AT** ___1237 MAIN ST., DALLAS___
(Street Address and City)

CHECK APPLICABLE BOXES:

☒ A. TERMITES: Buyer, at Buyer's expense (except at Seller's expense in VA transactions), may have the Property inspected by a Structural Pest Control Business Licensee to determine whether or not there is visible evidence of active termite infestation or visible termite damage to the improvements. If termite treatment or repairs are required, Buyer will furnish a written report to Seller from such Licensee within ___30___ days from the effective date of this Contract, but no treatment or repairs will be required for fences, trees or shrubs. Buyer's failure to furnish such report to Seller within the time specified shall constitute a waiver of Buyer's right to any treatment and repairs.

☒ B. INSPECTIONS: Buyer, at Buyer's expense, may have any of the items designated below inspected by inspectors of Buyer's choice. Repairs will only be required of items designated by this Contract for inspection and reported to be in need of immediate repair or which are not performing the function for which intended. Failure of Buyer to furnish written inspection reports and to designate the repairs to which Buyer is entitled by this Contract within the times specified below shall be deemed a waiver of Buyer's repair rights.

STRUCTURAL: Buyer requires inspections of the following: (check applicable boxes)

☒ foundation, ☒ roof, ☒ load bearing walls, ☒ ceilings, ☐ basement, ☒ water penetration, ☒ fireplace and chimney, ☒ floors,
☒ and ___STORAGE BUILDING___

Within ___30___ days from the effective date of this Contract, Buyer will furnish Seller written inspection reports with a designation of repairs if repairs are required.

EQUIPMENT AND SYSTEMS: Buyer requires inspections of the following: (check applicable boxes)

☒ plumbing system (including any water heater, wells and septic system), ☒ electrical system, ☒ all heating and cooling units and systems,
☒ any built-in range, oven, dishwasher, disposer, exhaust fans, trash compactor, ☒ swimming pool and related mechanical equipment, ☒ sprinkler systems,
☐ gas lines (inspection by private inspector) ☐ gas lines (inspection by gas supplier) ☐ and _____

Within _____ days from the effective date of this Contract, Buyer will furnish Seller written inspection reports with a designation of repairs if repairs are required.

☒ C. OTHER REPAIRS: Seller shall make the following repairs in addition to those required above: ___REPLACE BROKEN___
___OVERHEAD GARAGE DOOR___

All inspections shall be by persons who regularly provide such service and who are either registered as inspectors with the Texas Real Estate Commission or otherwise permitted by law to perform inspections. Repairs shall be by trained and qualified persons who are, whenever possible, manufacturer-approved service persons and who are licensed or bonded whenever such license or bond is required by law. Seller shall permit access to the Property at any reasonable time for inspection or repairs and for reinspection after repairs have been completed. Seller shall only be responsible for termite treatment and repairs to termite damage, repairs to items specifically designated above for inspection, and repairs specifically described in Paragraph C, subject to the provisions of Paragraph 7 of this Contract. Broker and sales associates shall not be liable or responsible for any inspections or repairs pursuant to this Contract and Addendum.

SELLER _____   BUYER _____

SELLER _____   BUYER _____

Fig. 20-6.

PROPERTY CONDITION ADDENDUM

ADDENDUM TO EARNEST MONEY CONTRACT BETWEEN THE UNDERSIGNED PARTIES CONCERNING THE PROPERTY AT _____
(Street Address and City)

CHECK APPLICABLE BOXES:

☐ A. TERMITES: Buyer, at Buyer's expense (except at Seller's expense in VA transactions), may have the Property inspected by a Structural Pest Control Business Licensee to determine whether or not there is visible evidence of active termite infestation or visible termite damage to the improvements. If termite treatment

or repairs are required, Buyer will furnish a written report to Seller from such Licensee within _____ days from the effective date of this Contract, but no treatment or repairs will be required for fences, trees or shrubs. Buyer's failure to furnish such report to Seller within the time specified shall constitute a waiver of Buyer's right to any treatment and repairs.

☐ B. INSPECTIONS: Buyer, at Buyer's expense, may have any of the items designated below inspected by inspectors of Buyer's choice. Repairs will only be required of items designated by this Contract for inspection and reported to be in need of immediate repair or which are not performing the function for which intended. Failure of Buyer to furnish written inspection reports and to designate the repairs to which Buyer is entitled by this Contract within the times specified below shall be deemed a waiver of Buyer's repair rights.

STRUCTURAL: Buyer requires inspections of the following: (check applicable boxes)

☐ foundation, ☐ roof, ☐ load bearing walls, ☐ ceilings, ☐ basement, ☐ water penetration, ☐ fireplace and chimney, ☐ floors,
☐ and _____

Within _____ days from the effective date of this Contract, Buyer will furnish Seller written inspection reports with a designation of repairs if repairs are required.

EQUIPMENT AND SYSTEMS: Buyer requires inspections of the following: (check applicable boxes)

☐ plumbing system (including any water heater, wells and septic system), ☐ electrical system, ☐ all heating and cooling units and systems,
☐ any built-in range, oven, dishwasher, disposer, exhaust fans, trash compactor, ☐ swimming pool and related mechanical equipment, ☐ sprinkler systems,
☐ gas lines (inspection by private inspector) ☐ gas lines (inspection by gas supplier) ☐ and _____

Within _____ days from the effective date of this Contract, Buyer will furnish Seller written inspection reports with a designation of repairs if repairs are required.

☐ C. OTHER REPAIRS: Seller shall make the following repairs in addition to those required above: _____

All inspections shall be by persons who regularly provide such service and who are either registered as inspectors with the _____ Real Estate Commission or otherwise permitted by law to perform inspections. Repairs shall be by trained and qualified persons who are, whenever possible, manufacturer-approved service persons and who are licensed or bonded whenever such license or bond is required by law. Seller shall permit access to the Property at any reasonable time for inspection or repairs and for reinspection after repairs have been completed. Seller shall only be responsible for termite treatment and repairs to termite damage, repairs to items specifically designated above for inspection, and repairs specifically described in Paragraph C, subject to the provisions of Paragraph 7 of this Contract. Broker and sales associates shall not be liable or responsible for any inspections or repairs pursuant to this Contract and Addendum.

SELLER _____   BUYER _____

SELLER _____   BUYER _____

Fig. 20-6. Cont.

that's included with the property, such as ''refrigerator and all window treatments to remain with property.'' Any personal property that looks like it is attached to the property, but which the seller will take with him, should be included here.

You can also show other terms of purchase or financing that don't fit anywhere else, such as ''First five payments on owner financing to be made in the amount of $250, to cover principal only. Interest to begin on the sixth month.''

Paragraph #12. To know which box to check here, the seller needs to know the status of his escrow account. If there is an excess of funds in it, the seller will be due a refund, and he'll want to check the first box. If there's an excess, you might want to check the second box so you can keep that excess. If there is a shortage, make sure the second box is checked. Generally, the escrow agent will require that any shortage be made up by the seller. You might want to put a provision in Paragraph #11 to make sure any shortages are made up by the seller.

Paragraph #21. There are two spaces at the end of this paragraph for the name of the buyer's or seller's attorneys. Write in their names if attorneys will represent either party. Often on simple transactions, attorneys will not be used and you'll mark out these lines.

On the blanks that ask for the date, fill in the effective date of the contract, which is when all parties have affixed their signatures.

PROPERTY CONDITION ADDENDUM FORM

The property condition addendum form allows the buyer the right to inspect the property. Figure 20-6 shows a completed sample addendum as well as a blank one you can use. Make sure you write the address of the property on the first blank to tie this form in with the main contract.

If you are buying the property at a substantial discount and don't expect repairs from the seller, and won't be inspecting the property, then don't use this form. On the other hand, if you want to be able to do a thorough inspection, *check all the boxes*, whether they apply to the property or not.

By checking all of the boxes, you are allowed to inspect the house. But that way the seller is more or less relieved of liability in case there are problems found after you move in equipment or areas you didn't inspect. Of course, if the seller has hidden structural or mechanical defects, there would be a basis for a lawsuit against him.

This form is self-explanatory. If you are buying a property in good condition, with exceptions for known defects, then you should leave blank those items that pertain to the problems, and *make a note of the problems* on one of the blank lines, stating that you acknowledge existence of the problem and are buying the house "as is" with respect to that problem.

Under C, if the seller will be doing repairs, make sure you state specifically what he will repair. The seller will want to put a limit on the amount to be spent on repairs. The seller might just give you credit in a lump sum of money so he doesn't have problems with cost overruns on the repairs. This won't work with some lenders, though. Often, if there are problems, the lender wants the problems corrected before he funds a loan. For example, if the roof leaks, the lender or the FHA or VA will want the roof replaced or fixed before closing. It's smart business on their part. Otherwise, if it never gets done, and they have to foreclose, they might have to do the repairs themselves.

21

Surviving
Buyers' Remorse

BUYERS' REMORSE IS AN ILLNESS THAT AFFLICTS ALMOST ALL PEOPLE WHO make the purchase of a large or expensive item, and a home is no exception. Buyers' remorse comes on when a buyer suddenly realizes a stupendous commitment has been made to either spend a large amount of cash, or to get into a long-term obligation for the steady outflow of a stream of payments. Buyers' remorse hits home buyers much more so than car or other big-ticket buyers. That's because, in a house purchase, the buyer has time to think about what he's done before the deal is actually consummated. Car dealers often don't let the buyer have that luxury. The car dealer wants the buyer financed, contract signed, and the buyer and car out the door as soon as possible. You can't take a car back. Once it's out the showroom floor, it's a used car. The buyer knows he can't take it back. Anyway, for the first few days, he's too infatuated with his new toy to want to give it back. If he gets buyers' remorse, there's no turning back.

The home buyer can turn back by forfeiting his earnest money, or using some of the back door tricks I talked about in the previous chapter. Some people are affected much more than others. It can happen that one spouse isn't affected, and the other falls apart from the little malady.

The more prepared you are for the purchase, the more confident you can be about the value of the property, and the less severe the case of buyers' remorse that you'll get. In fact, if you're very confident about value, you'll avoid getting buyers' remorse altogether.

Buyers who are bulldozed into signing a purchase agreement are the most susceptible to remorse. I have a competitor who's a tremendous closer. His favorite saying is, "I take no prisoners." He'll grab a buyer and not let go until he has a contract. He probably has a 98 percent contract rate. The problem with that high a contract rate is that too large a percentage of his buyers end up backing out. They back out because they get the idea they've not done their homework; that they haven't looked long enough, not made enough offers, that it was all too easy and perhaps—as is often the case—they've overpaid for the property.

You can avoid the urge to back out of a contract by doing your homework. Understand the market, understand the financing, be certain of what your real needs are, know house prices not simply from the assurances of a real estate agent, but from true knowledge of the market's prices. Study the house you're bidding on and place a limit on what you'll pay for it. Be certain the price is a reasonable bargain. Do all you can not to fall in love with a property, and above all, take your time in finalizing the contract. The only cure for buyers' remorse is to go back and determine again if the property meets the needs it was intended to fulfill, and if the value is still there.

22

The Closing

THE *CLOSING* IS WHERE AND WHEN THE SALE IS CONSUMMATED. THERE IS NO deal until the deal is closed *and funded*. Closing is when you and the seller sign all of the papers; funding is when the money is disbursed by the *escrow agent*, a disinterested third party who handles the closing for the buyer, seller, and lender. Only when the seller has his money, and you have the keys to the house, is there a purchase.

The closing can be done anywhere and at any time. An escrow agent does not have to do the closing. If you pay a seller cash for a property, or if you just assume his loan and give him some equity, you can simply hand him the money and he hands you a warranty deed and the keys to the property. Most situations will invariably be handled by an escrow agent, however. You'll not see an escrow agent if you simply assume someone's loan, pay him no money down because he's desperate to give his house away, and you don't want to spend the money it takes for a regular closing. In that case, you can check title by running a simple title search. You look at the seller's note and mortgage or deed of trust to see that the loan is assumable, and just take over where he left off.

PREPARING FOR THE CLOSING

Getting things ready for the closing means making sure all final papers reflect the seller's and the buyer's full agreement as stated in the contract. It also means making sure the lender's charges are in accordance with what was offered at loan application. You won't know that everything is as you understood the contract to say unless you read and *understand* the closing documents.

In order to be prepared, at least a day before the closing go to the escrow agent's office and review the documents. This chapter, and chapter 19 contain completed examples of the documents in a typical closing:

- **HUD Settlement Statement** (see Fig. 19-1). Study the back page first. The left column shows your expenses. The total of these expenses is taken forward to the left column of the front page. There, along with other charges and credits, is the balance due from the buyer. The right columns are the seller's.

- **Note** (see Fig. 19-2). This instrument is of prime importance to the lender, which can be a mortgage company or the seller.

- **Deed of Trust** (see Fig. 19-3). This is usually called a mortgage. It's used in states that don't use mortgages. If your state doesn't use a deed of trust, then you'll have a mortgage. Sometimes the Deed of Trust repeats the contents of the note and includes information pertinent to foreclosure.

- **Warranty Deed** (see Fig. 22-1). This transfers title from the seller to you. Make sure all names are spelled correctly. The seller is the only one that signs this instrument.

- **Deed of Trust to Secure Assumption** (see Fig. 19-4). When you take over someone's loan in an assumption situation this form is used to give the seller the right to foreclose on the buyer and keep the original loan in case the buyer defaults on his payments.

- **Contract for Deed** (see Fig. 22-2). When this is used, you probably won't see any of the other forms, except perhaps the closing statement. When there's a contract for deed, there's no title transfer, and quite often the closing is not done through an escrow agent but directly between buyer and seller.

- **Wraparound.** If you buy on a wraparound, it's not likely that there will be any preprinted forms used. An attorney or someone knowledgeable in this type of sale will prepare the papers. As with the examples shown here, there should be: 1. A closing statement; 2. A note; 3. A mortgage or deed of trust, and; 4. A warranty deed.

WARRANTY DEED
(LONG FORM)

THE STATE OF   Texas

COUNTY OF   Dallas

} KNOW ALL MEN BY THESE PRESENTS:

That Jack B. Nimble and wife, Sandy W. Nimble

(hereinafter called Grantor(s),

of the County of   Dallas   and State of   Texas   for and in

consideration of the sum of   ten and 00/100 ($10.00)----------------------- DOLLARS

and other valuable consideration to the undersigned paid by the grantee s   herein named, the receipt of which

is hereby acknowledged, and for the further consideration that the Grantee(s) hereby assume(s) and promise(s) to pay,

according to the terms thereof, all principal and interest now remaining unpaid on that one certain promissory note in the

original principal sum of $90,000.00   payable to the order of   Olive Oil's
Investment Company

and secured by a vendor's lien

retained in Deed of even date therewith recorded in Volume   388-456   Page(s)   197

of the Deed Records of the hereinbelow stated County, Texas, and additionally secured by a Deed of Trust of even date therewith

to   John Smith   Trustee, recorded in

Volume   397-455   Page(s)   216   of the Deed of Trust Records of said County, Tex, and

Grantee(s) assume(s) and promise(s) to keep and perform all of the covenants and obligations of the Grantor(s) named in

said Deed of Trust;

have GRANTED, SOLD AND CONVEYED, and by these presents do GRANT, SELL AND CONVEY unto

Lady N. Shoe, a single woman

of the County of   Dallas   and State of   Texas   , all of

the following described real property in   Dallas   County, Tex, to-wit:

All that certain lot, tract or parcel of land, described as follows: Being Lot 5, Block 9 of Forest
Park, an Addition to the City of Dallas, Texas, according to the Map
thereof recorded in Volume 188, Page 2179, Map Records of Dallas
County, Texas.

Fig. 22-1.

TO HAVE AND TO HOLD the above described premises, together with all and singular the rights and appurtenances thereto in anywise belonging, unto the said grantee   her   heirs and assigns forever; and we   do hereby bind   ourselves, our   heirs, executors and administrators to WARRANT AND FOREVER DEFEND all and singular the said premises unto the said grantee   her

heirs and assigns, against every person whomsoever lawfully claiming or to claim the same or any part thereof.

BUT IT IS EXPRESSLY AGREED that the Grantor(s) herein expressly reserve for themselves, their heirs and assigns, the Vendor's Lien as well as the Superior Title in and to the above described property, premises and improvements, until the note and indebtedness herein assumed by the Grantee(s) has been fully paid according to the face, tenor, effect and reading thereof, when this Deed shall become absolute, and to additionally secure the Grantor(s) herein in the payment of the note and indebtedness so assumed, the Grantee(s) ha executed and delivered a Deed of Trust to Secure Assumption of even date herewith conveying the herein described property.

EXECUTED this   12th   day of   November   , A. D. 19 87

———————————————————
Jack B. Nimble

———————————————————
Sandy W. Nimble

(Acknowledgment)

STATE OF TEXAS
COUNTY OF DALLAS

This instrument was acknowledged before me on the 12th day of   November   , 19 87
by Jack B. Nimble and wife Sandy W. Nimble

My commission expires: 4/30/91

———————————————————
Jack S. Doe, Notary Public

Fig. 22-1. Cont.

WARRANTY DEED
(LONG FORM)

THE STATE OF

COUNTY OF

} KNOW ALL MEN BY THESE PRESENTS:

That

(hereinafter called Grantor(s),

of the County of   and State of   for and in

consideration of the sum of   DOLLARS

and other valuable consideration to the undersigned paid by the grantee s   herein named, the receipt of which

is hereby acknowledged, and for the further consideration that the Grantee(s) hereby assume(s) and promise(s) to pay,

according to the terms thereof, all principal and interest now remaining unpaid on that one certain promissory note in the

original principal sum of   payable to the order of

and secured by a vendor's lien

retained in Deed of even date therewith recorded in Volume   Page(s)

of the Deed Records of the hereinbelow stated County,   , and additionally secured by a Deed of Trust of even date therewith

to   Trustee, recorded in

Volume   Page(s)   of the Deed of Trust Records of said County,   , and

Grantee(s) assume(s) and promise(s) to keep and perform all of the covenants and obligations of the Grantor(s) named in

said Deed of Trust;

have GRANTED, SOLD AND CONVEYED, and by these presents do GRANT, SELL AND CONVEY unto

of the County of   and State of   , all of

the following described real property in   County,   , to-wit:

All that certain lot, tract or parcel of land, described as follows:

Fig. 22-1. Cont.

TO HAVE AND TO HOLD the above described premises, together with all and singular the rights and appurtenances thereto in anywise belonging, unto the said grantee   heirs and assigns forever; and   do hereby bind   heirs, executors and administrators to WARRANT AND FOREVER DEFEND all and singular the said premises unto the said grantee heirs and assigns, against every person whomsoever lawfully claiming or to claim the same or any part thereof.

BUT IT IS EXPRESSLY AGREED that the Grantor(s) herein expressly reserve for themselves, their heirs and assigns, the Vendor's Lien as well as the Superior Title in and to the above described property, premises and improvements, until the note and indebtedness herein assumed by the Grantee(s) has been fully paid according to the face, tenor, effect and reading thereof, when this Deed shall become absolute, and to additionally secure the Grantor(s) herein in the payment of the note and indebtedness so assumed, the Grantee(s) ha   executed and delivered a Deed of Trust to Secure Assumption of even date herewith conveying the herein described property.

EXECUTED this   day of   , A. D. 19

_____

_____

(Acknowledgment)

STATE OF
COUNTY OF

This instrument was acknowledged before me on the   day of   , 19
by

My commission expires:

_____

Fig. 22-1. Cont.

Contract For Sale of Real Estate

1. PARTIES. This agreement, made and entered into by and between
_____, hereinafter referred to
as Seller, and _____, hereinafter referred to as Purchaser (whether singular or plural).

2. AGREEMENT. Seller agrees to sell and Purchaser agrees to buy under
the terms and conditions and for the consideration hereinafter set forth, the
following described real property situated in _____
County, _____, to wit:
_____, and more commonly
described as: _____, subject to
all easements, restrictions and mineral interests reserved of record, for a
total consideration of _____ dollars ($_____), payable as follows:
_____ cash down payment, the receipt of which is hereby acknowledged by Seller, and the balance of the purchase price to be paid in
monthly installments of $_____ each, including principal and interest at
the rate of _____ per cent per annum on the unpaid balance, plus a sum
equal to one-twelfth (1/12) of the estimated annual taxes, fire insurance premiums and extended coverage, which funds are to be held in escrow by
Seller and applied to the payment of such taxes and insurance as they
become due and payable. Said beginning reserve amount shall be
$_____. The total payment for principal, interest, taxes and insurance
at the beginning of this contract is $_____. The first such monthly
installment shall be due and payable on _____. A like
installment shall be due and payable on the first day of each succeeding
month thereafter until _____ when the entire purchase
price above stipulated, together with all accrued interest threon has been
fully and finally paid. Each installment when paid to be applied first to interest accrued to date, and the balance of the payment if any shall be applied
to the principal. In the event that the taxes or insurance premiums on the
property are increased from time to time, Purchaser shall increase his
monthly deposits by a sum sufficient to compensate for such increase, and
should the annual taxes or fire and extended coverage insurance premiums
exceed the amount on deposit in the escrow fund at such time as these
amounts are due and payable, Purchaser shall forthwith make good the
deficiency by paying to Seller the amount thereof. Purchaser agrees to
maintain the fire and extended coverage insurance policy and appropriate
extensions thereof to provide the Seller the protection provided by the existing policy.

3. DESTRUCTION OF IMPROVEMENTS. Should the improvements be
wholly or partially destroyed by fire, storm or other occurrence insured
against, Purchaser shall give prompt notice of such damage to Seller and to
the insurance carrier. Seller may make claim for loss if not promptly made by
Purchaser. Seller is hereby authorized to collect all monies due under such
policies of insurance, and to apply same to the restoration of said improvements if economically feasible, or to apply same to reduction of the above

Fig. 22-2.

described indebtedness whether then matured or not, deducting there from any expenses incurred in handling or collecting said sums. Purchaser may rebuild or repair the property only with insurer's permission and with Seller's prior approval of such repairs, and with Seller's prior approval of the building contractor who will perform same. If this Contract is cancelled as hereinafter set forth, all right, title and interest of the Purchaser shall pass to Seller in and to any insurance policies and the proceeds thereof resulting from damage to the property.

4. DEED. Seller agrees that upon punctual payment by the Purchaser of the total purchase price as herein above set forth in the manner herein above set forth, to execute and deliver a General Warranty Deed to the above described property. Said Deed shall be expressly made and accepted subject to the easements, rights of way, covenants, restrictions and mineral or royalty reservations or exceptions of record in _____ County, _____, affecting the above described property.

5. DEFAULT BY PURCHASER. Should Purchaser default in the payment of any monthly installment when due, or should he default in performance of any other agreement herein contained, or should he fail to keep the improvements in good repair, reasonable wear and tear excepted, Seller may cancel this contract and apply all payments made by Purchaser as liquidated damages, and as and for the agreed rental charge for the use and occupance of the above described property, it being expressly stipulated and agreed between the parties that the monthly payments herein provided are the reasonable rental value for the use of said property; and thereupon this contract shall become null and void, and of no further force and effect, and the parties hereto shall thereupon be fully and finally released herefrom. In the event of cancellation of this contract, Purchaser shall thereafter be a tenant of the premises. No failure of Seller to exercise such option at the time of any default shall be held to constitute a waiver of any rights hereunder, it being understood that written notice from Seller addressed to Purchaser at

_____

and deposited in the United States Mail shall be sufficient notice of the exercise by Seller of any option herein provided for.

6. PERSONAL PROPERTY. In the event personal property is abandoned in the above described premises after the termination of this agreement, Seller or his representative may enter the premises and remove all property of every kind found therein.

7. TRANSFER OF CONTRACT. If Purchaser transfers or assigns this Contract of Sale without the prior written consent of Seller, Seller shall have the option to declare all sums due hereunder to be immediately due and payable without further notice or demand.

8. PREPAYMENT. Purchaser may prepay the principal of this Contract at any time.

Fig. 22-2. Cont.

9. ATTORNEY'S FEES. If the holder of the indebtedness herein provided for shall at any time be required to place same in the hands of an attorney for enforcement or collection, or if the Seller shall otherwise be required to employ an attorney in connection with the enforcement of this contract, then the Purchaser agrees to pay to Seller the reasonable attorney's fees thereby incurred.

10. SUBORDINATION. Purchaser hereby specifically acknowledges, consents and agrees to the creation by Seller of any loan which Seller deems advisable, covering the above described property, to be secured in its payment by a mortgage, and in this connection Purchaser hereby subordinates the above described property to said indebtedness and the liens securing same, as well as any and all renewals and extensions thereof. Seller agrees that the sum of all liens shall not be for more than the balance of the amount due from Purchaser on this Contract.

11. CONVEYANCE TO PURCHASER. At any time prior to payment by Purchaser of the full purchase price, Seller, at his option, may execute a conveyance in the form of a Warranty Deed to Purchaser, reserving a Vendor's lien for the unpaid portion of the purchase price, payable as herein set forth, and Purchaser will, upon request, execute a Note and Deed of Trust evidencing such unpaid purchase price, such note to bear interest and be payable in the same monthly installments, and with the same prepayment provisions as provided herein. If Purchaser refuses to execute such Note and Deed of Trust, Seller may declare all unpaid balance of the purchase price immediately due and payable, and if such balance is not promptly paid upon demand, Seller shall have the same remedies herein provided for other default.

12. LATE PAYMENTS. At any time if the Seller has not received the full amount of the required monthly installment for principal, interest, taxes and insurance by the end of 7 calendar days after the date it is due, purchaser will pay a late charge to the Seller in the amount of 5% of the due monthly payment for principal, interest, taxes and insurance. Purchaser shall pay for this late charge only once on any late payment.

Witness our hands this _____ day of

_____, 19 _____.

_____
Purchaser

_____
Purchaser

_____
Seller

_____
Seller

Fig. 22-2. Cont.

REPRESENTATION AT THE CLOSING

In some states, it's common practice for buyer and seller to have their respective attorneys present at the closing. In other areas, the attorneys simply review the documents before the closing, but don't actually attend the closing. Check with a title or escrow company to see what the norm is in your state.

In your area, attorneys might rarely be involved. For simple transactions, there's no need for an attorney. If you understand the paperwork, which you should, then why pay someone to explain it to you? If the purchase is complicated by a wraparound or contract for deed that's been drawn by the seller's attorney, then the cost of an attorney might be cheap insurance. In this case, have him review the documents.

SELLER'S REVIEW OF THE DOCUMENTS

You'll avoid any problems at the closing if the seller reviews the documents and/or has his lawyer look at them. In fact, if you and the seller can look at the documents a day or two prior to close date, then you'll have a smooth closing. What you or the seller don't want on the final day is surprises. If any come, have them come up soon enough to work them out smoothly, without pressure on either party.

You certainly don't want to have all of your furniture, and have the seller's furniture, in a moving van on the day of closing only to find out there are additional settlement charges that neither you nor the seller agree on, or wording in the loan papers you aren't happy with. Be safe and look ahead.

THE CLOSING

Rarely do the buyer and seller close at the same time. One goes first, then the other. A good closer will go over the papers carefully with each party. It goes without saying that if both parties have studied the papers beforehand, then it's just a matter of signing on the dotted lines, getting the keys, and moving.

TAKING POSSESSION

The custom of possession differs in each state. In some areas, the seller hands the buyer the house keys at the closing, and the buyer has immediate possession. In other places, the seller gets anywhere from a day to a week to move out and hand possession to the buyer. Even if the custom is to give immediate possession, the seller might ask you to give him a week, a month, even a year to move on. Anything longer than a week should involve a written lease agreement, where the seller pays you rent, and there are provisions for the maintenance and repairs to the property at the time the seller finally moves out.

TAKING DUMPED PROPERTY

If you're merely taking someone's home where he's just dumping it in an effort to save his credit (in other words, he can't make his payments anymore, he can't sell the house, and giving you the house is better than just losing it in foreclosure), then neither you nor the seller need the expense of a title or escrow company, title insurance, or even a lawyer. The most important piece of advice I can give you here is that you take title to the property *subject to the loan. Do not* assume the loan. This means that you'll take title to the property and keep making the payments on the loan. The loan stays in the seller's name, which doesn't affect you since you have title and when the loan is finally paid in full there will be a release of the lien. With this method, if you have economic setbacks, or find that there were problems with title or additional liens on the property, then you simply quit making payments and walk away from the house. The seller's credit might be affected but yours won't be, because you didn't sign any papers with the seller or the lender guaranteeing payment of the note.

You should be able to have an abstract company or record company search the county records and, for less than $100, get a title search that will show all liens on the property, and who has legal title. If title is vested in the seller, and there are no liens other than those the seller has indicated he has, then make a copy of the blank warranty deed in Fig. 22-1 and fill it out like the completed sample I've included immediately before it.

Have the seller sign the deed in front of a notary and have it notarized. You can then take it to the county courthouse and file it at the County Clerk or County Recorder's office. There is a small filing fee, but there may be transfer stamps or transfer taxes to pay. In some states, transfer of property runs less than $15, depending on the length of the deed. In others, it can be a few thousand dollars.

23

The Tax Implications of Buying a Home

IF YOU'VE JUST SOLD YOUR PREVIOUS HOME, OR ARE ABOUT TO SELL IT, YOU'LL have to deal with the tax implications of a profit or loss on your income tax return, unless, of course, you've sold without a gain or loss. If this is your first time to purchase, then the information that follows on income taxes will be useful some time in the future.

This chapter just highlights the tax laws. For very detailed information on the tax implications of home selling, call your nearest IRS office and ask for advice. You can request that one or all of the following publications be sent to you, or you can pick them up free of charge at the local IRS office:

- Moving Expenses (#521)
- Basis of Assets (#551)
- Installment Sales (#537)
- Tax Information for Owners of Homes, Condominiums, and Cooperative Apartments (#530)
- Tax Information on Selling Your Home (#523)
- Tax Information for Homeowners Associations (#558)

Tax laws and rules change often, so update this information when you're about to make a decision that will affect your tax liabilities.

Two of the most frequently asked questions refer to the gain or loss on the sale of a home, and the exclusion of gain at age 55 or older.

GAIN OR LOSS ON THE SALE OF A HOME

If you sell or exchange your personal home at a profit, you're allowed to postpone paying the tax on all of the gain if, within two years before or two years after its sale, you buy and live in another home that costs *at least* as much as the adjusted sales price of the old home.

Being able to hold off on the profit is quite useful, but if you sell or exchange your personal home at a loss, you're not able to deduct the loss on your federal tax return. Most sellers make money on the sale of their home, but here the bad news is for those few who end up losing money.

EXCLUSION OF GAIN AT AGE 55

You might exclude from the gross income you declare an amount up to $125,000 of the gain on the sale or exchange of your principal home if you are aged 55 years or older on the date of the sale of the house.

You must have lived in your principal home for at least three years out of the five-year period ending on the date of the sale of the house. You or your spouse must never have excluded gain on the sale or exchange of a home after July 26, 1978.

This election can only be made once in a lifetime by either spouse. If your spouse has claimed it before your marriage, then neither one of you can claim that exemption again as long as you're married. As long as one takes it, or has taken it, then both are considered to have taken it.

TREATMENT OF GAIN

The tax on some or all of the gain, or profit, from the sale of your principal residence can be postponed. If you buy another home, and the purchase price of the new home is at least as much as the adjusted sales price of the old home, you might be able to postpone the tax on all the gain from the sale. If you don't buy another home, or if the purchase price of that new home is less than the adjusted sales price of the old home, you'll be subject to tax on some or all of the gain, unless you qualify to exclude the gain.

If you are on active duty in the armed forces, or if your tax home is outside the United States, the two-year period might be suspended.

PURCHASE PRICE LESS THAN SALES PRICE

If the purchase price of your new home is less than the adjusted sales price of your old home, and you buy and live in the new home within the time period given above, the gain taxed in the year of the sale is the lesser of the following:

1. The gain on the sale of the old home; or
2. The amount by which the adjusted sales price of the old home is more than the purchase price of the new home.

POSTPONING THE GAIN

You *must* postpone the gain if you replace your old home within the required period. If you have more than one home, you postpone the gain only on the sale of your *principal* home.

The tax on the gain is postponed, not forgiven, except for amounts that are excluded under the aged 55 and older rule. You subtract any gain that's not taxed in the year you sell your old home from the cost of your new home. This will give you a lower basis in the new home. If you sell the new home in a later year and again replace it, you can continue to postpone any tax on your gain.

Here's an example. Assume you sold your home in 1988 and had a $10,000 gain. Within 2 years, you bought another home for $90,000, which is more than you received for the old one. The $10,000 gain won't be taxed in 1988 (the year of sale), but you have to subtract it from the $90,000. This makes the basis of your new home $80,000. If you later sell the new home for $120,000, and don't buy and live in a replacement home within the required time, you're subject to tax on the $40,000 gain ($120,000 − $80,000) in the sale year.

SEPARATE FUNDS TO PURCHASE THE NEW HOME

You don't have to use the same funds received from the sale of your old home to buy or build the new home. Consequently, you can use less cash and increase the amount of your mortgage loan.

LOSS ON SALE

You might not deduct a loss on the sale or exchange of your home. The loss has no effect on the basis of your new home.

EMPLOYER REIMBURSEMENTS

Any reimbursements from your employer covering the losses on the sale or exchange of your home or for expenses on the sale or exchange if your employer transfers you, have to be included in your income. You can't include the payment as part of the selling price. Reimbursements are considered gross income as compensation for services.

ESTIMATED TAX PAYMENTS

If you have a gain from the sale of your home and don't plan to replace it, or don't meet the requirements for postponing the gain, then you might have to make estimated tax payments to cover the gain.

BASIS

Basis is a way of measuring your investment in property for tax purposes. It doesn't matter that you bought your home, hired a contractor to build it, you built it yourself, or received it in another way, it's important that you know its basis. The basis of property you buy is usually the cost or purchase price. But you must know its adjusted basis to figure gain or loss when you sell or otherwise dispose of it. You also have to know the adjusted basis at the time of a casualty to determine your deductible loss from the casualty.

If you change your home to rental or business use, your depreciation is based on the lesser of fair market value, or its adjusted basis at the time of the change.

PURCHASE

The original basis of a home you bought is the purchase price or cost of the property to you. This includes down payment and total loans such as a first or second lien—whether third party financed or seller financed. Certain settlement or closing costs are added or deducted from your basis. I'll cover that later.

NEW CONSTRUCTION

If you have the house built on land that you own, your original basis is your basis of the land plus the amount it cost you to complete the house. This includes the cost of labor and materials, or the amounts paid the general contractor (or all subcontractors if you did the contracting), any architect's fees, and charges for building permits, utility meters and connections, legal fees directly connected with building the home. If you built all or part of your house yourself, its original basis is the total amount it cost you to complete it. You can't include the value of your own labor or any other labor you didn't have to pay for. Only cash paid for materials and labor can be included.

GIFT

If someone gives you the home, its original basis to you is whatever the donor's adjusted basis was when the gift was made. If the donor's adjusted basis was more than the fair market value of the home at the time it's given to you, however, you have to use the fair market value as your basis for measuring any possible loss if you later sell or exchange the home. You can still use the donor's adjusted basis to measure any gain.

If the fair market value was more than the donor's basis at the time of the gift, your basis is the donor's adjusted basis at the time you received the gift. You can increase your basis by any federal gift tax paid on the gift for gifts made before 1977. However, this increase can never raise the basis to more than the fair market value of the home when it was given to you.

If you received a gift after 1976, your basis is the donor's adjusted basis increased by the part of the gift tax paid that's due to the net increase in value of the gift. This part is figured by multiplying the gift tax paid on the gift by a fraction where the numerator (top part) of the fraction is the net increase in value of the gift and the denominator is the amount of the gift. The net increase in value of the gift is the fair market value of the gift less the donor's adjusted basis. This is probably confusing even to the IRS. So if you're dealing with a large gift, professional advice can be cheap insurance.

INHERITANCE

If you inherited your home, the original basis of the home is its fair market value at the date of the decedent's death or the later alternate valuation date if that date was used for federal estate tax purposes. If an estate tax return was filed, the value listed there for the property is generally your basis. If no return was filed, use the best available objective evidence of fair market value. That means a professional appraisal or a valuation from someone expert enough to give you accurate current value.

TRADE

If you acquired your home in a trade for other property, the original basis of your home is the adjusted basis of the property you traded in, plus any gain or cash difference you paid, minus any loss or cash difference you received.

ADJUSTED BASIS

This is the original basis increased or reduced by certain amounts. You must increase your basis by the cost of improvements, additions, and other capital items. You can also add assessments, such as those for streets and sidewalks, to your basis. You must reduce the basis by any deductible losses from fire or other casualty payments you receive for any easements or rights-of-way you give up and any depreciation you claimed. You'd reduce the basis if you sold part of the land the house sat on.

If you claimed any residential energy credit before 1986 and the items for which you took the credit increased the basis of your home, you must reduce the amount of that increase by the credit you took on those items.

POINTS AND CLOSING COSTS

Points, fire insurance premiums, mortgage insurance premiums, or charges for services concerning occupancy of the house can't be added to the basis.

IMPROVEMENTS

Improvements increase the value of the home. They prolong its useful life or adapt it to new uses. Cost of improvements, which is added to the basis of your property, should not be confused with repairs, which you don't add to the basis. Repairs simply maintain a home in good condition. They don't add to the value or prolong its life.

Here are some examples of improvements: finishing the basement into a den, adding a bathroom or bedroom, putting up a fence, putting in new plumbing or wiring, installing a new roof, paving the driveway. On the other hand, repainting your house inside or outside, fixing gutters or floors, mending leaks or plastering, and replacing broken windows are examples of repairs. However, if items that would otherwise be considered repairs are done as part of an extensive remodeling or restoration of your home, the whole job is considered an improvement.

PURCHASE CREDIT

The tax credit on the purchase of a new home acquired and occupied after March 12, 1975, and before January 1, 1977, has no effect on its basis.

ENERGY CREDIT

You must reduce the basis of your home by the amount of the residential energy credit allowed for energy saving and renewable energy source items you installed before 1986. You should add the cost of the items to the basis of your home.

RECORDKEEPING

Save all receipts and expense records for all improvements, additions, and other items that affect the home's basis. Keep them at least three years after the year you sell or otherwise dispose of the home.

PRINCIPAL HOME

Usually, the home in which you live is your principal home (residence). The home that you sell and the one you buy to replace it must both qualify as your principal home.

HOUSEBOATS, MOBILE HOMES, AND CO-OPS

A houseboat or mobile home might be your principal home. Likewise, if you own a co-op, it can also be considered your principal home. Your basis in the apartment is the cost of your stock in the co-op housing corporation, which might include your share of a mortgage on the entire building.

CONDOMINIUMS

A condominium, just like a co-op, can be your principal home. Your basis is your cost, which might also include your share of the mortgage on the common parts of the development—land, pools, tennis courts—or the structure.

FURNITURE

Furniture, appliances, and other such items that are not fixtures permanently attached to the property are not part of your principal home. They're not considered real estate, but simply personal property. Appliances that are built-in are part of the home, however. These include dishwashers, central vacuum systems, ranges, etc.

LAND

If you sell the land on which your principal home is located, but not the house itself, as in the case of a mobile home lot, you might not postpone any gain you have from the sale of the land. If within the replacement period you buy another piece of land and move your house to it, then the sale of the land is not considered to be a sale of your principal home and you can't postpone any gain on the sale.

MORE THAN ONE HOME

If you have more than one home, you can only postpone the tax on the sale of the principal home. If you own and live in a house in town and also own beach property, which you use in the summer months, the town property is your principal home; the beach property is not.

If you have two homes and live in both of them, your principal home is the one you live in most of the time.

If you own a house, but live in another house for which you pay rent, the rented home is considered your principal home. You might temporarily rent out your principal home, however, before its sale without changing its character as your principal home.

OLD HOME

Your gain is the selling price minus the adjusted basis of the home. The selling price is the total amount received, including money, notes, mortgages, or other debts, and the fair market value of other property received.

AMOUNT REALIZED AND SELLING EXPENSES

The amount realized is the selling price minus selling expenses, which includes commissions, advertising, legal fees, and loan charges you've paid, such as loan placement fees or discount points. If your move is job related, some of the expenses of selling a home might be deducted as moving expenses.

TRADING HOMES

If you trade your old home for another home, the trade is treated as a sale and a purchase.

PROPERTY PARTLY USED AS YOUR HOME

You might use your property partly as your home and partly for business, such as a working farm on which your house is located, an apartment building in which you live in one unit and rent out the others, or a store building with an upstairs apartment in which you live. If you sell the entire property, you postpone only the tax on the part used as your home. This includes the land and outbuildings, such as a garage for the home, but not those for the business or the production of income. The sale should be treated as the sale of two properties: your home and the business property.

BUSINESS USE OF YOUR HOME

If, in the year of sale, you deduct expenses for the business use of your home, you cannot postpone the tax on the gain, on the part of the home used for business. In figuring the amount of gain you can postpone, make an allocation for the business-use portion of the home.

HOME CHANGED TO RENTAL PROPERTY

You cannot postpone tax on the gain on rental property even though it was once your principal home. Once you change its use, you have investment property.

TEMPORARY RENTAL OF PRINCIPAL HOME

It's different if you temporarily rent out your principal home before selling it, or your new principal home before moving into it and living in it. If it's only a matter of convenience, or for some other nonbusiness purpose, the gain on the sale of the property will qualify for treatment as the sale of a principal residence. Even if you place your home for rent, if it's not rented, it won't be considered business property.

CONDEMNATION

If your house is condemned for public use and you have a gain, you can either postpone paying tax on the gain, or you can choose to treat the transaction as an involuntary conversion. The replacement periods allowed under the two treatments might be different and you should compare the replacement periods under both:

If you treat the transaction as an involuntary conversion to postpone tax on the gain, you must buy within a specified period replacement property that costs at least as much as the net proceeds received from the involuntary conversion, or;

In a condemnation, or the threat or imminence of one, the replacement period begins on the date you disposed of the property or the date condemnation was threatened or was imminent, whichever is earlier. Generally, the replacement period ends two years after the close of the first tax year in which you realize any part of the gain on the conversion.

GAIN ON CASUALTY

The tax on a gain from fire, storm, or other casualty cannot be postponed.

OPTIONS

If you grant a potential buyer an option to buy your home, add the amount you receive for the option to the sale price of your home if the option is exercised. If the option is not exercised, then you simply report any money you received for the option as ordinary income for the year the option expires.

PROPERTY TAXES

You can deduct property taxes in the year of sale based on the number of days in the year that you owned the property. It doesn't matter what part of those taxes you actually paid. If the buyer paid delinquent taxes that you owed as part of the contract price of your home, the payment increases the amount you realized on the sale.

TRANSFER TAXES

You cannot deduct transfer taxes, stamp taxes, and other incidental taxes and charges on the sale of a home as itemized deductions on your income tax return. If you pay these amounts as the seller, they reduce the amount you realize on the sale. If you pay these amounts as the buyer, they are included in your cost basis of the property. If you deduct them as moving expenses, then you can't use the amount deducted to reduce the amount realized on the sale of the home or to increase the cost basis of the new home.

HOW INTEREST AND PROPERTY TAX DEDUCTIONS WORK

When you file your income tax return each year, you are allowed to reduce the amount of income you've made in your regular job or your business, by the amounts you've paid for interest on loans, as well as property taxes, on your principal residence and another residence, such as a beach house, a mountain house, or a house in the country, that you use as a secondary residence. It's a very unfair situation for tenants who pay rent and don't pay property taxes or home mortgage interest. But who said life was fair?

If you made $50,000 last year, and paid $7,000 in home mortgage interest, and another $1,000 for home property taxes, then your real income to report to the IRS is:

$50,000	Real income
− 7,000	Mortgage interest
− 1,000	Property taxes
$42,000	True income in the eyes of the IRS

Naturally, you don't do your reporting this way. Your tax forms will have blanks to fill in so you get credit for the mortgage interest and property taxes. This little provision of the tax code is what makes home ownership under the present laws so desirable. If you're in the 28 percent tax bracket, a $9,000 reduction in reportable income is a tax savings of $2,520. If you divide that by 12 months, your monthly savings is $210.

If you were previously paying rent of $750, and you purchase a house with a PITI payment of $750, and you're saving $210 on your income taxes every month, then it's like paying only $540 in rent. Plus, you get to keep the house after you're done paying for it.

This is a little oversimplification, because there are some breaks tenants get that you won't get, all depending on income, mortgage interest, and property tax payments. But the saving is real and there's nothing wrong with lawmakers encouraging home ownership with laws that give tax breaks to homeowners.

CO-OP AND CONDO TAX BREAKS

As a co-op or condo owner, you're treated the same way as a single family home-owner. You might hold a different type of ownership to your property than the folks who own single family detached homes, but nevertheless, you are a home-owner and are able to deduct interest and property tax payments from your income taxes.

Because you might pay these costs indirectly, you'll have to figure out what part of your payment goes to interest and taxes. This is especially true in the case of a co-op.

PROPERTY TAXES

All individual personal property real estate is taxed in one form or another by any, or all, taxing authorities such as the following:

- Counties or parishes
- Cities
- School districts
- Hospital districts
- Water districts
- College districts
- Certain utilities

Oftentimes, taxing authorities are grouped together for tax simplification. You might have a bill from the county that includes not only the county taxes, but those for the hospital and college districts as well.

EXEMPTIONS TO PROPERTY TAXES

Each state has laws that give certain groups of people exemptions on some of their property taxes, such as homestead exemptions for example. They give homeowners—as opposed to investors—an exemption on a certain percentage of the taxes due on their property. There are exemptions for older homeowners and other individuals who need some relief in their property taxes.

If you've never owned a home before, call your taxing authorities to get an idea of what exemptions you might be entitled to. While you're on the phone, ask how property is assessed, and what the tax rate is in your locality so you can figure out what taxes will run in your price range. With that information, you can not only figure principal and interest payments on a loan, but taxes as well. Once you know taxes plus principal and interest, all you'll need to figure PITI on a loan is a figure for homeowners insurance, which you can get from your insurance agent.

Appendix Table A

Mortgage Payment Table A
Payment factors for each $1,000 of a loan

Term of Loan in Years

Rate	5	10	15	20	25	30
5.0%	18.8712	10.6066	7.9079	6.5996	5.8459	5.3682
5.5%	19.1012	10.8526	8.1708	6.8789	6.1409	5.6779
6.0%	19.3328	11.1021	8.4386	7.1643	6.4430	5.9955
6.5%	19.5661	11.3548	8.7111	7.4557	6.7521	6.3207
7.0%	19.8012	11.6108	8.9883	7.7530	7.0678	6.6530
7.5%	20.0378	11.8702	9.2701	8.0559	7.3899	6.9921
8.0%	10.2764	12.1328	9.5565	8.3640	7.7182	7.3376
8.5%	20.5165	12.9386	9.8474	8.6782	8.0523	7.6891
9.0%	20.7584	12.6676	10.1427	8.9973	8.3920	8.0462
9.5%	21.0019	12.9398	10.4422	9.3213	8.7370	8.4085
10.0%	21.2470	13.2151	10.7461	9.6502	9.0870	8.7751
10.5%	21.4939	13.4935	11.0540	9.9838	9.4418	9.1474
11.0%	21.7424	13.7750	11.3660	10.3219	9.8011	9.5232
11.5%	21.9926	14.0595	11.6819	10.6643	10.1647	9.9029
12.0%	22.2444	14.3471	12.0017	11.0109	10.5322	10.2861
12.5%	22.4979	14.6378	12.3252	11.3614	10.9035	10.6726
13.0%	22.7531	14.9311	12.6524	11.7158	11.2784	11.0620
13.5%	23.0098	15.2274	12.9832	12.0737	11.6564	11.4541
14.0%	23.2683	15.5266	13.3174	12.4352	12.0376	11.8487
14.5%	23.5283	15.8287	13.6550	12.8000	12.4216	12.2456
15.0%	23.7899	15.1335	13.9959	13.1679	12.8083	12.6444
15.5%	24.0532	16.4411	14.3399	13.5388	13.1975	13.0452
16.0%	24.3181	16.7513	14.6870	13.9126	13.5889	13.4476
16.5%	24.5845	17.0642	15.0371	14.2890	13.9824	13.8515
17.0%	24.8526	17.3798	15.3900	14.6680	14.3780	14.2568
17.5%	25.1222	17.6979	15.7458	15.0494	14.7753	14.6633
18.0%	25.3934	18.0185	16.1042	15.4331	15.1743	15.0709
18.5%	25.6662	18.3417	16.4652	15.8190	15.5748	15.4794
19.0%	25.9406	18.6672	16.8288	16.2068	15.9768	15.8889
19.5%	26.2164	18.9952	17.1947	16.5966	16.3801	16.2992
20.0%	26.4939	19.3256	17.5632	16.9882	16.7845	16.7102
20.5%	26.7729	19.6582	17.9335	17.3815	17.1901	17.1218
21.0%	27.0534	19.9932	18.3061	17.7764	17.5966	17.5340
21.5%	27.3354	20.3303	18.6808	18.1728	18.0041	17.9467
22.0%	27.6189	20.6697	19.0576	18.5706	18.4124	18.3598
22.5%	27.9039	21.0112	19.4362	18.9697	18.8215	18.7734
23.0%	28.1905	21.3548	19.8166	19.3700	19.2313	19.1873
23.5%	28.4785	21.7004	20.1988	19.7715	19.6417	19.6015
24.0%	28.7680	22.0481	20.5827	20.1741	20.0527	20.0160
24.5%	29.0589	22.3977	20.9682	20.5777	20.4643	20.4308
25.0%	29.3513	22.7493	21.3553	20.9822	20.8763	20.8458
25.5%	29.6452	23.1027	21.7438	21.3876	21.2888	21.2610

Glossary

abstract of title A brief history of the previous ownership of property, including all liens or encumbrances and any claims against the property.

acceleration clause A term of a home mortgage loan that gives the lender the right to call all sums owed immediately due upon a certain event, such as the sale of the home.

acceptance Favorable approval of an offer or purchase contract by the seller. Acceptance of an offer means that both parties have signed a binding contract.

acre A measure of land area which equals 43,560 square feet. An acre lot is approximately $210' \times 210'$.

adjustable rate mortgage A method of calculating interest payments by home mortgage lenders that was established for federally chartered savings and loan companies. ARMs give lenders virtually unlimited power to vary a loan's interest rate from month to month to keep pace with current market rates.

agent An authorized representative acting in behalf of a client and usually working under the legal responsibility of a real estate broker.

amenities Natural or man-made attractions that increase the value of property such as trees, nearby parks, a beautiful view, a marble tub, a swimming pool, etc.

amortization The paying off of a loan, in installments, normally in equal monthly payments. The payments are made large enough to pay both interest and part of the principal, so the debt is gradually reduced and completely paid off at the end of the loan period.

appraisal   An estimate of the value of a property on a given date.

appreciation   An increase in the value of property caused by changes in economic conditions, improvements in the neighborhood, time, etc.

appurtenances   Property rights, privileges, or improvements. Although they are not strictly a part of the land, they go with the title to the new owner, such as easements, right of way, orchards, etc.

assessed value   A value placed on property for the sake of tax collection.

assessment   A government-imposed tax for a specific purpose such as a street improvement, a sewer, etc. The assessment is levied against those who benefit mostly from the improvement.

assumptions   Taking over payments of, and primary responsibility for, an existing loan under all of its terms, without the loan being renegotiated.

balloon payments   Payment of a loan in one lump sum after a predetermined period of time in which smaller, regular payments have been made.

bench mark   A permanently fixed marker in the ground, such as a metal marker, that surveyors use to establish property lines and elevation. Also called a monument.

binder   A short-term agreement by which the buyer and seller tentatively agree on the terms of a contract.

breach   The act of breaking a contract.

broker   A person licensed by the state who sells real estate for a commission. A broker is usually hired by the seller.

buy-down   A creative financing method to decrease the interest rate or reduce the payment for the first three to five years on a home mortgage loan.

buyer's market   A market in which the buyer has better negotiating leverage than the seller. As a rule, this occurs when there are more houses than there are buyers.

carrying charges   The money it costs to own property, including mortgage payments, insurance, taxes, and maintenance. This is equivalent to the rent one would pay for an apartment or house.

caveat emptor   Let the buyer beware. The buyer purchases real estate in an *"as is"* condition and must investigate and take the risks that go with any purchase. The seller cannot be held responsible for the quality of the property unless guaranteed in a warranty.

chattel mortgage   A mortgage on personal property.

chattels   Personal property.

close of escrow (closing)   Signing of final papers and exchange of funds for the sale of a home.

closing costs   The miscellaneous charges, over and above the cost of the house, paid by the buyer and the seller at closing when the deed to the property is transferred from the seller to the buyer.

collateral   Security such as bonds, jewelry, real estate, or other marketable items pledged for payment of a loan.

commitment   A promise made by a lender to make a specific loan to a specific person.

community property   Property acquired by a husband, a wife, or by both together that is considered to be jointly owned and equally shared. Community property laws are valid in only a few states.

condominium   A unit within a multiple-unit dwelling. The owner of the unit has full title to the unit and has joint ownership in the common grounds of the complex with the owners of the other units.

contingency   A point or condition of a contract that has not yet been accepted by both parties to the contract.

contract   A legal agreement between or among two or more parties that binds each to fulfill a specific promise or promises.

contract for deed (sale on contract)   A creative real estate transaction method that allows a buyer to purchase property without qualifying for a loan, and without receiving a deed to the property.

conventional loan   A mortgage which is not insured by the FHA nor guaranteed by the VA. The loan rates and conditions are set by the lender, subject to some controls by the government.

conveyance   The transfer of ownership of real estate by deed from one party to another.

counteroffer   An offer proposed in response to an original offer that was not completely satisfactory to the original party making the counteroffer.

covenant   A promise or agreement between two parties usually applied to specific promises in a deed.

creative financing   An unconventional method of obtaining funds to purchase property.

credit unions   A cooperative association of members (employees) of a company formed to save money, make loans and share profits. A cooperative bank.

deed   A document which describes property and is used to transfer ownership of that property.

deed of trust   Used in some states in place of a mortgage. The buyer deeds the property to a third party (a trustee), who holds the deed in trust to guarantee that the buyer will repay the loan to the lender.

default   The failure to meet a promise on a contract, including not paying money when due, or not complying with other provisions of the contract.

deposit   A small down payment given by the buyer when the buyer makes an offer to purchase. The deposit can become the earnest money when the contract is signed, or the buyer might have to add money to the deposit to constitute the earnest money.

depreciation   The decrease in value of property caused by age, wear and tear, and changing neighborhood conditions, etc.

down payment   The money a buyer must pay in cash on a house before being granted a loan.

earnest money   A payment made as evidence of a serious buyer's intent to go through with the purchase of real estate, usually between 1 percent and 2 percent of the purchase price. It is given by the buyer on the signing of a contract for the sale of real estate. If the buyer defaults in carrying out the contract, the money might be forfeited to the seller.

easement   The right, privilege, or interest which one party has in the land of another owner.

eminent domain   The right of the government to take over part or all of a person's property for public use. This can be done with or without the owner's consent. The government must pay the owner the fair price for his property.

encroachment   A trespass or invasion over the property line of another person, such as a fence, a building overhang, etc.

equity   The interest or value an owner has in real estate over and above the remaining mortgages. The equity is the difference between the selling price of the house and the unpaid mortgage(s).

escalation clause   A clause written into some loan agreements that permits the lender to raise or lower the interest rate without the borrower's consent as business conditions change. The right of a lender to force the borrower to prepay the entire principal balance because of conditions in the note and mortgage or deed of trust.

escrow   A third, neutral party that holds and processes documents, initiates necessary paperwork, collects money due, pays out money due, etc. Also, the amount a lender collects from the owner and uses to pay taxes and insurance on the owner's property.

et al   Legal doubletalk for ''and others.''

et ux   Legal doubletalk for ''and wife.''

exclusive listing contract   A contract between the seller of a home and his real estate agent that gives that agent exclusive rights to represent him and the buyers of the home.

existing loan A loan that is currently active.

Fannie Mae Federal National Mortgage Association, a real estate lender that buys groups of mortgages from lenders that originate the loans.

fee simple Ownership of real estate, free from all conditions and limitations. Complete ownership of land.

FHA The Federal Housing Administration, an agency of the federal government.

FmHA The Farmers Home Administration, an agency of the federal government.

first mortgage The principal mortgage that is the first lien on the property. This has first claim (after delinquent taxes, if any) on the money realized in a foreclosure.

fixed-interest rates Loan interest rates that will not change during the life of the loan.

fixture Personal property that has become real property because it is attached to the real property, or agreed by both parties to pass with the property, or because of local custom.

foreclosure When a lender (by legal proceedings) forces the sale of a mortgaged property in order to recover the loan money remaining when a borrower defaults on a loan.

Freddie Mac Federal Home Loan Mortgage Association, a real estate lender that buys groups of mortgages from lenders that originate the loans.

graduated payments Mortgage payments in which initial payments are less than they would be for a standard amortized loan, but in which payments increase after five to seven years to levels slightly higher (sometimes substantially higher) than they would have been for a standard amortized loan.

GI mortgage A VA mortgage.

grantee The buyer of real estate. The term often used in a deed.

grantor The seller of real estate. The term often used in a deed.

guaranty A promise to answer for performance of an obligation.

hard money Cash borrowed under stringent payback terms such as high interest rates, an advance fee, and a short-term payback date.

impound account A trust account that is established by a lender to accumulate monies to cover the cost of items such as taxes and insurance policy premiums. The money usually is collected at the time regular payments are made for the loan. Also called an escrow account.

installment sales A real estate transaction wherein the seller carries the secondary financing on the home (becoming a lender to the buyer) and takes payments on that loan over a period of two or more tax years.

interest rate The percentage of the principal amount of a loan that is charged for the use of the money.

joint tenancy Property jointly owned by two or more persons who can assume full title to the property if the other dies. It avoids probate.

land lease See contract for deed.

lease/purchase option A contract under the terms of which one party (the prospective seller) gives to another party (the prospective buyer) the possession and use of property for a fixed payment and fixed time period. At the end of that time, the prospective buyer has the right to exercise an option to buy the property at a predetermined price.

lien A hold or legal claim a person has on the property of another as security for a debt, such as a mortgage, mechanics lien, unpaid taxes.

listing contract A contract authorizing a real estate agent or broker to sell a home on behalf of a seller.

market value The amount buyers will pay for a given property at a given time. The value of property on an open market.

marketable title A title to a property, not completely clear, but with only minor objections which a court would require a buyer to accept.

mechanic's lien A hold or claim on the property of another as security for an unpaid bill of a building contractor, material supplier or workman.

MIP Mortgage insurance premium.

mortgage An instrument, recognized by law, that secures payment of a debt.

mortgagee The institution or individual that lends the money.

mortgage insurance An insurance policy that protects the lender's loan in case of borrower default.

mortgagor The person who borrows the money, using property as security.

note A written agreement, sometimes secured by a mortgage or deed of trust, by which the borrower acknowledges the debt and promises to pay it in a specified time. A home buyer usually signs a note as well as a mortgage at closing. Also called a promissory note.

offer A document signed by the buyer offering to buy certain real estate at a specific price. The signed acceptance of the seller makes it a contract if all of the essential items are covered.

open-end mortgage A mortgage clause that permits a homeowner to refinance the mortgage in the future to raise funds without having to rewrite the mortgage and pay closing costs again.

open house Opening a home that is for sale for public inspection without appointment.

option The right to buy property at a specified price within a stated time. If an owner receives consideration (e.g. money) the owner is bound to honor the option.

origination and processing fees Fees lenders charge for granting a mortgage and processing a loan, which could include points if money is tight.

personal property All types of movable, tangible items that people can own.

PI Principal and interest.

PITI Principal, interest, taxes, and insurance.

plat A map showing the planned use of land, such as the layout of lots on a tract of land.

plot plan The architectural plan showing the location of a house in relation to the lot.

points One point is one percent of the principal amount of a loan.

prepayment penalty A clause in a loan contract that allows the lender to charge an interest penalty if the borrower pays the loan in full prior to the end of the loan's lifetime.

PMI Private mortgage insurance.

principal The seller or the buyer. Also, the base amount of money owed on a loan.

private mortgage insurance An insurance policy issued by a private insurance company as opposed to one by the FHA.

promissory note See *note*.

qualify To meet the financial requirements of a lender when applying for a loan.

quit claim deed A legal instrument that transfers the property title without warranties. It conveys whatever interest the owner has in the property. The buyer is responsible for any claims brought against the property.

real property or real estate The land and everything built or growing on it or attached to it.

realtor A person licensed by the state to sell real estate and who is also a member of The National Association of Realtors, a trademark of that association.

recording Placing a transaction into the public records at the county courthouse.

refinance   Acquiring a new loan to pay in full a current loan that is due.

restrictive covenants   An agreement limiting the use of property. It is usually used by land developers or neighborhood property owners to preserve open space or to prevent undesirable businesses or non-residential activities.

sale by owner   The sale of a home by the owner/seller without the services of a real estate agent.

second mortgage   Also second lien. A mortgage given in addition to the first mortgage. The holder of the second mortgage has second priority on the funds realized in case of a foreclosure and sale of the property.

setback   The distance (specified by a zoning ordinance or restrictive covenant restriction) that must be left between a building and the boundaries of the lot.

short-term loan   A loan that has a payback date shorter than is normal for most real estate loans.

simple interest   A method of computing interest rates making interest due based on the unpaid balance of the principal at the end of each pay period. Most home mortgages are of this type.

single-family dwelling   A single structure for one family, on a separate lot.

square footage   A measure of area. Multiply the length times the width (both in feet) to obtain the square footage or living space of a room, house or lot. The square footage of a house is figured using the exterior structure dimensions.

sub-escrow   A second, nonconcurrent escrow completed on a house in order to skirt lender rules that do not allow secondary financing.

subsidized loan   A loan wherein interest rates are supplemented from a secondary source (as in buydowns).

survey   The process of determining the precise location and boundaries of a piece of land.

tax shelter   A financial investment, such as the purchase of real estate, made in order to have deductible expenses to reduce one's income taxes.

tenancy-in-common   Where two or more parties (as co-buyers) share the ownership of a property, without the right of survivorship. If one dies, the other does not assume full ownership of the property. Each partner has the right to will his or her portion of the property to another party.

tender   An offer of money.

third mortgage   A loan that is obtained for the purchase of a home, in addition to the first and second loans acquired for its purchase.

tight money market A time in which loan money is scarce, usually when there is inflation and high interest rates.

timesharing Property bought in blocks of time. Condominium units are usually sold by the week. The buyer purchases only those weeks during which he or she intends to use the unit, thus becoming the co-owner of a single unit with several other buyers.

title A document evidencing a person's ownership rights to a particular piece of property.

title insurance A policy written by a title company that guarantees the title to property. If the title becomes clouded because of a claim of prior ownership by someone else, the title company must make good any losses arising from these defects.

title search An examination of public records to find out the ownership history of a property and to determine the legal status of a property.

transfer A change of ownership of property.

trust deed See *deed of trust*.

usury Interest rates charged in excess of that permitted by law.

VA Veterans Administration. The Department of Veterans Affairs.

valuation An estimate of a property's worth.

vendee The buyer of real estate.

vendor The seller of real estate.

waiver Voluntarily giving up a claim, right, or privilege.

walk-through A home buyer's final inspection of the property prior to the close of escrow.

warranty A guarantee by the seller that the title is conveyed as stated in the deed.

wraparounds A creative financing method wherein the sellers continue to make payments on their original bank loan and receive payments from the buyers for that loan and for the secondary financing that the sellers are carrying. The two loans are "wrapped" together for one monthly payment by the buyer.

zoning Municipal laws that regulate how land can be used.

About the Author

MAURICE DUBOIS GRADUATED FROM TRINITY UNIVERSITY IN SAN ANTONIO, Texas with a major in home building. During the past 22 years, he has designed and built several hundred homes, developed a half-dozen subdivisions, and designed and built countless remodeling projects. He has sold hundreds of resale properties, and during one six-month period, he personally sold more than 40 single-family homes. He has had building and real estate experience in Illinois, Iowa, and Texas.

He is a licensed, Texas real estate broker and currently owns and manages a real estate company with offices in the Dallas/Fort Worth area. His company specializes in the sale of distressed, foreclosed, and owner-financed property throughout the Dallas/Fort Worth metropolitan area.

Dubois owns and manages rental property, and has written other books, including a home building manual, a home selling guide (*Sold By Owner*, Liberty Hall Press #30016), and two novels.

Index

Look for These and Other TAB Books at Your Local Bookstore

To Order Call Toll Free 1-800-822-8158

(in PA, AK, and Canada call 717-794-2191)

or write to TAB BOOKS, Blue Ridge Summit, PA 17294-0840.

Title	Product No.	Quantity	Price

☐ Check or money order made payable to TAB BOOKS

Charge my ☐ VISA ☐ MasterCard ☐ American Express

Acct. No. _____ Exp. _____

Signature: _____

Name: _____

Address: _____

City: _____

State: _____ Zip: _____

Subtotal $ _____

Postage and Handling
($3.00 in U.S., $5.00 outside U.S.) $ _____

Add applicable state and local
sales tax $ _____

TOTAL $ _____

TAB BOOKS catalog free with purchase; otherwise send $1.00 in check or money order and receive $1.00 credit on your next purchase.

Orders outside U.S. must pay with international money order in U.S. dollars.

TAB Guarantee: If for any reason you are not satisfied with the book(s) you order, simply return it (them) within 15 days and receive a full refund. **BC**

Other Bestsellers of Related Interest

LENDING OPPORTUNITIES IN REAL ESTATE:
A High Profit Strategy for Every Investor
—James C. Allen
Earn high yields at low risk by making short-term secured loans! This book offers specific advice and procedures for investing in short-term loans secured by real estate. Samples of actual forms involved are included. Topics addressed cover: preparing a personal financial statement, sources of free advice, borrowing investment capital, setting rates and terms in any market, advantages of smaller notes, avoiding foreclosure, and "prospecting" made easy. 192 pages, 42 illustrations. **Book No. 30019, $14.95 paperback, $24.95 hardcover**

THE NO-NONSENSE LANDLORD
—Richard H. Jorgensen
This is a realistic, no-hype guide to making money in real estate. Here Richard Jorgensen presents his proven methods of shrewd financing and management—methods that even seasoned landlords will find invaluable. You'll find helpful expert advice on: selecting good tenants, making low-cost repairs, exploiting every benefit allowed by the new tax law, collecting rents, problem tenants, keeping records, and handling complaints. 204 pages, Illustrated. Book No. 30032, $14.95 paperback, $22.95 hardcover

THE PERSONAL TAX ADVISOR:
Understanding the New Tax Law
—Cliff Roberson, LLM, Ph.D.
How will the new tax law affect your tax return this filing season? Any reform is certain to mean a change in the way your taxes are prepared. But you don't have to be an accountant or a lawyer to understand the new tax laws . . . use this easy-to-read guide and learn how to reduce your income taxes under the new federal rules! 176 pages. **Book No. 30134, $12.95 paperback only**

SOLD BY OWNER! Secrets of Selling Your House
without a Broker's Fee—Maurice Dubois
This practical guide gives you all the information you need to sell your home, coop, or condo *without* a real estate broker. Packed with information, *Sold by Owner!* provides step-by-step instructions outlining the entire process. You'll learn how to: size up the local housing market, use creative financing options, advertise, and complete necessary legal forms and contracts. 240 pages, 32 illustrations. **Book No. 30016, $13.95 paperback only**

AVOIDING PROBATE: Tamper-Proof Estate Planning
—Cliff Roberson
Discover how to hand down everything you own to anyone you choose without interference from courts, creditors, relatives, or the IRS. In this easy-to-read planning guide, attorney Cliff Roberson shows how you can avoid the horrors of probate court. Sample wills and trust agreements and checklists for every chapter make planning each step easy. *Avoiding Probate* covers: living trusts, life insurance, specific property, wills, family businesses, valuing your estate, estate taxes, and more. 263 pages. **Book No. 30074, $14.95 paperback, $29.95 hardcover**

ESTATE PLANNING MADE EASY—Herbert F. Starr
"Worth your reading" **—Consumer Newsweekly**
"If control over one's financial destiny is the goal, [this] is a good place to start."
—National Association of Life Underwriters
Practical and well-organized, this handbook explains, in a down-to-earth language, what everyone should know about: living trusts, buy-sell agreements, state and inheritance taxes, legal and administrative costs, the revocable living trust, life insurance, probate and taxes, the U.S. estate tax, and more! 160 pages. **Book No. 30047, $14.95 paperback only**

FAMILY INSURANCE HANDBOOK: The Complete
Guide for the 1990s—Les Abromovitz
Les Abromovitz provides you with an in-depth look at every type of insurance offered on the market today, including travel insurance, vacation insurance, dread disease insurance, even pet insurance. He explains in easy-to-follow language how to analyze policies, what coverage to take and what to avoid, how to file claims, and what to do if a company denies coverage. Other timely topics include changes in tax and Medicare laws and the California voter revolt against high premiums. 240 pages. **Book No. 30057, $17.95 hardcover**